A Climate Agenda for System Change: From Theory to Social Transformation

Diana Stuart
Brian Petersen
Ryan Gunderson

Published by Mayfly Books. Available in paperpack
and free online at www.mayflybooks.org in 2023.

ISBN (Print)   978-1-906948-68-9
ISBN (PDF)   978-1-906948-69-6

may fly

A Climate Agenda for System Change: From Theory to Social Transformation

Diana Stuart
Brian Petersen
Ryan Gunderson

Contents

Acknowledgements

This book represents a synthesis and significant expansion of our collaborative and independent work on social theory and responses to climate change. In several of the chapters, we tie together and update key discussions from our previous work. In other chapters, we extend our work into new terrain as we focus specifically on how a new "system changing" climate agenda might be conceived and achieved. Compared to our previous work, this book moves well beyond a critique of techno-capitalist strategies and engages in new discussions about what system change to minimize global warming might look like and how it might come to fruition. We would like to acknowledge the role of our previous work and the publishers of the articles below that we authored prior to writing this book. We applied ideas and adapted or revised sections of text from these articles in specific chapters as follows:

The introduction includes revised text and key ideas from:
Petersen, B., Stuart, D., & Gunderson, R. (2019). Reconceptualizing climate change denial: Ideological denialism misdiagnoses climate change and limits effective action. *Human Ecology Review*, 25(2), 117-141.

Chapter 1 contains portions of adapted text and updated discussions from:
Gunderson, R., Stuart, D., & Petersen, B. (2019). The political economy of geoengineering as plan B: Technological rationality, moral hazard, and new technology. *New Political Economy*, 24(5), 696-715.

Gunderson, R., Stuart, D., & Petersen, B. (2021). In search of plan (et) B: Irrational rationality, capitalist realism, and space colonization. *Futures*, 134, 102857.

Stuart, D., Gunderson, R., & Petersen, B. (2020). Carbon geoengineering and the metabolic rift: Solution or social reproduction? *Critical Sociology*, 46(7-8), 1233-1249.

Chapters 2 and 3 includes text, expanded discussions, and further elaborated ideas found in:

Stuart, D., Petersen, B., & Gunderson, R. (2022). Articulating system change to effectively and justly address the climate crisis. *Globalizations*. DOI: 10.1080/14747731.2022.2106040.

Chapter 4 contains portions of revised and adapted text from:

Gunderson, R. (2016). Environmental sociology and the Frankfurt School 2: ideology, techno-science, reconciliation. *Environmental Sociology*, 2(1), 64-76.

Gunderson, R., Stuart, D., Petersen, B., & Yun, S. J. (2018). Social conditions to better realize the environmental gains of alternative energy: Degrowth and collective ownership. *Futures*, 99, 36-44.

Chapter 5 features adapted text and further elaborated discussions from:

Stuart, D., Gunderson, R., & Petersen, B. (2020). Overconsumption as ideology: Implications for addressing global climate change. *Nature and Culture*, 15(2), 199-223.

Chapter 6 includes portions of adapted text from:

Stuart, D., Gunderson, R., & Petersen, B. (2020). The climate crisis as a catalyst for emancipatory transformation: An examination of the possible. *International Sociology*, 35(4), 433-456.

Chapter 7 features revised sections of text from:

Gunderson, R. 2022. Powerless, stupefied, and repressed actors cannot challenge climate change: Real helplessness as a barrier between climate concern and action. *Journal for the Theory of Social Behaviour.* DOI: 10.1111/jtsb.12366.

Stuart, D. (2020). Radical hope: Truth, virtue, and hope for what is left in extinction rebellion. *Journal of Agricultural and Environmental Ethics*, 33(3), 487-504.

Introduction:
Beyond Ideological Denial

[T]he insanity of the whole absolves the particular insanities and turns the crimes against humanity into a rational enterprise.

— Herbert Marcuse (1964: 52)

Despite overwhelming evidence and increasingly dire predictions, world leaders have yet to initiate meaningful and sufficient responses to address the climate crisis. While warming has already occurred and more warming is inevitable, the outcomes associated with a 2 °C versus a 4 °C warmer future are dramatically different with increasing loss and suffering associated with each fraction of a degree warmer. Yet, with everything at stake, we still do not see the bold actions necessary to minimize warming. For decades, action was stymied by climate change denial propagated by "vested interests," or those invested in and profiting from the fossil fuels-based system (e.g., see McCright and Dunlap 2000, 2003, 2010, 2011). Arguments that climate change is not occurring or is not caused by humans confused the public and delayed concern, a deliberate tactic used by fossil fuel interests, lobbyists, and conservative think tanks as part of a climate countermovement (Ferrell 2016). While some people continue to believe that climate change is a hoax or poses no threat, and organized denial efforts have continued and increased over the past few decades (Stoddart et al. 2021), the majority of people are now concerned about climate change (de Bruin 2022). Even in the United States (US), 60% believe the government should do something to address global warming and 70% believe environmental protection is more important than economic growth (Marlon et al. 2019). Yet, denial also exists in new forms that hinders the actions necessary to minimize warming.

There is widespread denial about the extent of change necessary to minimize warming or even avoid some of the worst outcomes of climate change. Using bolder language than ever before, in 2018 the Intergovernmental Panel on Climate Change (IPCC) called for significant changes to our social, economic, and energy systems to address the climate crisis, specifically stating that "rapid, far-reaching and unprecedented changes in all aspects of society" are necessary (IPCC 2018). With a 1.1° C average global temperature increase thus far, we are already seeing serious impacts including unprecedented fires, floods, and hurricanes; and much more severe impacts are projected as warming continues. Ripple et al. (2021: 1), representing the Alliance of World Scientists, identify "disturbing" vital signs of climate impacts that they state "clearly and unequivocally" illustrates we are in a "climate emergency."

Now is the time to identify what scientists mean by pronouncing that we need "rapid, far-reaching and unprecedented changes in all aspects of society." Beyond the IPCC, other scientists are providing a clearer picture as to what kind of changes are necessary. Green and Cato (2018: 1), representing nearly 100 scientists, argue that governments have betrayed us "in failing to acknowledge that infinite economic growth on a planet with finite resources is non-viable." Steffen et al. (2018: 5-6) argue that "[t]he present dominant socioeconomic system... is based on high-carbon economic growth and exploitative resource use" and we need "changes in behavior, technology and innovation, governance, and values." Ripple et al. (2019: 4) state that:

> Excessive extraction of materials and overexploitation of ecosystems, driven by economic growth, must be quickly curtailed to maintain long-term sustainability of the biosphere... Our goals need to shift from GDP growth and the pursuit of affluence toward sustaining ecosystems and improving human well-being by prioritizing basic needs and reducing inequality.

More and more scientists are calling for changing our economy to curtail never-ending economic growth. For some time, scientists have known that a 1% increase in GDP equals a 0.5–0.7% increase in carbon emissions (Burke et al. 2015) and that the most notable greenhouse gas (GHG) emissions reductions have occurred during economic recession due to a reduction in production and consumption (Feng et al. 2015). Based on their analyses of carbon budgets, scientists Anderson and Bows (2011, 2012) find that overall reductions in economic growth are *required* to stay within global climate targets. As the United Nations biodiversity chief Paşca Palmer explains, this means that "[w]e need a transformation in the way we consume and produce" (Conley 2019). Scientists continue to illustrate positive linkages between economic growth, energy consumption, and carbon emissions (e.g., Chen et al. 2022); bringing to attention the absolute necessity to transform our economy to avoid social and ecological breakdown.

Yet, we do not see the far-reaching changes in our economic system that scientists continue to state are necessary. Transformation remains stymied by political and social barriers, including new forms of denial: denial about the scope of social change required. This denial conceals the underlying drivers of climate change and therefore what is necessary to minimize warming. Drawing from critical theory, we call this denial an *ideological* form of denial (Petersen et al. 2019), which fixes attention on minor tweaks to the current system rather than the "rapid, far-reaching and unprecedented changes" necessary. Even many environmentalists and those deeply concerned about the climate crisis have succumb to ideological denial, failing to grasp the extent of social change required.

Minimizing or even significantly reducing global warming will indeed require *radical* societal change. Radical, from the Latin *radicalis*, means relating to the root. Action is needed to address the root causes of the climate crisis, not only to treat the symptoms. As scientific evidence continues to illustrate, the root drivers are related to our growth-dependent economic system. However, the extent of change required continues to be concealed by widespread ideological denial – a pattern of thought that veils awareness of the necessity of radical system change and social transformation.

What do we mean by "ideological" denial? The term ideology dates to the French Revolution (Lichtheim 1967), when it had a positive connotation associated with scientific rigor in the study of ideas. Here we apply a Marxist negative conception of ideology (Larrain 1979), one grounded in an understanding of social contradictions. In an early formulation, Marx and Engels (1977) referred to ideology as a sublimation of material life in ideas that justify and naturalize the interests of the ruling class. More specifically, ideology serves to obscure or mask contradictions in society that dispel actions towards social change. A contradiction refers to "two seemingly opposed forces [that] are simultaneously present within a particular situation, an entity, a process or an event" (Harvey 2014: 1) and ideology refers to "ideas and practices that reproduce contradictory social relations" (Gunderson 2017: 271). Ideology ranges from extravagant theological and ethical systems that justify contradictory social conditions to, more commonly and elusively, the unthinking daily practices that reproduce these contradictions by taking the social world for granted. Ideology is both reified, taken-for-granted practices that conform to social structures and the beliefs and "common sense" that assume these structures to be necessary or natural. The defining characteristic of all ideology is leaving the contradictory and historical nature of society unexamined by ignoring social contradictions. While the effect of ideology is to conceal contradictions, this does not imply that ideology exists because of its effect (Larrain: 1983: 42) - though ideologies have been and continue to be manufactured for this very purpose (e.g., Bell and York 2010).

Although ideology is sometimes a veil created by elites to distract the masses from seeing reality clearly and realizing their true interests, ideology is far more often the implicit, tacit assumption, rooted in everyday practices that conform to existing institutions—institutions that dominate humans and the environment rather than conform to rational goals—and accepted as "just the way things are," as well as the normative, ethical, and political ideas that emerge from this originating assumption. Althusser (1971: 165ff) makes the case that ideology is not only false consciousness or immaterial, subjective beliefs, but has an actual material existence in "un-reflected, merely lived practical activity" (Jay 1984: 404), activities governed by rituals within specific institutions, or, "Ideological State Apparatuses" (see also Žižek 1994: 12ff). In the case of the climate crisis, "ideological denial" indeed has a material existence, in ineffective climate action, structured by institutions. Gramsci (1971) built on Marx and Engels' conception of ideology to show how culture can create social acceptance of ideas that ultimately prevents social change. These conceptions of ideology showcase "how the ideas of elite political and economic actors come to be seen as common sense to the general public, and how control in modern societies is maintained though consent to 'ruling ideas' rather than through direct imposition of force" (Norgaard 2011: 11). This conception of ideology, as contradiction-concealing ideas and practices that reproduce existing social conditions, also lends itself to a comparison with the notion of denial.

We argue that ideology gives life to forms of denial that dramatically limit the suite of options seen as viable solutions to climate change. Due to this widespread form of denial, even among those concerned about climate change, we must now "preach to the choir," coaxing the already concerned to understand that, due in part to ideology, they have both misdiagnosed the problem and are relying on so-called solutions that will not solve our problems related to climate change. Prominent proposed solutions are not radical in the sense that they fail to address the root drivers of climate change. Those who neglect to see this deny the reality of the problem and the needed social transformations to address it.

We recognize that this argument may be interpreted as polemical and accusatory, which can sometimes undermine rather than build the solidarity needed to create social change. Indeed, both terms that make up the organizing concept—ideology and denialism—are historically polemical concepts. No one wants to be accused of being an ideologue or a denialist, let alone both. Our goal is not to engage in counterproductive name-calling, which, when the goal is to sway opinion, tends to do the opposite. Nor is our goal to suggest that everyone who disagrees with us must be an ideologue or a denialist. Indeed, this critique transcends individuals, suggesting instead that ideology manifests in society broadly, leading to individuals taking actions or believing in certain "truths" that reproduce rather than challenge the social order. A tension of hoping-turned-belief— combined with material interests in continuing existing social institutions and, as discussed later, the lack of a powerful movement to successfully address climate change—is often how ideological denialism functions long before it underpins coherent climate policies and debate. In other words, our goal is not to dismiss ideas by labelling them with pejorative terms, but, instead, to bring to light ideas and practices, ideas and practices the authors are not immune from, that delay serious climate action despite good intentions.

Although climate action remains stymied, when a window of opportunity opens for bold climate policies and programs, it is critical to understand the scope and scale of the changes that are now required. This involves overcoming all forms of climate denial and embracing the transformation necessary. In this book, we begin by addressing this denial in order to focus on the alternatives – the more radical changes necessary to get at the root of the climate crisis and most effectively and justly minimize associated impacts.

Ideological Denial

Denialism has received significant attention due to how it influences society's responses to climate change. Norgaard's (2011) study, looking at climate change perspectives in Norway, reveals how denial emerges through social interaction. Rather than focusing on the psychological realities that limit humans from viewing climate change as an immediate risk that requires action, Norgaard develops the idea of "socially organized denial," in which individuals distance themselves from information based on "norms of emotion, conversation, and attention" (Norgaard 2011: 211). This leads to individual apathy and a situation where people "find real change unnecessary" (Norgaard's 2011: 225). Cohen (2001) identifies three denial variants: literal, interpretive, and implicatory. Literal denial refers to someone asserting something is not true despite evidence to the contrary. Interpretive denial focuses on contesting or distorting facts and evidence in an attempt to change the meaning associated with ideas or events. Lastly, implicatory denial, the variant that Norgaard (2011) focuses on, conceals information such that individuals, and society in general, do not act upon it.

John Bellamy Foster (2010, 2015) also draws on the concept of denial to diagnose why society has failed to adequately address climate change. Foster focuses attention on dominant views held by those convinced climate change is happening. He contributes to this line of thought by identifying prominent strategies put forth by environmentalists as denial. Mainstream strategies are labeled a form of denial because the strategies remain woefully inadequate to address the systemic factors causing climate change. Recently, Foster has said that "the willful delusions here are in some ways more dangerous than that of straight-out climate deniers, since they are subtler and infect those who are ostensibly on the side of change" (quoted in Ferguson, 2018). He marshals evidence that climate change poses significant threats to society, notes that the current trends represent an unsustainable pathway, and suggests the only means by which to address the situation requires radical alternatives.

Still, environmental discourses refrain from engaging the gravity, scope, and extent of the drivers causing climate change. Foster (2010: 4) explains:

> However, rather than addressing the real roots of the crisis and drawing the appropriate conclusions, the dominant response is to avoid all questions about the nature of our society, and to turn to technological fixes or market mechanisms of one sort or another. In this respect, there is a certain continuity of thought between those who deny the climate change problem altogether, and those who, while acknowledging the severity of the problem at one level, nevertheless deny that it requires a revolution in our social system.

Further elaborating Foster's notion of social denial (2015), we (Petersen et al. 2019) define ideological denial as ideas and practices underlying responses to climate change that:

1   Acknowledge that climate change is real and primarily driven by human activities, and that we should take immediate action to mitigate its current and projected serious harms.

2   Implicitly or explicitly misdiagnose the underlying social drivers of climate change, and that this misdiagnosis is embedded in the ineffective prescriptions, actions, and laws.

3   Limit the suite of effective actions that could be adopted to challenge the social drivers of climate change. These limits are erected by either: (a) assuming that an ineffective strategy (e.g., lifestyle changes) are "realistic" and effective themselves or (b) adopting ineffective strategies (e.g., carbon markets) in order to suppress strategies that would challenge the social drivers of climate change (e.g., Lohmann 2005).

4   Maintain, rather than challenge, the current social order that drives climate change.

While a few remaining dissenters may continue to deny the existence of climate change and some neo-skeptics may deny the severity of the consequences of global warming (Perkins 2015), ideological denial now represents a major obstacle to effectively addressing the climate crisis. Ideological denial, as we describe here, can take a variety of forms. These forms relate to faith in partial or false solutions that divert attention away from the real changes necessary that would actually "engage the nature of society" (Foster 2010). These beliefs in false or partial solutions deter the necessary recognition of the radical extent of change that is required. Ideological denial exists in different forms as people support a range of minor tweaks to the current system, believing they will be sufficient to address the climate crisis. These forms include faith in: (1) individual behavior change without system-level transformation, (2) market mechanisms, (3) "green growth" or being able to "green" an ever-growing economy, and (4) technological solutions/techno-fixes divorced from social change. Here, we summarize these four variants of ideological denial, noting that they are not mutually exclusive.

Individual Behavior Change

It is not surprising that many people and major media outlets continue to focus on what individuals can do to reduce their personal carbon emissions. Responses to climate change, particularly in the US, often focus on individual actions. Norgaard (2011: 192) attributes this to the fact that "Americans are so immersed in the ideology of individualism that they lack the imagination or knowledge of alternative political means of response." The underling belief is that individuals can solve the climate crisis through making different consumption choices that reduce GHG emissions. This involves buying items such as energy efficient appliances and lightbulbs, hybrid cars, "green" household products, and rooftop solar panels.

Why is a focus on individual behavior change to address the climate crisis a form of ideological denial? On the one hand, it is undeniable that many individuals, especially the rich (Nielsen et al. 2021), will have to make significant behavior changes if we are to reduce emissions. However, this transformation requires changing the social structures in which individual behaviors adapt to. Unfortunately, most calls for individual behavioral change exclude analysis of how to change these social structures, thereby drawing attention to a partial and inadequate solution pathway. In fact, the probable reason fossil fuel companies have spent millions of dollars on promoting individual behavioral changes as the solution to climate change is to insulate their own actions from regulation (McFall-Johnsen 2021). Or, in the language of ideology critique, they are concealing the underlying structural drivers of climate change to maintain current power relations. Assuming that changes in individual actions are sufficient or adequate to address the climate crisis is a dangerous notion, as the data is clear that systemic change is required to reduce the majority of GHG emissions. Here, we summarize a few studies to illustrate the limitations of focusing on individual actions as the solution to the climate crisis.

The estimates regarding the potential contributions of individual behavior changes vary, but all confirm that the majority of emissions come from companies and states, not individuals (Heede 2014). According to the US Department of Energy, residential use only represents 34% of total energy use in the US with commercial and industrial sectors using the majority of energy (EIA 2018). Dietz et al. (2009) estimate that individual and household-level changes may be able to reduce GHG emissions by around 7%. More recently, Moran et al. (2018) estimate that a shift to green consumption could reduce European GHG emissions by 25%. Williamson et al. (2018) estimate that the widespread adoption of 30 different behavioral changes could mitigate from 19% to 36% of global GHG emissions between 2020 and 2050. Yet, global emissions need to be roughly halved by 2030 and reach net zero by 2050 in order to stay within 1.5°C (IPCC 2018).

The initial reduction in global GHG emissions due to the

Covid-19 pandemic was around 17%. While some claimed this reduction showed how individual changes can really add up, scientists explained that "at the same time, 83% of global emissions are left, which shows how difficult it is to reduce emissions with changes in behaviour... Just behavioural change is not enough" (Harvey 2020). Despite a global pandemic, which led to worldwide lockdowns, a halt to most air travel, drastic reductions in commuting and car travel more broadly, and significant reductions in travel and entertainment, GHG emission levels in 2020 reached record highs and have continued their upward trend throughout the pandemic. In other words, because the majority of emissions lie outside the control of individuals, behavioral and lifestyle changes alone will not come close to reducing emissions at the rate and scale necessary to keep global temperature increases within 1.5°C or even 2°C.

The current growth-oriented system also constrains the emissions reduction potential that could be achieved through individual behavior changes. A key relationship that undermines the effectiveness of green consumerism is that in most cases production and marketing drive consumption (Wiedmann et al. 2020). In other words, consumer choices rarely reshape production. As explained by many scholars, the idea of "consumer sovereignty" is largely a myth as increased production and advertising create demand (Gailbraith 1958, Schnaiberg 1980). In addition, the state continues to allow widespread advertising, including advertising aimed at children and also subsidizes production industries and encourages consumption to stimulate the economy. This creates a context in which constantly consuming is the norm as well as consuming more over time – thus production and consumption *per person* has increased over time in affluent nations (Wiedmann et al. 2020). Even if there were widespread education programs to promote a low-carbon lifestyle, increasing production levels, advertising to sell products, and a materialist culture would continue to encourage high consumptive living and undermine the (already limited) potential of individual mitigation efforts. We return to this dynamic in chapter 5.

While individual consumption and behavioral changes alone are insufficient, this does not mean that they should not be pursued. There are clear ethical reasons to pursue a lower personal carbon footprint (for a discussion, see Stuart 2022). The danger in focusing on individual actions, divorced from prescriptions for social change, is if they result in less attention and effort to address the majority of emissions that must be reduced to avoid catastrophic warming. While some people may be able to pursue both individual lifestyle changes and demand systemic change, evidence suggests that in other cases adopting personal and household actions to reduce GHG emissions can result in reduced support for climate policies (Werfel 2017). And, as fossil fuel companies have clearly realized, focusing more on individual actions takes attention away from the structural drivers of emissions.

Market Fundamentalism

A second form of ideological denial relates to market fundamentalism. Thus far, the dominant government responses to climate change have focused on market mechanisms. The Kyoto Protocol led to the creation of the first international carbon market in the European Union (EU). Climate change has been referred to as a market failure, most famously by Nicholas Stern (2008), who called it the "biggest market failure the world has seen." A market failure arises when "firms have not met the full cost of their production and have imposed significant costs arising from pollution on society generally" (Andrew 2008: 394). Market-based solutions, thus, attempt to correct this failure. However, as the EU's Emissions Trading Scheme (ETS) and other emissions trading programs have shown, carbon trading prioritizes economic outcomes first and foremost and have had little success curbing emissions. Analyses of trading programs continue to conclude that without a meaningful cap on emissions and with significant levels of fraud, price volatility, and speculators, such programs have failed to result in significant emissions reductions (Tapia Granadas and Spash 2019, Stoddard et al. 2021).

Supporting carbon markets as a solution embodies denialism as it presents a small tweak to a broken system, rather than acknowledging the system is broken and must be remade. Market approaches thus far have also been designed with a focus on how to economically benefit from climate change rather than how to most effectively cut GHG emissions. Lohmann (2010: 237) suggests that "carbon markets isolate and objectify a new product that is difficult to define," and in so doing separates emissions from their political roots leading to seemingly apolitical actions. Carbon markets create a market-based approach to a problem that dissolves the need for political and social action. Focusing on carbon markets also prevents and delays alternatives with the potential for transformative reductions in emissions. For example, Lohmann (2005) provides evidence that this happened in the context of the Kyoto Protocol. After the US introduced the idea of emissions trading, this redirected intellectual and financial resources from innovations and social changes that had the potential of reducing emissions. Environmental criticisms of Kyoto's emphasis on establishing a carbon market were scorned as taking a "do-nothing" stance, input and ideas from nonprofessional and noncorporate groups were minimized, and alternative pathways were marginalized. The corporate watchdog non-profit Corporate Europe Observatory (2015) argues that the existence of the EU ETS has undermined the ability of new emissions regulations to take hold and its negligible targets act as a "ceiling" rather than a "floor" for national climate policies. In short, another function of emissions trading is to deter more direct and effective action.

The creation of carbon markets as a response to climate change represents a defensive maneuver to preserve the status quo and to also further the accumulation of capital to the wealthy few (Klein 2014). Supported by Wall Street, it is a political strategy influenced by substantial financial interests (Bryant 2016). The further commodification of carbon creates profits, and the vast majority of these profits are going to the same people already profiting from the current system. Lohmann (2010) details how carbon markets are dominated by the same institutions active in derivatives trading, including Goldman Sachs and other big banks. Carbon markets are controlled by speculators and supported by the largest actors in finance as well as industry, who prefer a more flexible and capitalist mechanism to address GHG emissions (Kaup 2015). Large banks and corporations are already reaping substantial profits from trading carbon, as carbon markets represent a way to further financialize the environment (Stoddard et al. 2021).

Markets offer an easy way for those benefiting from the current system to slightly tweak it to "solve" climate change while still reaping increasing levels of profit. However, due to the underlying structural drivers of the crisis, market mechanisms will be unable to adequately address climate change. As stated by Hoffmann (2011: 13) regarding the EU ETS and similar schemes: "While well intentioned at first sight, such measures run the risk that they perpetuate the systemic flaws of the system." Further expanding markets to fix problems with markets has resulted in an effective wealth accumulation strategy, not an effective climate mitigation strategy. Focusing on market-based solutions perniciously provides the illusion that we can address climate change while still expanding markets and economic growth.

Green Growth

Faith in green growth represents a firm denial that we must significantly shift the goals and processes of our economic and social relations to address the climate crisis. Widely touted as a "win-win" approach, green growth attempts to achieve ongoing economic growth and environmental goals simultaneously. Green growth has emerged as a central framing in climate and broader environmental discourses (Lorek and Spangenberg 2014). The promise of green growth relies on decoupling environmental harm from economic activity and growth. This means continuing to increase GDP growth (and associated production of goods and services), while decreasing total GHG emissions at the pace and scale necessary to meet climate targets. Such decoupling has not yet materialized.

While many studies show examples of "successful" decoupling, looking carefully at these studies reveals that they are typically focusing on certain sectors or countries and often on relative rather than absolution decoupling. Relative decoupling traces environmental impacts per unit of economic activity while absolute decoupling emphasizes overall reductions (Jackson 2009). To address the climate crisis, decoupling would need to be (1) absolute, (2) global, and (3) permanent. According to recent analyses, decoupling in these terms has not occurred and is very unlikely to occur (Parrique et al. 2019, Hickel and Kallis 2019, Vaden et al. 2020).

In a review of the literature surrounding green growth and its challenges, Parrique et al. (2019: 3) summarize their findings: "not only is there no empirical evidence supporting the existence of a decoupling of economic growth from environmental pressures on anywhere near the scale needed to deal with environmental breakdown, but also, and perhaps more importantly, such decoupling appears unlikely to happen in the future." They pinpoint seven reasons to be skeptical of the future possibility of sufficient decoupling:

1   *Rising energy expenditures* – The amount of energy and resources invested in the extraction of cheap resources and energy will likely increase.

2   *Rebound effects* – The potential environmental benefits of efficiency gains are often totally or partially compensated by reallocating saved resources or money in consuming the same given resource or another resource.

3   *Problem shifting* – Focusing on technological solutions to environmental problems often creates new environmental problems (e.g., nuclear power).

4   *The underestimated impact of services* – The service economy does not replace the material economy; the former is built "on top" of the latter and has numerous environmental impacts.

5   *Limited potential of recycling* – Recycling rates are low, require energy and resources, and, even if optimized and expanded, cannot provide sufficient inputs for a growing economy.

6   *Insufficient and inappropriate technological change* – Changes in productive technologies do not tend to reduce environmental pressure, do not displace many ecologically undesirable technologies, and are not fast enough to permit speedy absolute decoupling.

7   *Cost shifting* – Some purported instances of decoupling are achieved by externalizing environmental impacts via trade.

The viability of the case for green growth requires total reductions in *global* GHG emissions despite increasing economic growth (absolute decoupling). While evidence of decoupling depends on what is measured and over what time period (some trends are temporary), decoupling remains far from global and, in some cases, national "success" stories relate only to production-based emissions (produced in the specific nation) and fail to include significant consumption-based emissions (emissions from imported goods). A recent review of national-level decoupling trends found that evidence of absolute decoupling of carbon emissions from GDP was identified in 32 counties for production-based emissions, 23 countries for consumption-based emissions, and in only 14 countries for both production and consumption-based emissions – with the authors concluding that "[e]ven countries that have achieved absolute decoupling are still adding emissions to the atmosphere thus showing the limits of 'green growth' and the growth paradigm" (Hubacek et al. 2021). In addition, Haberl et al. (2020) state that, while absolute decoupling of both production and consumption-based emissions can be found in some cases, it is not occurring globally or at the rates necessary:

> We conclude that large rapid absolute reductions of resource use and GHG emissions cannot be achieved through observed decoupling rates, hence decoupling needs to be complemented by sufficiency-oriented strategies and strict enforcement of absolute reduction targets.

To summarize, there has "never been a global pattern of absolute decoupling of CO2 from economic growth" (Parrique et al. 2019: 24). Further, if economies continue to grow, the likelihood of absolute decoupling occurring at the scale and pace necessary to meet climate targets is very low (Hickel and Kallis 2019; cf. Anderson and Bows 2012). Given the lack of absolute decoupling of GHG emissions from economic growth, Schor and Jorgenson (2019: 322) argue that meeting climate targets likely requires that we abandon the "growth-at-all-costs mentality." Thus, relying on hypothetical future decoupling remains a very risky gamble.

Green growth represents a denial of the fundamental relationship between economic growth and GHG emissions, which remains an empirically illustrated positive correlation (Stern 2006, Jorgenson and Clark 2012, York et al. 2003). Green growth denies this relationship and therefore fails to focus on the root cause of climate change: a society structured around ever-increasing production and economic growth. Green growth remains a useful myth to support ongoing economic growth and profit accumulation for those most benefiting from the current fossil fuel-based and profit-oriented system. This is largely the wealthiest 10% of the world's population who, as of 2020, has been responsible for nearly half of all emissions since 1990, with the wealthiest 1% of the global population responsible for more than twice the emissions as the poorest 50% of the global population (Kartha et al. 2020). Green growth also relies heavily on techno-optimism, or the belief that technologies—and, in many cases, non-existing, hypothetical future technologies—will be able to decouple growth from GHG emissions. Without evidence that decoupling is possible in a way that is absolute, global, and permanent, a reliance on green growth lead by techno-optimism remains a dangerous path.

Techno-Optimism

Technological change is an essential lever for climate mitigation; however, technology alone will not be enough in a system that continues to use more materials and energy per person over time. Having faith that technology alone will solve the climate crisis is another form of denial – denying that systemic changes are necessary. As we will explore in a later chapter, applying certain technologies *in a new social order* would be a highly effective way to minimize global warming. While energy efficiency and renewable energy can play a key role in climate mitigation, in a system with increasing material and energy use, faith in these technologies as the solution to the climate crisis represents ideological denial.

Energy use plays a significant role in GHG emissions. As a result, a commonly proposed climate solution focuses on energy efficiency improvements with important policy implications (Alcott 2005). Although conceptually intuitive, the realities of energy use and efficiency do not represent a panacea. Long ago, William Stanley Jevons (1865) interrogated the relationship between efficiency gains and resource use in the context of coal. Jevons showed that efficiency in coal use decreased its costs and led to increased consumption, a relationship now known as the "Jevons Paradox." This paradox has been empirically illustrated as it relates to climate change. York and McGee (2015) show that countries with greater efficiencies generally have higher rates of GHG emissions, energy use, and electricity consumption. In addition, York (2006) shows how vehicle efficiency in the US did not lead to reduced fuel consumption, in part due to changes in vehicle weights and types, drivers, and miles driven.

The counterintuitive outcome of efficiency gains being partially or fully consumed by increased resource use has been termed the "rebound effect." For example, Freire-Gonzalez (2017) analyzes the rebound effect in households using energy efficiency improvements in the 27 countries of the European Union. The results from the analysis shows that seven countries had rebound effects above 100%, in which more energy is consumed than prior to implementing improvements, and most countries show at least a 50% rebound, meaning the rebound effect neutralized half the efficiency gains. Santarius (2012) delineates financial, material, psychological and cross-factor rebound effects. Recent evidence supports these findings, showing large rebound effects in energy consumption from energy efficiency efforts at all levels, from national to household scales (York et al. 2022). These and other examples provide insights into how and why the rebound effect greatly undermines the emission reduction potential from energy efficiency. This evidence suggests that despite widespread support, energy efficiency alone will not be an effective solution to climate change. Its false promise helps to support the continuation of business as usual. Faith in energy efficiency, therefore, represents a form of technological optimism supporting a denial of the necessary social changes.

A focus solely on switching to renewable energy sources, without systemic change, also represents a similar form of denial. Few solutions to climate change have received as much attention as switching to renewable energy. The United Nations Development Programme (n.d.) states: "The role of renewable energy solutions in mitigating climate change is proven." Jacobson et al. (2015) provide a "roadmap" for each state in the US, arguing that renewables can power the entire country. The focus on renewable energy development is understandable: it presents an opportunity to displace fossil-fuel based energy with less carbon-intensive sources. Doing so would enable society to meet energy demand without contributing to climate change. Despite its seeming potential, however, renewable energy development embedded in current social conditions has not materialized into an effective mitigation response to climate change.

The idea that renewable energy development alone will reduce GHG emissions relies on the assumption that renewable energy production will displace fossil fuels. Empirical analyses suggest displacement does not occur and that renewable energy production may, in some cases, counterintuitively increase overall energy use and emissions, an outcome known as the "energy boomerang effect" (Zehner 2012). York (2012) conducted a cross-national study to assess whether increases in alternative energy production led to fossil fuel displacement. This analysis showed minimal displacement: "the average pattern across most nations of the world over the past fifty years is one where each unit of total national energy use from non-fossil-fuel sources displaced less than one-quarter of a unit of fossil-fuel energy use and, focusing specifically on electricity, each unit of electricity generated by non-fossil-fuel sources displaced less than one-tenth of a unit of fossil-fuel-generated electricity." Later, York (2016) further found that increases in total energy and electricity production have occurred in conjunction with carbon intensity reductions from renewable energy. Expanding renewable energy thus does not necessarily displace fossil fuels and could lead to increases in development and energy consumption (Zehner 2012, York and Bell 2019). Thombs (2017) has coined the term "renewable energy paradox" to describe the counterintuitive outcome that renewable energy has little influence on GHG emissions in developed countries, which he attributes to outcomes associated with the treadmill of production. The treadmill of production theory, developed by Schnaiberg (1980), suggests that capitalist economies demand perpetual growth and expansion, which requires ever more production. This production, which never ends, also involves increasing material throughput and concomitant energy demands. Renewable energy development in current social conditions, according to Thombs and supported by York and others, merely creates *additional capacity for production* rather than displacing fossil fuel-based energy consumption. Within current growth-oriented social relations, renewable energy is limited to marginal

GHG emission reductions, with increases in total energy use and GHG emissions in conjunction with increased renewable energy production (Adua et al. 2021).

This evidence suggests that reliance on renewable energy development without social change is insufficient to meet GHG emission reduction targets. Trends and realities raise additional concerns. York (2016) has additionally shown that decarbonizing energy supplies and reducing carbon intensity, including increasing renewable energy capacity, is associated with both higher energy use and electricity production. World energy use is expected to increase by 28% and natural gas consumption by 43% by 2040 (IAE 2017). Renewables are currently dominated by hydropower and, although wind and solar are projected to increase proportionally over this timespan, they will still only account for roughly 10% of total energy production. The increase in overall energy consumption will rely heavily on fossil fuels. Even without the boomerang effect, emission reductions from renewables would be minimal. With the boomerang effect they will remain marginal. Failing to recognize these relationships represents a denial of the limitations of renewables without necessary social changes that reduce overall energy use.

In the next chapter, we will discuss techno-optimism further in terms of the techno-capitalist climate agenda: a future scenario that could emerge as climate impacts increasingly threaten the capitalist economic system and social order. This agenda includes technological "solutions" that involve risky interventions, attempting to reduce or avoid climate impacts while also increasing economic growth and wealth accumulation (for the already wealthy few). While the evidence indicates that faith in technology to solve the climate crisis is misplaced, techno-optimism remains a powerful and comforting narrative, especially for vested interests.

Beyond Ideological Denial

Denialism, and ideological denialism in particular, obscures the root causes of the climate crisis by focusing on solutions that explicitly or implicitly deny the need for social-structural change, thereby contributing to the reproduction of the structural drivers of global warming. Each form of denial outlined above has a distinguishing characteristic in common: they all directly or indirectly focus on, maintain, or support continued economic growth and capital accumulation. These forms in aggregate represent ideological denial, a refusal to diagnose the root causes of climate change and what makes currently proposed solutions ineffective (Petersen et al. 2019). Ideology, manifested through ideas and practices, reproduces social contradictions (Gunderson 2017). These contradictions cannot be overcome through technology, markets, or individual actions alone. The structure of capitalist social relations and hegemony of economic growth have created social norms and worldviews that continue to conceal these contradictions and limit viable climate solutions.

A common thread uniting the strategies that emanate from ideological denialism is an inability to envision alternative social futures, or an alternative to our current economic system. Marcuse (1964) calls this "one-dimensional" thinking, or an outlook that is blind to possibilities latent in present social conditions, with a consequence captured in Murray Bookchin's (1990) statement that the "assumption that what currently exists must necessarily exist is the acid that corrodes all visionary thinking." Many remain trapped in what Fisher (2009) calls "capitalist realism," failing to see that alternative systems are possible. What is required to minimize global warming is to recognize the possibility of and to pursue an alternative system, or what Bonneuil and Fressoz (2017) call "alternative realism." In other words, we need to focus on what other systems are possible, what they might look like, and how they might be achieved.

By negating the ability to visualize social alternatives that would effectively and justly address climate change, ideological denialism is both an outcome of, and reinforcer of one-dimensionality and capitalist realism. Importantly, this denial has kept environmentalists and others who actively want to reduce GHG emissions from promoting effective solutions to the systemic problems causing climate change. This includes policymakers, academics, and everyday citizens who have difficulty visualizing alternatives outside the growth-based capitalist economic order. Rather than merely focusing attention on converting non-believers into climate activists who will fight for renewables, energy efficiency, and market-based strategies while neglecting the need to shift societal priorities in meaningful ways, significant effort is necessary to overcome ideological denial and increase public support for the systemic changes necessary. Only by creating social awareness and solidarity around the need to organize society around wellbeing, instead of economic growth for the sake of growth, can we have any hope for drastically reducing climate change impacts in a just way.

Book Overview: Toward a Climate Agenda for System Change

Things can also be otherwise.

– Ernst Bloch (1968: 274)

This book begins where ideological denial ends. We begin with an understanding that bold system change is necessary and proceed to articulate what a system-changing climate agenda might look like. While many environmentalists remain in denial that system change is necessary, seduced by one or more forms of ideological denial, an increasing number are calling for "system change, not climate change." Yet, at the same time, they often fail to articulate specific demands or pathways to achieve system change. A large gap remains between the complaints and discontent with the current system and any agenda that would result in meaningful change (Stoner and Melathopoulos 2015). As explained by Spash (2020), these "generalized complaints" about the failures of the current system remain unspecific and therefore the agenda of environmental activists remains "disconnected and incomplete." A *system-changing climate agenda* is necessary. This agenda requires overcoming ideological denial and acknowledging that bold systemic change is necessary. It also must go beyond generalized calls for change and demand specific policies, programs, and pathways for social transformation.

Calls for "system change" must get louder, but also *much* more specific – focusing on strategic ways to move away from the economic growth paradigm and capitalist logic that currently undermine all climate mitigation efforts. An understanding of specific structural changes to create a new system remains a crucial, yet missing, element in the climate movement. Like Frase (2011), we are interested in what futures could be birthed from the current order, though we narrow our focus to alternative, nearer-term futures that are explicit positive pathways to address the climate crisis. Through adopting a transformative *theory- and evidence-based agenda*, we believe society already has the ideas and means to justly minimize warming. Climate change is already occurring and will continue to occur, but there is still a chance to minimize the extent of climate impacts and associated loss, suffering, and tragedy. Negative climate impacts are unavoidable, but we can still act boldly to minimize the extent of global warming.

In this book, we draw from theory, ideas, and proposals associated with ecosocialism and degrowth to support an agenda with the potential to bring about systemic change and minimize global warming. This agenda represents a collection of ideas grounded in social theory and also supported by empirical social science research. Crossing over academic and intellectual silos, we draw from diverse scholars and scientists to evaluate this agenda and illustrate how it could specifically be used to minimize warming. This book is largely inspired by the many ecosocialist, degrowth, and other post-capitalist thinkers who have not only identified serious problems with the current system, but who have also worked to identify specific strategies that could aid in a just transition to a more sustainable social order. We will synthesize key proposals, add additional insights, and piece together key evidence supporting specific strategies. We will also go further and discuss possible pathways to achieve social transformation as well as the many challenges that would need to be overcome.

Throughout the book, we also draw inspiration from mid-century Western Marxist thinkers who were deeply concerned about the priorities and trajectories of the dominant system and imagined more rational and sustainable alternatives. Many of these individuals offer insightful critiques of the capitalist social order. However, some also offer more optimistic visions of alternatives and even specific pathways towards a more equitable, just, and sustainable future. We especially focus on insights from Herbert Marcuse and André Gorz, as their work, in particular, includes visions of a better future as well as thinking through specific social changes to achieve this better future. Marcuse and Gorz each collectively reimagined systems of work and production in order to reduce both human repression and negative environmental impacts. Both thinkers' work guides our critique of the technocaplitalist climate agenda as well as our discussions of what a climate agenda for system change might look like. Here, we briefly introduce Marcuse and Gorz as we will refer to their work throughout the book.

Herbert Marcuse was a first-generation member of the Frankfurt School who wrote extensively about production, work, human repression, and the irrationality of the current social order. He is well known for his critique of "one-dimensional thinking" that traps society in instrumental and economic rationality, overlooking the harms and contradictions in the system (Marcuse 1964). This type of thinking limits the realm of the possible and in terms of climate change, places us on a clear trajectory for a highly risky techno-capitalist climate agenda rather than addressing the root causes of the crisis. He also offers clear insights regarding changes to work and production that are needed to alleviate human repression and increase well-being. Marcuse (1964) points out how capitalism has negative impacts on nature, stating that overproduction not only wastes resources but leads to our own destruction. He argues that the capitalist system "has treated Nature as it has treated man—as an instrument of destructive productivity" (Marcuse 1964: 245) and that worker-consumers in this system are unknowingly "working with and for the means of destruction" (Marcuse 1964: 246). While Marcuse acknowledges ecological destruction, Gorz took these ideas further, recognizing the increasing risks of environmental degradation and the gravity of the climate crisis.

André Gorz in many ways represents a continuation of Marcusean thinking, but his work engages more deeply with the idea of ecological limits. He was a radical philosopher and proto-ecosocialist, who is cited as being the first person to use the term degrowth (*décroissance*) (Kallis et al. 2015, Demaria et al. 2019) and also proposed the use of policies representing "non-reformist reforms" (Gorz 1967) to transition society out of capitalism. Gorz was one of the early voices calling for reorganizing the social order to stay within ecological limits, stating that "human activity finds in the natural world its external limits" (Gorz 1980: 13). Thus, systems of work, production, and consumption must be reshaped to fit within these external limits. In an essay first published the year of his death (2007), Gorz (2010) specifically acknowledges the catalyzing power of the climate crisis, stating that "[i]t is impossible to avoid climate catastrophe without a radical break with the economic logic and methods that have been taking us in that direction for 150 years." Later in the essay, Gorz explains that the transition out of capitalism *has already begun* and is now unavoidable, yet whether it will be planned and civil or a tragic disaster is still yet to be determined. A civil transition will require visionary thinking, planning, and solidarity. In addition, it will require well-thought-out policies, grounded in theory and supported by evidence.

This book begins with a necessary discussion of the possible techno-capitalist future that would emerge if the status quo is not significantly altered. This is important to understand as the techno-capitalist agenda involves high-risk strategies not supported by evidence that would leave the majority of humans to face extensive suffering and loss. After painting a picture of a techno-capitalist future in chapter 1, we focus the remainder of the book on identifying and advancing a system-changing climate agenda guided by insights from the ecosocialist and degrowth literatures. While it is key to identify *what* specific strategies and programs would likely be most effective, it is also essential to examine *how* system change to minimize warming might be achieved. All of these discussions are informed by theory, drawing from the Frankfurt School and Western Marxists, and also supported by evidence from a growing number of social scientists who have examined specific strategies, policies, and pathways for social transformation.

Chapter 2 describes ecosocialism, degrowth, and their similarities and differences. We believe that the ideas associated with ecosocialism and degrowth have the greatest potential to guide an effective and just response to the climate crisis. Ecosocialism is a democratic socialism that recognizes natural limits and abandons the vision of socialism as an extension of capitalist productivism. It supports an economy based on the production of *use values* that meet human needs and promote human flourishing within ecological limits (Kovel 2000, Löwy 2007). Degrowth entails reduced material and energy throughput in the economies of wealthy or over-consuming nations to a steady state of sufficiency, while also helping nations in the Global South to more sustainably achieve an improved quality of life (Kallis 2017). Degrowth aims to address the environmental crisis while improving social wellbeing. While the changes required to reduce total material and energy throughput would contract the economy and reduce GDP (Hickel 2019), a well-planned economic contraction with social policies and protections would be very different compared to an economic recession. According to ecosocialist and degrowth thinkers, it is not a matter of *if* the economy will contract but *when*. Only forethought, planning, and social changes initiated now can make this inevitable transition more civil and less brutal.

In chapter 3, we identify a suite of strategies that we believe in concert would represent a powerful agenda of "non-reformist reforms" with the potential to justly minimize global warming and transition to a new socio-economic order. Based on the evidence, this agenda represents a less risky, more just, and more effective path compared to the techno-capitalist climate agenda. We identify a climate agenda with six key strategies: (1) economic democracy, (2) energy democracy/energy cooperatives, (3) work-time reduction, (4) advertising restrictions and sufficiency measures, (5) redistributing wealth, and (6) nationalizing and phasing out fossil fuel companies. We believe the climate movement could greatly benefit from adopting specific demands based on this agenda. While there are clearly stigmatisms and issues associated with using the terms ecosocialism and degrowth, this agenda and the individual strategies outlined can be discussed and promoted without using these terms. What is of increasing importance is to share that alternative strategies, pathways, and systems are possible and worth pursuing.

Chapters 4 and 5 then explore how the adoption of this climate agenda would likely increase the effectiveness of other strategies for social and ecological sustainability. As non-reformist reforms, these strategies would reshape the landscape of what else is possible and achievable. In chapter 4 we examine how in a new social order— catalyzed by a system-changing climate agenda—technologies to mitigate climate change could be used much more effectively to minimize global warming. In a different social context with different goals, technologies along with structural and policy changes have great potential to aid in a civil transition to a low-carbon, post-capitalist future. In chapter 5, we examine how the culture of overconsumption in wealthy countries can be partially addressed through key non-reformist reforms, but also how we must confront the ideology of overconsumption that has become so pervasive. Both structural and ideological transformations are necessary to curb excess consumption trends.

The final chapters of the book focus on a key question that is often overlooked in discussions about system change: what are the actual pathways to bring about the desired change? In other words, how do we actualize a climate agenda for system change? This relates to confronting the forces preserving the status quo and challenging power in the political sphere. In chapter 6, we discuss the role of the climate movement and potential pathways to challenge power and trigger a more rapid adoption of a bold climate agenda. Chapter 7 focuses on a more personal aspect of this question: what can one do to bring about a more sustainable and just future? We examine the struggle to find authentic hope to motivate action in the face of a political-economic system that in many ways renders individuals helpless. Identifying the obstacles hindering system change is necessary to understand how to overcome these obstacles and to pursue the pathways for change that remain or become accessible. In the short concluding chapter, we return to the work of Marcuse and Gorz and discuss how current struggles are critical to forge a pathway for a civil, rather than barbarous, transition out of capitalism. Minimizing global warming requires a transformation from a social order prioritizing economic growth and wealth accumulation to a social order prioritizing ecological and social wellbeing.

A civil pathway to a more sustainable and just future is still possible but faces many challenges. The first remains overcoming denial that system change is necessary. To erode this denial, we not only need to increase calls for system change, but to articulate what system change would entail and what it could look like. Identifying the specific pathways for change is key. As Speth (2015: 25) explains, when events open pathways for system change we must be ready – which "means having those initiatives well-developed and supported by large and active constituencies." We must continue to advance the awareness that alternatives are possible and increase support for specific system-changing strategies. With everything at stake, it is essential to continue to challenge denial and to identify and pursue alternatives for a more livable future.

Chapter 1:
The Techno-Capitalist Climate Agenda

Contemporary positivism… define[s] and filter[s] the universe of discourse for the use of technicians, specialists, and experts who calculate, adjust, and match without ever asking for whom or for what.

– Herbert Marcuse (1989: 122)

The current trajectory of global responses to climate change includes increased investments in renewable energy, energy efficiency, and technological development to mitigate global warming while continuing to increase levels of production and consumption to support a growing economy. However, as we explained in the introduction, there is a clear and widely recognized positive correlation between increasing levels of production and GHG emissions. As currently supported strategies prove ineffective at limiting warming, additional technological "solutions" will very likely be developed, considered, and deployed. Before we focus on the development of an alternative climate agenda based on ecosocialism and degrowth, we must first understand the possible implications and outcomes associated with the current trajectory.

Kellner (2002) uses the term *techno*-capitalism to describe capitalism's increasing reliance on science, computers, automation, and information technology to accumulate capital, thereby increasing growth. We develop this notion of techno-capitalism, focusing on how capitalism increasingly relies on developing and marketing technologies as *solutions* to the contradictions caused by its own internal dynamics – climate change, for example. These technological solutions must fit within the constraints of the capitalist system and promote, or at least not hinder, economic growth. Promoting technological solutions to problems caused by *social* forces remains a social reproduction strategy consistent with capitalist realism. A techno-capitalist system, in terms of the climate crisis, maintains the goals of production for the sake of economic growth and wealth accumulation and attempts to use technology to reduce the impacts of climate change. It aims to address climate change—or at least to pretend to address climate change—while keeping the production/consumption engine running at full steam.

As warming continues, the techno-capitalist climate agenda will include additional technological responses, likely geoengineering and even space colonization. These strategies represent an extension of the current capitalist system and, in lieu of social transformation, a suite of technological "silver bullets" to attempt to address, or literally escape, the climate crisis. Already we see a rise in proposed techno-fixes to the climate crisis, and some dangerous trajectories have emerged. Geoengineering strategies are being taken seriously, with the IPCC holding an "Expert Meeting on Geoengineering" in 2011 and IPCC reports increasingly discussing geoengineering for climate change mitigation (IPCC 2012, 2014, 2018). Geoengineering includes both *carbon geoengineering*, most often referring to "carbon dioxide removal" that aims to sequester atmospheric carbon dioxide, and *solar geoengineering* or "solar radiation management" that aims to deflect solar radiation to reduce global temperatures. Both forms of geoengineering are receiving increased attention and funding for development. In addition, space colonization research is being funded and developed with clear intentions to create (elite) human settlements when Earth becomes inhospitable due to climate change and escalating ecological degradation.

Carbon geoengineering is now considered essential in limiting warming due to increasing levels of GHG emissions. The effectiveness of geoengineering strategies in mitigation depends on negative emissions technologies (NETs) – strategies that result in the net movement of carbon from the atmosphere into the Earth's surface. However, many carbon geoengineering strategies being promoted as climate solutions fail to result in negative emissions. Others have yet to be proven effective or viable at the scale necessary. Yet this has not stopped investment, development, and the promotion of carbon geoengineering strategies – touted as "win-win" solutions for business and the environment. Some carbon geoengineering strategies are supported by fossil fuel companies, as they also represent a means to rationalize or justify continued fossil fuels use.

Increasing attention is being given to solar geoengineering strategies that aim to reflect solar radiation away from Earth, yet could cause famine in the Global South, among other serious risks. Stratospheric Aerosol Injection (SAI) has received the most attention, promoted as a way to create a dimmed and cooler Earth. This strategy is supported by those who see systemic change through political action as unrealistic or unlikely and, thus promote SAI as a back-up plan. It is also supported by those who wish to master and dominate nature, maintain the status quo, and/or stave off any transformative social-structural changes that might be proposed in response to the climate crisis. Increasingly, SAI and related technologies have become part of Plan A for techno-capitalists, who prioritize technological rationality and profit-maximization over addressing the root drivers of the climate crisis.

In addition, space colonization is supported by powerful billionaires as an exciting next step for humans – one that could provide a new place to live when Earth becomes inhospitable. Colonizing space to avoid a future catastrophe that social systems are still causing (and *can* still be reorganized to reduce or minimize) represents one of the many irrational aspects of space colonization, given that it is also more expensive, riskier, and exclusionary – only some people would likely be able to join the new colonies. A concerted effort to rapidly reduce GHG emissions on Earth is a much more just and effective approach if the goal is saving humans and other forms of life. Thus, additional reasons to colonize space emerge including conquest and control, the possibility of off-planet profits, and, once again, vested interests in protecting the current system.

In this chapter, we first discuss relevant insights from Marcuse that serve to contextualize the techno-capitalist climate agenda. These patterns of using science and technology to maintain the status quo and master nature, rather than liberate humanity and bring it into a sustainable relationship with nature, are not new and were discussed in depth by Marcuse. A focus on the means of techno-scientific achievement often overshadows any concern for consequences and can be used to reinforce current power dynamics and social relations. In addition, these trends make the techno-capitalist climate agenda appear neutral, rational, and even inevitable, as the only path forward, obscuring the possibility of alternatives that would have more just and sustainable outcomes. The bulk of this chapter examines geoengineering and space colonization in this context – as specific techno-scientific solutions used to maintain current power relations and the status quo. We focus on geoengineering and space colonization because both proposals represent the extreme yet conceivable lengths that the techno-capitalist climate agenda may go to sustain business as usual despite social alternatives with far fewer risks. Although the strategies discussed below may seem farfetched, they are actively researched and promoted, and some of the technologies have already been developed and applied. Exploring the risks associated with techno-capitalist strategies reveals a pathway that would economically benefit the already powerful few, while leaving the majority of the global population to face increased harm, suffering, and loss.

Science, Technology, and Social Reproduction

Marcuse (1964) offers a nuanced perspective on technology that is neither technophobic nor Promethean. In his view, technology is mediated by society and vice versa. Technology is neither inherently good or bad, but outcomes depend on the purpose of development and use. Domination and mastery (of nature and humans) have shaped much of technological development and use. Specific technical achievements can reinforce or alter the ways in which domination takes place. Marcuse also points out how technological rationality tends to focus on *means* rather than *ends*. In other words, it is more focused on questions of how technological endeavors can be achieved rather than the outcomes and consequences of technological use. In this way, the techno-scientific project is often centered around desires for scientific achievements and progress without considering what can sometimes be destructive outcomes (cf. Horkheimer 1947). The inability of reason to justify the ends of action leads to a number of interrelated contradictions, including the inversion of means and ends and the undermining of the organizing aim of instrumental reason: species survival. The inversion of means and ends is a byproduct of a society in which capital and technology dominate the lives of humans. Despite massive gains in productivity and the fact that we have the technical capacity to meet all basic survival needs today, the vast majority of humans are living to survive rather than surviving to live because capitalist relations of production continue to be structured around the profit motive.

Of particular relevance is Marcuse's work linking the use and development of technology to ruling interests and the maintenance of the current social order which supports those interests. Science and technology are not independent, autonomous forces, but are organized in societies to serve the dominant interests and the interest of capital. "Technology is always a historical-social project," Marcuse (1968: 223-24) claims, and "in it is projected what a society and its ruling interests intend to do with men and things." Marcuse argues that technical achievements can be used to support giant industries benefiting from the status quo and prevent actions that could usher in a qualitatively different society – one that may improve social and ecological wellbeing. In other words, specific technologies are developed, promoted, and utilized because they preserve the existing system in ways that benefit powerful actors.

Most perniciously, these forces act to diminish and undermine alternatives that may have more just and sustainable outcomes. The inability to contrast what is possible with what is actual and to, instead, accept the actual as necessary or the best of all possible worlds—what Marcuse (1964) calls "one-dimensional thinking"—continues today. This relates to capitalist realism (Fisher 2009: 2), which creates a narrow mindset where it is "impossible even to *imagine* a coherent alternative." Captured by capitalist realism, there seems to be no real alternative to the current social order: "[c]apitalism seamlessly occupies the horizons of the thinkable" (Fisher 2009: 9). On the one hand, capitalist realism assumes that any environmental problem can be solved within the bounds of capitalist processes (e.g., new techno-fixes without simultaneous social changes) and always assumes that resources are infinite. On the other hand, the real prospects and consequences of environmental catastrophe for capitalism are "too traumatic to be assimilated into the system" (Fisher 2009: 18) precisely because environmental problems like climate change are endemic to the basic processes of capitalism, namely its need for constant growth (see also Foster et al. 2010; Stuart et al. 2020).

Here we examine how the techno-capitalist climate agenda focuses on the use of science and technology as a means to maintain the current growth-oriented economy, to protect and advance fossil fuel interests and others vested in the capitalist system, and to diminish or extinguish any efforts to recreate the social order – even if it would more effectively and justly minimize global warming. Focusing attention on *how* to further master nature (geoengineering) and dominate new places (colonization of space), overlooks the extensive risks involved and the injustices associated with these solution pathways when compared to alternatives. The techno-capitalist climate agenda is seductive because it promises to offer techno-fixes that further human "progress," yet as we will illustrate, evidence indicates that many of these promises are misleading or false and serve to benefit powerful interests while putting the vast majority of people as well as the planet at great risk.

Carbon Geoengineering: Imaginary Negative Emissions and Increased Profits

Carbon geoengineering, in contrast to solar geoengineering (discussed below), comprises negative emission technologies and interventions that directly remove carbon dioxide from the atmosphere. Included in the majority of integrated assessment models used to guide climate policy and international agreements, carbon geoengineering has taken on greater importance in climate change discussions. However, as we will illustrate, most of these strategies do not result in negative emissions as promoted. Therefore, without evidence that these strategies can effectively remove carbon on a wide-scale, carbon geoengineering remains a risky techno-optimist gamble. Assuming that carbon removal will play a significant role in addressing climate change is a key component of the techno-capitalist climate agenda, as it justifies maintaining the current fossil fuel-based capitalist system grounded on an assumption that we will later be able to use technology to remove enough carbon to avoid catastrophic warming.

Many strategies are associated with carbon geoengineering, but they vary greatly in their approach, aims, and results. Like others (e.g., Robock 2008, Matthews 2010), we include carbon capture and storage (CCS) as a geoengineering strategy, though some argue that it is more accurately defined as a mitigation strategy (e.g., Vaughan and Lenton 2011). Post-combustion CCS is a widely discussed and promoted strategy, yet it is not a NET. It refers to capturing CO_2 at sources of fossil fuel combustion, such as coal or gas-fired power plants (Pires et al. 2011, Leung et al. 2014, Wennersten et al. 2015, de

Coninck and Benson 2014). Post-combustion CCS can theoretically result in carbon neutrality for fossil fuel-based power plants. However, recent evidence suggests CCS remains "net-additive" (Sekera and Lichtenberger 2020).

Despite the potential for carbon neutral energy production, very few post-combustion CCS examples exist. Scientists and engineers have been developing post-combustion CCS technology since the 1950s (Keith et al. 2018); however, it was not until the late 1990s and early 2000s that industrial scale post-combustion CCS projects began to emerge (de Coninck and Benson 2014). To date only a handful of demonstration projects exist and after decades of research have yet to show that these projects are economically viable: they cost approximately $1 billion and, without carbon pricing or technology mandates, both private and government investment has remained minimal (Reiner 2016). While post-combustion CCS could be designed to create carbon neutral power plants with direct storage, development of this strategy has largely stagnated (National Academy 2018). This is primarily due to the remaining challenges to commercial use involving high energy consumption and high operating and capital costs, yet scientists continue to explore alternatives to address these challenges (Otitoju et al. 2021).

Even more misleading is the promotion of CO_2 enhanced oil recovery (CO_2-EOR) as a technological solution to climate change. CO_2-EOR involves injecting CO_2 into near-depleted oil and gas reserves in order to extract otherwise unrecoverable reserves (Leung et al. 2014). It has been used for decades in the oil and gas industry. CO_2-EOR continues to be promoted as part of the solutions portfolio to address climate change (Biello 2009, IEA 2015). The "net" carbon storage referred to by proponents of CO_2-EOR is defined within the boundaries of the stand-alone EOR project and fails to consider the CO_2 emitted from the combustion of the oil recovered (Jaramillo et al. 2009). With related GHG emissions from life-cycle assessment, EOR projects at best remain a strategy to reduce emissions but are not NETs (Mavar et al. 2021). As explained by Farajzadeh et al. (2020): "From a thermodynamics point of view, CO_2 enhanced oil recovery (EOR) with CCS option is not sustainable, i.e., during the life cycle of the process more energy is consumed than the energy produced from oil."

Despite this evidence, CO_2-EOR continues to be promoted as an effective and profitable CCS solution. For example, the profitability of CO_2-EOR was highlighted by the International Energy Agency (2015) in their report titled *Storing CO2 through Enhanced Oil Recovery: Combining EOR with CO2 Storage for Profit*, stating that, "[n]ovel ways of conducting CO_2-EOR could help achieve a win-win solution for business and for climate change mitigation goals." They encourage "co-exploiting the storage of CO_2 with oil extraction to generate more profits." These arguments fail to consider the total increase in GHG emissions from the fossil fuels extracted through EOR. EOR is not an NET (Tanzer and Ramiere 2019), and its misleading promotion as a climate change "solution" is being used strategically to support the continued extraction of fossil fuels.

Bioenergy with CCS (BECCS) is the strategy most widely incorporated into current integrated assessment models used to guide climate policy and international climate agreements. The National Academy (2018) explains that the inclusion of BECCS rather than other strategies in integrated assessment models is a result of BECCS's potential affordability and that models for other removal technologies remain undeveloped. As described by Fridahl and Lehtveer (2018), BECCS involves carbon being sequestered in plants (trees, shrubs, grasses) that are then harvested and burned for power generation, while capturing and storing the carbon emissions from combustion. BECCS has the potential to result in negative carbon emissions (Pour et al. 2017), however, it remains primarily theoretical as the technology has not been deployed at scale – only partially or experimentally.

Analyses of BECCS illustrate that it may not be as effective as hoped and there are many challenges involved with widespread deployment. Finding suitable land, storage basins, and biomass availability limits potential negative emissions, as well as issues related to the transportation of biomass and CO_2 and social and political barriers (Baik et al. 2018, Fridahl and Lehtveer 2018, Turner et al. 2018). Plants or crops grown for energy also could compete with food crops for available agricultural lands (National Academy 2018) and modelling indicates that BEECS is likely to result in negative consequences for the environment (Fajardy et al. 2018). To date, there has been no "at scale" implementation of BECCS, and it remains an "effective" strategy only in theory. Based on their analysis, Fajardy et al. (2019: 10) find that BECCS "cannot deliver the scale or negative emissions required in current emissions projections" and can be expected to offer only limited contributions to meeting climate change targets. Given the evidence, the reliance of BECCS in emissions scenarios and policy formulation is highly risky and diverts attention away from other mitigation strategies. A blind reliance on BECCS as a future NET can be used as yet another justification to continue to use fossil fuels.

Direct air capture (DAC) and storage has been called the only high-tech carbon geoengineering strategy that could be truly carbon negative (Siegel 2018). It has substantial negative emissions potential. However, it requires a significant amount of energy: one estimate states that DAC requires 0.3 megawatt-hours per metric ton of captured CO_2, roughly equivalent to 35% of the total output of a typical power plant (Senftle and Carter 2017). Total negative emissions, therefore, depends on the source of energy used. As explained by the National Academy of Sciences (2018), DAC remains energy intensive, even if using renewable sources: one study found that DAC would require up to one quarter of global energy supplies (Realmonte et al. 2019). Stone (2018) explains that DAC may have the most potential for negative emissions, but it remains largely undeveloped due to higher costs and no profitable product for sale. Therefore, the companies that have created DAC facilities (including Carbon Engineering, Climeworks, Global Thermostat, Infinitree, and Skytree) have focused on converting CO_2 into a usable product for sale, or direct air capture and utilization (National Academy 2018, Siegel 2018).

Direct air capture and utilization (DACU) turns the captured carbon into a usable product. The degree of carbon sequestration depends on what kind of product is produced. Products are only carbon-negative if atmospheric CO_2 is used to make a solid material for long-term storage. Otherwise, products in the form of chemicals or fuels offer only temporary storage and are therefore carbon neutral (Bui et al. 2018). However, due to the higher costs associated with conversion into a solid (Keith et al. 2018), most DACU projects involve turning CO_2 into a short-lived liquid product. The most developed use is turning CO_2 into fuel products, reusing carbon to substitute for extracted fossil fuels (Bruhn et al. 2016). Start-up firm Carbon Engineering has been working on a "low-cost" method to turn CO_2 into usable fuels or "carbon-neutral hydrocarbons" (Keith et al. 2018; Meyer 2018). As stated by Bui et al. (2018), in the current political and economic system, DAC is not a rational investment and therefore remains limited to producing a product and carbon neutrality, rather than representing a NET.

Propagating the belief that carbon geoengineering strategies can be successful and widely deployed NETs reduces motivation for rapid emissions reduction and increases potential climate risks (Markusson et al. 2018). In addition, there are potentially negative environmental and political impacts of carbon geoengineering related to storage, land use, and food production (e.g., de Coninck and Benson 2014, Carrington 2018, National Academy 2018), as well as the continuation of fossil fuel-based electricity generation, with all its direct and indirect consequences. Relying on future NETs also remains highly risky: a report from the European Academies' Science Advisory Council warns that policy depending on NETs instead of cutting emissions could fail and result in severe warming (Carrington 2018). The clearest potential economic benefit of carbon geoengineering for the fossil fuel industry is that it "provides a vision" of a "carbon-constrained future" that still allows for fossil fuel use (Stephens 2009: 36).

While carbon geoengineering remains an unreliable "solution" to climate change, what we do know is that promoting these strategies allows companies and governments with fossil fuel resources to continue to reap profits and accumulate wealth (Kruger 2017). Therefore, some forms of carbon geoengineering are supported by governments and fossil fuel companies. Recent studies show increasing financial support from fossil fuel companies for CCS projects (Chalmin 2021). As a key part of the techno-capitalist climate agenda, companies are already profiting from carbon geoengineering projects. In addition, CCS in particular is falsely promoted as a solution and used by the fossil fuel industry to justify status quo maintenance: the application or anticipated application of a technology to reproduce fundamental processes and social structures – or *social reproduction*. Fossil fuel companies explicitly state that CCS can be used as a way to expand or maintain their business and associated profits (Gunderson et al. 2020). Thus, propagating faith in carbon geoengineering strategies represents a defensive maneuver used by those vested in fossil fuels as well as those who stand to financially benefit from the techno-capitalist climate agenda through other means. While narratives of being able to keep burning fossil fuels now and remove GHG emissions from the atmosphere later appeals to many people as an easy solution, evidence does not support that this is a realistic scenario. Thus, beliefs that these approaches can effectively address the climate crisis are shortsighted and extremely risky.

Solar Geoengineering: "Plan A" for Techno-Capitalists

As stated by Surprise (2020), "solar geoengineering is not a futuristic 'plan B,' but a rapidly developing pillar of capital's climate 'plan A.'" While once on the fringe of the climate change discussion, solar geoengineering is receiving increasing funding and much more serious attention as a viable option to the worsening climate crisis. The US National Academy of Sciences released a report in March 2021 in support of federal funding to advance geoengineering research, along with new plans for outdoor experiments from

Harvard University's Bill Gates-supported Solar Geoengineering Research Program (Biermann et al. 2021). Not only is solar geoengineering associated with catastrophic risks and possibly unjust consequences, it also reinforces a system of concentrated wealth and power, perpetuating power imbalances and associated global injustices (Stephens and Surprise 2020).

Solar geoengineering is most often discussed in the context of stratospheric aerosol injection (SAI), generally, or stratospheric sulphate injection (SSI), using sulphur specifically (Markusson et al. 2014, Horton 2015, Sillmann et al. 2015, Fragnière & Gardiner 2016). This geoengineering strategy was first put forth by Crutzen (2006) based on evidence from volcanic eruptions. Volcanic eruptions have provided a way to assess the effect that sulphur particles in the atmosphere have on incoming solar radiation and global temperature. The Mt. Pinatubo eruption in 1991 led to dimming that cooled the earth by 0.5°C for a year (Robock et al., 2010). Injecting sulphur particles (sulphur dioxide, hydrogen sulphide, sulphuric acid) into the stratosphere represents an attempt to emulate this process. Aerosols can be put into the stratosphere by release from planes, balloons, or ground canons. For example, one estimate would use "95 aircrafts flying 41 flights per day (60,109 flights per year) from four 'bases' to deliver 1.5 million tons of sulphur" (Stephens and Surprise 2020). Once in the atmosphere the particles combine with dust and water, creating aerosols that increase atmospheric albedo. Aerosols would likely last for about one year; therefore, this strategy requires continued sulphate deposition (Keith 2013).

Scientists have long warned of likely and possible risks associated with an SAI strategy. It remains unclear how SAI may affect weather patterns, especially precipitation and therefore ecological and agricultural systems (Robock 2008). Pumping aerosols into the stratosphere may result in drought in South America, Asia, and Africa (Ferraro et al. 2014). As stated by a leading geoengineering scientist (Keith 2013: 58): "used recklessly, geoengineering could threaten billions with starvation." Others have highlighted how aerosols do nothing to address ocean acidification and could exacerbate the ozone hole problem, increase acid rain and air pollution, have unknown impacts on plants and clouds, and reduce radiation for solar power –in addition to risks associated with human error, commercial control, military use, and many other possible risks (see Robock 2008, Robock et al. 2009, Boucher et al. 2013, Ciais et al. 2013).

Perhaps the most significant risk associated with SAI relates to continued GHG emissions during SAI activities and the likely consequences of a future cessation of these activities, known as the "termination effect." SAI could reduce incoming solar radiation and global temperatures, allowing for continued GHG emissions. If the intervention works initially but falters or if the project cannot be maintained, temperatures could increase rapidly due to a build-up of background GHG emissions (Robock et al. 2010). One modelling study found that implementing SIA for 25 years and then stopping aerosol deposition could rapidly increase temperatures by 4°C, with severe impacts to agriculture and biodiversity (McCusker et al. 2014).

Despite the risks, SAI has been discussed and framed for decades as a necessary "Plan B" to employ if mitigation efforts focused on emissions reduction failed. In its simplest form, the Plan B frame presents geoengineering as a backup plan to address climate change in case there is a failure to sufficiently reduce GHG emissions (Plan A). The frame can be thought about as part of a larger family of "insurance" frames of geoengineering ("last resort," "backup plan," etc.) (Fragnière & Gardiner 2016). Two other geoengineering frames are regularly used along with the Plan B frame: the "emergency measure" and "need for research" frames (Harnisch et al. 2015). The "emergency measure" or "argument by emergency" frame (Nerlich & Jaspal 2012) calls for geoengineering as Plan B because there may be a climatic emergency if Plan A fails (e.g., Crutzen 2006). The prescription either implicit or explicit in the Plan B and emergency measure frames is a call for research on geoengineering now in preparation for the climatic emergency if Plan A fails, or even to "arm the future" to tackle climate change when Plan A fails (Gardiner 2011). Although SAI research is promoted through diverse frames—even as a way to provide humanitarian relief to the world's poorest in the Global South (Horton and Keith 2016)—the most common "story line" for SAI runs as follows: "although risky (as mitigation is likely to fail to prevent dangerous climate change), CE [climate engineering] could be needed to prevent a climate emergency, and that research into the risks and benefits of CE is needed *now* to allow informed decisions about deployment if a climate emergency situation arises" (Harnisch et al. 2015: 61-62). This narrative is "condensed" in the Plan B frame. While the Plan B frame continues to be used to support research, this research is already underway and as GHG emissions continue to rise, SAI is shifting from Plan B to a key part of Plan A (Surprise 2020).

In our previous analysis of SAI, we identified several other primary rationales for pursuing SAI rather than less risky alternatives to address global warming (Gunderson et al. 2018, Gunderson et al. 2019). Corresponding with previously mentioned insights from Marcuse, we find that SAI allows for three objectives of the techno-capitalist agenda to be pursued simultaneously: (1) the further domination and conquest of nature, (2) a status quo maintenance strategy – reinforcing and furthering power and wealth inequalities, and (3) using irrational techno-rationality to suppress and thwart alternatives that might challenge power dynamics and support a less warm and more just future.

Focusing on domination, conquest, and scientific achievement, many in support of SAI focus more on *how* it can be achieved than the possible risks, let alone less risky alternatives. Although David Keith (2013: 173-174) is aware of the risks, he states: "We may use these powers for good or ill, but it is hard not to delight in these newfound tools." The development of geoengineering technology represents the advancement of scientific achievement and progress. Those promoting and funding geoengineering are often techno-optimists who believe that humanity can invent its way out of all problems. Keith (2013) also argues that humans have a long history of successfully using techno-fixes to address problems and suggests SAI is the next big techno-fix. Bill Gates is the world's leading financial supporter of geoengineering innovations and is known for viewing climate change as a technical problem that can be fixed through innovation. Gates donates to Harvard's Solar Geoengineering Research Program and has invested in geoengineering technology companies. Companies including Silver Lining, Carbon Engineering Ltd, and Intellectu all have Gates' name on at least one geoengineering patent. Gates has dismissed or belittled approaches relying on renewable energy, calling these strategies "cute" with solar power being the "cutest" (quoted in Romm 2010), and supports efforts to discover technological breakthroughs that will transform our relationship with the climate (Romm 2011). For Gates and other techno-optimists, society can address climate change simply through identifying the appropriate high-tech fixes. Scientists and entrepreneurs are also discussing moving beyond geoengineering as a way to address climate change, exploring how to use geoengineering technology to tailor the climate and create the desired and optimal climatic conditions (Hamilton 2013).

SAI as a status-quo maintenance strategy becomes clear if one investigates who supports SAI, its funding, and future development and possible deployment. As Hamilton (2013) revealed almost a decade ago, some geoengineering supporters have ties to the oil and gas industry, including Royal Dutch Shell, British Petroleum, and Exxon Mobil. The Geoengineering Monitor (2021) has highlighted that ExxonMobil, for example, has a senior scientific advisor who focuses on geoengineering. They have much to lose if world leaders decide to aggressively reduce GHG emissions. This explains their participation in campaigns to counter climate science and deny that climate change is occurring (McCright and Dunlap 2011). Geoengineering represents an approach to address climate change while continuing fossil fuel extraction and consumption. Geoengineering may buy these companies time to extract the remaining accessible fossil fuel resources (especially new sources in the arctic) and maximize profits from this extraction. At the very least, geoengineering discussions could further delay emissions reductions approaches. SAI allows unfettered capitalism to continue potentially indefinitely. Modifying human behaviour could address climate change but the policy intervention necessary to support these changes threatens free market ideology, a core conservative belief (Klein 2011). Keith (2013: 143) asks in his book: "Must we fix capitalism in order to fix the climate?" While he does not see a direct connection between capitalism and environmental degradation, others have answered this question with a resounding "yes." GHG reduction would require significant political and economic changes, changes that remain very undesirable to vested interests.

Finally, SAI undermines the possibility of other more transformative responses to mitigate climate change. The "moral hazard" argument is a common case against geoengineering research, which runs as follows: "major efforts in geoengineering may lead to a reduction of effort in mitigation and/or adaptation because of a premature conviction that geoengineering has provided 'insurance' against climate change" (Royal Society, 2009, p. 39). Because society is "insured" by geoengineering research and that the hazards associated with climate change may be reduced by geoengineering, societies are (1) less likely to implement emissions reduction strategies, (2) invest fewer resources in adaptation strategies (Royal Society 2009: 44-45), and/or (3) increase GHG emissions above business-as-usual projections (Hale, 2012). A critical theoretical position casts the moral hazard argument in a different light: because the purpose of SAI is to reproduce the current social order, it redirects attention from alternative social futures that have the potential to reduce emissions. The same background conditions and form of rationality that caused climate change are the same that make SAI a viable option: prioritizing a growth-dependent and resource intensive economy that serves powerful interests. Indeed, the primary geoengineering proponents frame the problem so as to not engage with the social dimension. Harvard's Solar Geoengineering Research Program (n.d) states on its website: "Carbon geoengineering seeks to remove carbon dioxide from the atmosphere, which would address the root cause of climate change – the accumulation of carbon dioxide in the atmosphere." But as we argue above, this misdiagnoses the root cause as a merely technical issue rather than an outcome of a social system. This subtle, yet profound, change in framing dramatically shifts how climate change is perceived and, thus, how society seeks solutions to address it.

Alternatively, the social-structural changes required to minimize warming would be much less risky and more effective. Powerful interests continue to successfully undermine these alternatives, proposing options such as SAI instead. Indeed, what sense would it make to inject millions of tons of sulphate aerosols into the stratosphere in a society capable of casting off growth-dependence, organizing production to meet needs, and interacting with the biophysical world in non-destructive ways? SAI attempts to treat the symptoms of climate change, while leaving the root driver in place. Marcuse would view SAI as an inept—and, of course, highly risky—means to solve problems through the same instrumentality that helped cause them.

Despite increased funding, support for funding, and ongoing research, solar engineering projects continues to face opposition. In June of 2021, Scandinavian indigenous groups challenged and deterred Harvard's research group and the Swedish Space Corporations' plans to test solar geoengineering technology in Sweden. In addition, in an open letter, Frank Biermann and 18 other scientists criticized increasing support for SAI research and proposed an International Non-Use Agreement on Solar Geoengineering (Biermann et al. 2022). The authors' main arguments focus on how solar geoengineering at a global level is not governable in a just and inclusive way and that recent normalization of these strategies is dangerous as the risks and efficacy are poorly understood, based on models, and are therefore impossible to know.

Both solar and carbon geoengineering strategies allow climate change deniers a means to paradoxically refute the reality of the seriousness of climate change while also embracing a response to the climate crisis. By supporting geoengineering, techno-capitalists may be able to protect free market capitalism while still appearing to be addressing the increasingly visible impacts of climate change. Thus, certain conservative groups began simultaneously denying climate change and supporting geoengineering. As explained by Kintisch (2010), geoengineering offers a strategic middle ground for climate change deniers to finally agree that the world is getting hotter but to continue to argue that this is not caused by humans, or more importantly, fossil fuels. To counter warming they can propose a low–cost geoengineering strategy while at the same time dismiss critics for opposing what they claim will be a quick and effective solution. As Stephens and Surprise (2020) explain, those who benefit most from the current fossil fuel-based capitalist system are deeply threatened by prospects of radical change to reduce emissions, thus geoengineering approaches are attractive to not only preserve and reinforce current wealth and power dynamics but also because they offer an opportunity to increase profits and further power imbalances.

Space Colonization: Furthering the Reach of Capital

Lastly, we examine techno-capitalist support for, and increasing steps being taken toward, space colonization. While the idea of space colonization may seem in the realm of science fiction to some people, others believe that a trajectory for space colonization has already begun and that colonies on Mars, the Moon, or on giant space stations are an inevitable part of the future. There are multiple proposals being seriously considered, invested in, and developed for space colonization, including ones led by billionaires Elon Musk and Jeff Bezos.

Elon Musk and his company SpaceX aim to make humans a multiplanetary species (SpaceX 2020). Musk envisions starships carrying cargo to Mars in up to 1000 trips per year. These starships could carry around 100,000 people every 26 months when the Earth and Mars are best aligned for the 6-month journey. The vision is a Martian city with over a million people. Musk describes abundant jobs, solar powered hydroponic farms, direct democracy, and fewer laws. The self-sustaining city will be covered by a glass dome so people can walk around without a space suit to enjoy its "outdoorsy, fun atmosphere." SpaceX had planned to send an unmanned rocket to Mars with cargo by 2022, but various factors precluded that goal. More recently, Musk has set a 2029 goal to send a crew to Mars (Torchinsky 2022). Musk has stated that by 2050, he will send a million people to Mars (Locke 2020). Musk has also stated that such colonies will be necessary to save the seeds of human civilization in the face of "another dark age" or planetary apocalypse (Carson 2018).

Amazon CEO Jeff Bezos is also moving forward plans for space colonization with his company, Blue Origin. Bezos imagines multiple space colonies orbiting Earth holding over a trillion people. As described by Foer (2019), the space stations would be colonized with soil and biodiversity from Earth, allowing up to trillions of people to live in flourishing societies. Blue Origin plans to first land on the moon, bring in cargo loads, and create a lunar settlement to extract resources. In addition to fulfilling a life-long dream, creating space colonies for Bezos represents a way to address humanity's growing energy and resource demands. Bezos has stated that if we have to stop growing, "that will be a very bad future," and that "[w]e have to go to Space to save Earth" (quoted in Foer 2019).

Space colonization as a means to avoid species extinction from catastrophe on Earth is not a new concept. This notion follows what Abney (2019) calls the "interstellar doomsday argument": if something is going to destroy Earth, we must move off-planet. Thus, engaging in space colonization represents a morally obligatory risk mitigation strategy: not putting all your eggs (humans) in one basket (Earth). Both quotes from Musk and Bezos indicate that the interstellar doomsday argument is likely one of their motivations, or least one of their stated reasons, for pursuing space colonization. Musk, Bezos, and others continue to work towards space colonization. Both of their companies, Blue Origin and SpaceX, received government contracts in 2020 to work on lunar landers for a 2024 mission to the Moon (Scheetz 2020).

It is unlikely that the sole motivation of those promoting space colonization is saving a portion of the human race from catastrophe. Space colonization is also seen as a tremendous human achievement. As Bas Londrom has states, "[i]f humanity can send humans to Mars, is there anything we cannot do?" (MarsforMany.com, cited in Stoner 2017). Elon Musk explains that staying on Earth is not a "bright future" and that "the thing that is super important in the grand scale of history is, are we on a path to becoming a multi-planet species or not?" (Marino 2019: 15). With current space projects, we also see motivations that include "gaining political and economic leadership" (Schwarz 2019: 56). Firms are already competing to see who will receive government contracts and who will be the first to take key steps toward building a space colony. DeVito (2019:54) explains that one force pushing space colonization is "the egos of some people." Others believe that through space colonization humans will "make the universe a better place" (Green 2019: 37). Yet, how can we make the universe a better place when we cannot address the problems here on Earth?

Digging even deeper into the rationale for space colonization we find that it represents an irrational response to the climate crisis and a byproduct of capitalism's need to expand. We previously highlighted (Gunderson et al. 2021) the following three arguments:

(1)   That alternatives to Earth are obviously far more inhospitable for human life than Earth and, thus, preserving Earth is more instrumentally rational.

(2)   If the goal of space colonization is to preserve the human species, then it is more instrumentally rational to save many more lives on Earth than create space colonies for a small population who can afford the ticket; and, most importantly.

(3)   There is reason to predict that humans would take an irrational rational logic with them to space, the same rationality that oversaw the destruction of Earth and brought them to space in the first place.

Supporting the first reason, Stoner (2017) explains (specific to a colony on Mars) that the same risks as well as new risks make the colony very dangerous and protective measures would be immensely expensive in a cost-benefit analysis. In other words, it is not rational in economic terms or in terms of protecting people from harm:

> If the goal is species survival, and given that the Martian environment is much less survivable than even a post-strike Earth would be, then there is no remotely realistic budget point at which the marginal dollar would be more effectively spent on Mars colonization than on protecting Earth and the creatures and civilizations that evolved to live within its shelters.

Second, only a portion of Earth's population would be able to escape Earth and live in space as it seems unlikely that all would be invited or able to go. As depicted in Adam McKay's 2021 movie, *Don't Look Up*, a possible scenario is economic elites leaving behind the vast majority of humans on an inhospitable Earth. Billings (2019: 45) wonders,

> how many poverty-stricken Bangladeshis, how many sub-Saharan Africans, how many permanently displaced Syrian refugees, how many disabled and unemployable workers could come up with $200,000—or $2,000,000 for that matter—to move to another planet and start a new life. What are the ethics

of giving the rich yet another advantage over the poor? What are the ethics of ignoring the need to check the rapid pace of climate change on our own planet?

As Kovic (2021: 6) states, "[g]iven these acute problems, pursuing space colonization today could be a misguided use of limited resources." He poses the following questions: If the goal is to save as many lives as possible and to maximize overall wellbeing, then why focus on an alternative that only benefits a very small group, while the vast majority struggle to survive or perish? Given the rate of climate change, how much time is there to develop this technology and transport all people and enough other organisms off-planet? If the goal is species survival, the time and resources could be spent in more effective ways to benefit *all* people and species.

Lastly, if humans colonize space with techno-capitalist rationality and goals, these colonists are very likely to find themselves in a very similar situation in time. As Marino (2019: 15) explains (emphasis added),

> [i]n Musk's view we need a back-up planet. But he doesn't acknowledge that we ourselves are the cause of this dire situation. And therein lies the problem and the reason we, as a species, have no business trying to colonize another planet. Musk's reason for wanting to colonize Mars is to *save ourselves from ourselves* and it is self-evident that this alone recommends *we should not be going anywhere.*

There is no reason to assume that societies that colonize space will adopt a new social order that prioritizes wellbeing over profits and increases their chances of survival. There is no indication that any new civilizations in space would ultimately result in better outcomes, when the same system and drivers continue to dominate the social order.

Not only could a space colony unintentionally recreate the same social conditions that lead to its formation, but there is evidence that this may be precisely why space colonies would be formed in the first place. For example, Jeff Bezos envisions the Moon as the future "manufacturing sector of the universe" (Liberto 2019). Or take the case of keeping a Martian colony warm: fossil fuels extracted on Earth could be burned in space transport and at colony sites, increasing fossil fuel profits. Relatedly, there are plans to mine Mars and the Moon for minerals to increase wealth accumulation (Dello-Iacovo and Saydam 2022). In addition, the companies working on space colonization projects are private companies with "pecuniary reasons" for their projects beyond saving (some of) humanity (Kovic 2021: 5).

The case for space colonization is a social-reproduction strategy in the sense that, if successful, it could maintain the current system and even allow those profiting from the current system to continue to benefit as Earth faces increasing threats. It also detracts attention from social alternatives that have the potential to actually address the ecological crisis. Like other "false solutions" to climate change that deter attention and resources from the need for systemic change to reduce emissions (Stuart et al. 2020b), hopes of escaping Earth's problems through a future ticket to a space colony weakens the case for solving Earth's problems. Why not trash the planet if a Golden Ticket to Musk's Mars awaits? In summary, the case for space colonization is another silver bullet narrative that is shortsighted, illogical, risky, and serves to benefit the wealthy few. As with carbon and solar geoengineering strategies described earlier, we believe a focus on space colonization also detracts attention, resources, and energy away from the need to rapidly adopt systemic changes to minimize global warming.

A Techno-Capitalist Agenda for Whom and for What?

If there is no alternative to capitalism, then the only path forward is to use technology to attempt to fix or escape the increasing harms of capitalism. This rationality is a one-dimensional thinking where the only options are to pursue within-system strategies. Thus, carbon engineering, solar geoengineering, and space colonization become the "rational" responses to the climate crisis. Any viable solutions must support increasing levels of production, consumption, and economic growth. If it fails to do this, it is not considered a viable or feasible strategy – it just won't work. If one is stuck in capitalist realism, which remains despite capitalism's contradictions being on full display, then this is acceptable and rational. However, if one examines the likely consequences and outcomes of these strategies, one will realize that remaining stuck in one-dimensional, capitalist thinking leaves the majority of humans facing repeated, extensive, and escalating catastrophes and tragedies. As put by Marcuse (1989: 122), we remain surrounded by "technicians, specialists, and experts who calculate, adjust, and match without ever asking for whom or for what." Yet, focusing on techno-capitalist climate "solutions" distracts us from the horrific implications of this trajectory. Indeed, the focus on *how* these technological feats could be achieved overshadows questions regarding for *whom* and *for what* ends these technologies will serve.

First, let us briefly discuss *for whom*. While support for geoengineering and space colonization among elites does not mean that all elites support these strategies, or that these strategies are necessarily supported for vicious reasons, it lends evidence to the argument that these strategies appeal to those who have a vested interest in continuing business as usual (i.e., burning fossil fuels for capitalist expansion). Regardless of the personal motivations for pursuing space colonization and geoengineering, we predict these strategies will gain support for structural reasons: capitalism's need to expand, an aim fueled by fossil fuel combustion. The rulers of this system, economic and political elites, will benefit the most from the techno-capitalist climate agenda. In other words, this is *whom* the techno-capitalist agenda serves. This also includes the same people who have most contributed to climate change, as the wealthy in the Global North have contributed by far the most GHG emissions and continue to do so. Here are some figures to consider: the richest 10% of the global population are responsible for *half* of all GHG emissions, the poorest *half* of the global population is responsible for 12% of GHG emissions (World Inequality Report, 2022), and the richest 1% of the global population uses 175 times more carbon than the poorest 10% (Oxfam 2015).

Second, to what end or *for what* end is the techno-capitalist agenda leading us toward? Techno-capitalist strategies seem very unlikely to "save humanity" as there are significant risks involved in geoengineering, and space colonization (also risky) would likely only save a small and select portion of humanity. Instead, it serves to advance "progress" and domination through techno-scientific achievements and to increase wealth accumulation for vested interests. The techno-capitalist agenda would thus result in a widening of current wealth and power imbalances. Climate change is predicted to dramatically increase global poverty, disease, famine, and death, especially for the world's most marginalized people and the techno-capitalist agenda holds the potential to worsen these impacts. Meanwhile, those who can profit from climate disaster or climate techno-fixes will seek out every opportunity to do so. The techno-capitalist agenda would likely result in what the United Nations (Carrington 2019) calls a "climate apartheid," where wealthy people may be able to avoid (and even financially benefit from) some of the impacts of climate change while others face the full burden of loss and suffering. That means the inability to escape deadly heat waves, floods, hurricanes, mudslides, famine, and more. At the same time the wealthiest individuals will have the ability to move to safer locations, build safer places to live, and possibly even escape Earth to space colonies. The outcomes of the techno-capitalist agenda could very possibly involve the loss of most of humanity as well as the collapse of global ecosystems. While these techno-fixes are appealing to many people, they are not supported by evidence and remain extremely risky. There are real alternatives that would be less risky, more effective, and much more just.

Although we think some carbon geoengineering strategies have the potential to help address climate change if embedded in different social conditions (see chapter 4), we reject the idea that capitalism can continue to grow in the long-term while addressing the negative climatic impacts of growth through technological development (i.e., the techno-capitalist agenda). The remainder of this book defies capitalist realism and one-dimensional thinking by imagining and describing in detail alternatives already existing in current conditions that can offer much more just and sustainable outcomes. Embracing the possibilities for social transformation, we draw from scholarship related to ecosocialism and degrowth to articulate an alternative trajectory, one that can still involve the use of technologies to mitigate global warming, but uses technologies for the specific purpose of protecting people and ecosystems – not for domination or increasing capital accumulation. While we will return later to the challenges and obstacles that must be recognized, confronted, and overcome to create this alternative path, first we need to understand the specific goals, strategies, and social-structural changes necessary to minimize warming and create a more just and livable future.

Chapter 2:
Ecosocialism and
Degrowth

[T]he ecological perspective is incompatible with the rationality of capitalism.

– André Gorz (1980: 18)

Leading up to the 2021 United Nations Climate Change Conference (COP26), we heard calls for bold change from world leaders intermingled with statements indicating that very little will change. Representatives from the US may illustrate some of the clearest examples of this contradiction. For example, the US Special Presidential Envoy for Climate, John Kerry, said that the climate crisis is an "existential" threat and the "test of our time" requiring world leaders to step up and make bold changes (quoted in Harvey 2021). Yet Kerry also claimed that the American "quality of life" need not change because we can rely on untested future technologies to reduce half of necessary carbon emissions (quoted in Murray 2021). This clearly illustrates continued ideological denialism and a techno-capitalist agenda, using faith in future technology as a rationale for minimal changes now and maintaining the current system.

Among climate movement groups calling for "system change," such as Extinction Rebellion (XR) and Fridays for Future (FFF), a large gap remains between the complaints and discontent with the current system and any agenda that would result in meaningful change. These complaints without agendas to reach alternatives leaves environmental concerns open to manipulation, dilution, and cooptation by those actively maintaining the current system. Leading up to COP26, XR activists organized to express their demands to world leaders. Yet, XR's demands remain "beyond politics" as they call for governments to tell the truth about climate change and act boldly to reduce emissions without supporting any specific policies or programs. As pointed out by Spash (2020), these generic calls for change fail to connect with any agenda or program to facilitate change and fail to confront the very real political powers that continue to protect the status quo.

These two challenges—(1) denial that system change is necessary and (2) failure to articulate what system change involves—both stem from a societal inability to adequately engage with the fact that different socio-economic systems exist and are possible to create. This inability is partly a response to ineffective political structures and insufficient social mobilization to create change, barriers discussed later in the book, and partly a failure of imagination. As stated in the introduction, we are trapped in the "pervasive attitude" of "capitalist realism" (Fisher 2009), where most people implicitly affirm or explicitly believe that there is no alternative. Instead, we must embrace what Bonneuil and Fressoz (2017) call "alternative realism," focusing on *what could be* and the possible alternatives that could bring about a more sustainable and just future. To change our system in ways that minimize harm to current and future generations, the majority must shift from the captivity of capitalist realism to the open-mindedness of alternative realism. There is a critical need to connect alternative realism—knowledge of alternatives, why they are desirable, and how they can be achieved—with the climate movement. Those trapped in the belief that system change is unnecessary will remain in denial, especially if those calling for system change do not advocate for specific policies and present rough blueprints of alternatives. Again, we argue that calls for "system change" in the climate movement must not only get louder, but also *much* more specific. Gorz (1964) gives the same argument about calls for socialism: generic calls for socialism would not be enough without a clear idea of the specifics, tangible intermediate goals and improvements, and clear strategies for positive change.

In the footsteps of critical theorists, we aim to identify alternative social futures that exist in the cracks of current contradictions. With the threat of catastrophic climate change on the horizon, this involves searching for specific strategies and pathways to create a less warm, more just, and sustainable future. Critical theory can play a role in this. As Marcuse (1967) states:

> By logical inference from the prevailing conditions and institutions, critical theory may also be able to determine the basic institutional changes which are the prerequisites for the transition to a higher stage of development: "higher" in the sense of a more rational and equitable use of resources, minimization of destructive conflicts, and enlargement of the realm of freedom.

André Gorz's work also examines the potentialities for a better society, linking theory to specific reforms that could catalyze a social transition out of capitalism. As a predecessor to both ecosocialist and degrowth thinking, Gorz (1980) grounds his arguments in a new sense of realism, what he calls "ecological realism." Ecological realism acknowledges the external limits of the biophysical world and that we must change our system to protect current and future generations from the destruction that ensues from ignoring these limits. Gorz's (1980: 77) position on growth in these terms is clear: "the logic of profit has led it to produce for the sake or production, to demand growth for the sake of growth, to waste irreplaceable resources, to plunder the planet."

In this chapter, we examine ideas and proposals associated with ecosocialism and degrowth to identify prerequisites, concrete pathways, and specific key levers for the "system change" required to minimize global warming. Negative climate impacts are now unavoidable, but governments and global movements can still act boldly in an attempt to minimize the extent of global warming and the associated loss and suffering. Yet this will require overcoming ideological denial that systemic change is necessary and *also* connecting calls for system change to specific policies, programs, and strategies. We first briefly describe the origins and primary positions associated with ecosocialism and degrowth, acknowledging that this review captures only a fraction of the plurality of views that exists within each area of scholarship. We then focus on the synergies or overlapping ideas supported by both ecosocialists and degrowth thinkers.

Ecosocialist Visions and Strategies

While holding and governing resources in common are prehistoric practices and socialistic ideas are recorded in ancient and Medieval texts, modern socialism and its many branches emerged following the French and industrial revolutions (for overviews of early modern socialism and the emergence of anarchism and Marxism, see Cole 1953, 1954; Kołakowski 2005: ch. 10). The word "socialism" was first used in print in 1832 by Pierre Leroux, a devotee to the doctrines of the French socialist Saint-Simon (Cole 1953, Kołakowski 2005). Early on, socialism referred to the

> collective regulation of men's affairs on a co-operative basis, with the happiness and welfare of all as the end in view, and with the emphasis not on 'politics' but on the production and distribution of wealth and on the strengthening of 'socialising' influences in the lifelong education of the citizens in co-operative, as against competitive, patterns of behaviour and social attitudes and beliefs. (Cole 1953: 4-5)

Despite general agreement on some essential points (see below), socialism has always been, and still is, a diverse politics (Wolff 2019), with two centuries worth of discussion and disagreement over fundamental questions, including:

1) Should, or can, the state be abolished or, instead, used as an instrument to transition to socialism? If the latter, will state power be won through the ballot or through force? Can incremental reforms build socialism, or is revolution necessary?

2) What social groups will play a key role as historical subjects for building socialism?

3) What will socialism look like, and will it be a transition to a "higher" social stage of communism?

4) Is socialism a natural inevitability built into the laws of history or a collective choice?

5) Can socialism be built in one country or region, or is its international spread a prerequisite for success?

The wide-ranging answers to these and related questions accounts for why socialism is a broad political label adopted by seemingly opposed political factions, from moderate social democrats interested in securing a more robust welfare state, without aspiring to socialize property, to insurrectionary anarchists who seek to abolish the state and private property through revolution. These questions are being revisited today due to a growing and relatively widespread interest in socialism, especially among young people, a renewal rising out of the multiple crises created and sustained by capitalism (Foster 2020).

Despite its many variations, socialism was united from the start by the conviction that the uncontrolled concentration of wealth and unbridled competition were bound to lead to increasing misery and crises, and that the system must be replaced by one in which the organization of production and exchange would do away with poverty and oppression and bring about a redistribution of the world's goods on a basis of equality. (Kołakowski 2005: 150)

This early conviction is echoed in a definition of socialism proposed in a recent popular primer:

[Socialism is an] egalitarian political tradition characterized by its skepticism of wealth inequality and private, for-profit ownership. There are many strands of socialist philosophy, including Marxism, anarchism, and the less radical "Fabian" socialisms. Some are in favor of centralized states, some are against the state entirely. Some are revolutionary and some are reformist. Some believe that markets, money, and some private ownership will be necessary, while others believe the world should be held in common and shared by all. But each has a radical vision for a more fair and equal social/economic landscape, and is trying to shift control of the production of goods and services from rich owners to ordinary workers. You are not a socialist if you do not aspire to drastic changes in the existing arrangement of economic power, meaning it is not enough simply to affirm vague rhetorical support for "equality." (Robinson 2019: 139-140)

Common though not universal themes and goals in socialism include the abolition of private property (not personal property) through its "socialization," which ambiguously refers to nationalization and/or democratization/cooperatization; the democratization of the workplace; the reduction of inequality; wealth redistribution through high progressive taxes and welfare programs; the realization of freedom and equality; and using technological progress to reduce working hours.

No one has had a more acute and sustained intellectual influence on socialism than Karl Marx. His writings and debates with, and critiques of, leading socialists of his time, such as the anarchists Mikhail Bakunin and Pierre Proudhon and the socialist Ferdinand Lassalle, set the stage for the international development of socialist doctrine and strategy. For Marx, "socialism means more... than a welfare society, the abolition of competition and want, the removal of conditions that make men an enemy to man: it is also, and above all, the abolition of the estrangement between man and the world, the assimilation of the world by the human subject." (Kołakowski 2005: 183). Marx's ideas were central to the codification of socialist doctrine during the Second and Third Internationals and many major socialist parties and states have claimed to follow Marxism. Given that many of the horrors committed by failed and still-existing "socialist" states that officially adhered and adhere to Marxism, some readers are likely and understandably skeptical of socialism, let alone Marxism. Further, readers are likely aware of some of the ecological devastation caused by "socialist" states.

On the one hand, it is misleading to conflate the many socialist experiments of the twentieth century, from Stalin's Russia to Yugoslavia's experiments with democratic workplaces, in the same box and to overlook the massive gains in education, literacy, welfare, housing, and medicine experienced by many "socialist" states (see Saed 2021). Wright (2010), argues that the applications of socialism in authoritarian examples is not socialism at all, but what he calls undemocratic and oppressive "statism." These examples missed the mark and failed to be directed by the people for the benefit of the people. Many socialists today modify socialism with "democratic" to unambiguously communicate a commitment to democracy and anti-authoritarianism (Robinson 2019: 140). Relatedly, contemporary socialists who are committed to saving the environment from what they see as the inherently anti-ecological dynamics of capitalism often call themselves "ecosocialists." It is these two overlapping variants of socialism—democratic socialism and ecosocialism—that we summarize below.

The Democratic Socialists of America (DSA) (2021), the largest socialist organization in the US, defines democratic socialism as "a system that extends bottom-up democracy to our workplaces, neighborhoods, and society." One of DSA's founding members, Michael Harrington (1989: 9, emphasis removed) similarly conceives of socialism as "democratic control from below by the people and their communities," in contrast to what currently exists: top-down capitalist control. Bhaskar Sunkara (2020), editor of *Jacobin*, a popular democratic-socialist US-based magazine, supports social-democratic reforms but believes they are only a starting point to transition to democratic socialism. Along with guaranteed public jobs and strong social welfare programs, democratic socialism entails the end of labor and capital markets while retaining markets for goods and services. The goods and services are produced by nationalized firms that are simultaneously governed by their workers, despite being owned by the state. In a thought experiment Sunkara (2020: 20) describes it this way: "Collectively you and your coworkers now control your company. You're more like citizens of a community than owners. You just have to pay a tax on its capital assets (the building and the land it's on, machinery, and so forth), in effect renting it from society as a whole." He argues that democratic socialism is well-placed to counter capitalism's attempt to expand infinitely despite the finite limits imposed by nature:

> There are reasons to believe that democratic socialism would do far better at keeping humanity flourishing along with the wider ecology in which we're enmeshed. Worker-controlled firms don't have the same "grow or die" imperative as capitalist ones. A more empowered citizenry, too, would be better able to weigh the costs and benefits of new development. At the very least, more democracy means a better chance to argue for a politics that defends the interests of our children and grandchildren. (Sunkara 2020: 241)

Further, public ownership of firms allows for technological changes to be used to reduce work hours rather than increase profits. The ecological significance of this is discussed further in the next chapter in terms of work time reduction policy.

Although Sunkara (2020) is clear that democratic socialism would better allow for society to address climate change, some of the details of how this would be achieved remain unclear. These details are important because some democratic socialists maintain a techno-optimistic, Cornucopian wish-image of a socialist future as one of endless excess and abundance (for critique, see Foster 2017). In contrast, ecosocialists argue that it is capitalism's inherent growth imperative that lies at the root of the ecological crisis (e.g., Foster et al. 2011):

> Capital... is nothing but self-expanding value, and is indistinguishable from the drive to accumulate on an ever-increasing scale... This ceaseless drive for the amassing of greater and greater wealth, requiring more and more throughput of energy and resources, as well as reserves of labor, generating more waste, constitutes "the absolute general law of environmental degradation under capitalism [Foster et al. 2011]." Today the scale of the human economy has become so large that its everyday activities, such as carbon dioxide emissions and freshwater use, now threaten the fundamental biogeochemical processes of the planet. (Foster and Clark 2020: 246-247)

Although there are differences between ecosocialists like Ted Benton, James O'Connor, Joel Kovel, John Bellamy Foster, and others (e.g., see White et al. 2017; Foster and Clark 2020: ch. 8), two common strands running through ecosocialism include (1) the argument that capitalism is inherently unsustainable (see above) and (2) a prescriptive case that socialism would allow society to produce to meet human needs within ecological limits. Others have shown that these arguments stretch back to Marx's analysis of the "rift" capitalism ruptures in biogeochemical cycles and the need to build a society in which "socialized man, the associated producers, govern the human metabolism of nature in a rational way… accomplishing it with the least expenditure of energy" (Marx 1981: 959, see Foster 2000, Saito 2017).

As an alternative to capitalism's structural necessity to increase energy and material throughput, ecosocialism has been defined as:

> [A]n attempt to provide a radical civilizational alternative to what Marx called capitalism's 'destructive progress'. It advances an economic policy founded on the non-monetary and extra-economic criteria of social needs and ecological equilibrium. Grounded on the basic arguments of the ecological movement, and the Marxist critique of political economy, this dialectical synthesis… is at the same time a critique of 'market ecology', which does not challenge the capitalist system, and of 'productivist socialism', which ignores the issue of natural limits. [The aims of ecosocialism] require: (a) collective ownership of the means of production ('collective' here meaning public, cooperative or communitarian property); (b) democratic planning, which makes it possible for society to define the goals of investment and production, and (c) a new technological structure of the productive forces. (Löwy 2007: 294)

In this definition, ecosocialism is a democratic socialism that recognizes natural limits and abandons the vision of socialism as an extension of capitalist productivism. Collective ownership and democratic planning open the possibility of, though do not guarantee, an economy based around the production of *use values* that meet human needs and promote human flourishing within ecological limits (see Kovel 2000). The guiding assumption is that democratically controlled firms free from the profit motive who collectively and discursively decide, with surrounding communities (Löwy 2007), what should and should not be produced—as opposed to leaving these choices to supply and demand and a tiny elite—will be better positioned to take ecological impacts and social welfare into consideration. As Lawrence (2022: 21) states boldly in *Planet on Fire: A Manifesto for the Age of Environmental Breakdown*, we need to replace the economics of extractivism with a twenty-first-century ecosocialism: the collective effort to democratise our economic and political institutions, repurposing them towards social wellbeing and individual flourishing, rooted in an abundant and thriving natural world... If you do not like the word 'ecosocialism', then use something else.

Degrowth Visions and Strategies

While it does not date back as far as socialist thinking, degrowth is not a new concept. It is widely described as having emerged from a question posed by Gorz in the early 1970s (Kallis 2015a, Paulson 2017). Giorgos Kallis' book *Degrowth* (2018) includes a detailed history of the evolution of degrowth that we will not repeat here, but it should be noted that key contributors to degrowth's development include Gorz, radical Catholic priest and philosopher Ivan Illich, bioeconomist Nicholas Georgescu-Roegen, radical economist and political-scientist Serge Latouche, as well as Joan Martinez-Alier, Herman Daly, Tim Jackson, Peter Victor and other ecological economists. Barcelona, Spain, has become an epicenter for current degrowth research, education, and activism, as the Autonomous University of Barcelona is home to prominent degrowth scholars and now offers a graduate program in degrowth. The academic collective "Research & Degrowth" also coordinates networking among degrowth scholars and activists and holds an international degrowth conference at least every other year in various locations.

The primary goal of degrowth is to equitably reduce total resource and energy use to a sustainable level that provides enough for everyone and corrects for the current level of ecological overshoot causing our environmental crisis. Kallis (2017: 10), one of degrowth's most prolific scholars, defines degrowth as "an equitable down-scaling of production and consumption that increases human wellbeing and enhances environmental conditions." Degrowth entails reduced material and energy throughput in over-extended economies to reach a steady state of "enough" or sufficiency, while at the same time helping nations in the Global South to more sustainably achieve an improved quality of life (Kallis 2017).

Degrowth faces many challenges as a movement (Liegy and Nelson 2020) and is still widely misunderstood as simply a decrease in GDP and, therefore, misinterpreted as recession. The overall goal of degrowth is not to reduce GDP; however, the changes required to reduce total material and energy throughput to stay within planetary limits would most likely result in a contraction of the economy and a reduction in GDP (Hickel 2019). Yet, degrowth is planned and is therefore not the same as an economic recession. The "degrowth hypothesis" posits that through prioritizing distribution, equity, and having enough, wellbeing and quality of life can improve even as total material and energy throughput decreases (Kallis 2018). With an increasing number of new degrowth books written for a general audience (e.g., Hickel 2021, Liegy and Nelson 2020, Schmeltzer et al. 2022) and associated media coverage, interviews, and lectures; degrowth is receiving increased attention. And in 2022, for the first time, an Intergovernmental Panel on Climate Change (IPCC) report mentioned degrowth 15 times in discussions of pathways to stay within climate targets (Parrique 2022).

As capitalism is growth dependent, degrowth represents an anti-capitalist position. Kallis (2015:1) explains that "[d]egrowth challenges not only the outcomes, but the very spirit of capitalism. Capitalism knows no limits, it only knows how to expand, creating while destroying." Degrowth values and principles challenge key components of neoliberal capitalism including consumerism, individualism, and greed and, instead, focuses on sufficiency, sharing, common resources, relationships, conviviality, and care (Kallis 2018). In addition, rather than supporting a culture of always needing more and more material goods (largely propelled by advertising and a constantly expanding production engine), degrowth promotes a "culture of self-limitation" that values restraint to enhance social and ecological wellbeing (Kallis 2019: 270). In all these ways, degrowth in theory and practice is incompatible with capitalism, which remains dependent on economic growth and increasing levels of production and consumption.

While degrowth scholars and activists have developed diverse interpretations of degrowth (Chertkovskaya 2019, Liegy and Nelson 2020), much of the literature illustrates clear overlapping principles and agendas. For example, Jarvis (2019: 7) states that

> a degrowth perspective can be identified in the literature with respect to four transformations: extending human relations instead of market relations; deepening democracy; defending ecosystems; and realizing a more equal global distribution of wealth.

Gabriel and Bond (2019: 328) identify three primary agendas associated with degrowth: (1) to decrease material and energy throughput, (2) to emphasize social justice, wellbeing, and inclusion, and (3) to create voluntary democratic channels to participate in decision-making. Degrowth thrives on the multiplicity of perspectives and approaches, yet core values include "care, cooperation, mutual aid, solidarity, conviviality, autonomy, and direct democracy" (Barca et al. 2019: 4). Kallis (2018) emphasizes several key principles of degrowth: equality, democracy, relocalization, diversifying economic forms, decommodification, care, sharing, building relationships, conviviality, celebration, and, of course, reducing throughput. Others similarly describe degrowth as reorienting priorities from growth to wellbeing (Paulson et al. 2020).

Casting off the hegemonic capitalist goal of GDP growth is a prerequisite for degrowth. However, the call to abolish GDP as an indicator of progress is coming not only from supporters of degrowth, but also from an increasing number of scholars, economists, and political pundits. As explained by Nobel laureate and economist Joseph Stiglitz (2019): "If we measure the wrong thing, we will do the wrong thing" and currently what we are measuring and prioritizing is leading us further into global crisis. GDP has failed to be a good indicator of wellbeing and quality of life

(O'Neill 2012, Stiglitz 2019). Alternative indicators, including the Index of Sustainable Economic Welfare, Gross National Happiness, and the General Progress Indicator, illustrate that GDP remains a poor indicator of social progress in terms of health, education, wellbeing, and happiness. However, degrowth entails much more than simply abandoning the use of GDP as a metric of progress. It also requires changing the way we live, work, and organize our societies. From household behavior to global governance, everything must change. Scholars have outlined degrowth-oriented policy proposals for national and international-level structural changes as well as strategies and programs to guide community-level planning to reduce material and energy use.

Degrowth living requires a shift away from consumer culture and toward a culture of sufficiency where quality is valued over quantity and new forms of abundance emerge. This cultural transition is in line with what Juliet Shor (2010) calls *Plentitude* and involves simple living yet feeling satisfied with enough rather than always wanting more. Degrowth involves a cultural and paradigmatic shift where collective social and ecological values are placed before personal wealth accumulation (Brossman and Islar 2019). It also involves fostering a "culture of self-limitation" that, in contrast to austerity, is chosen through self-awareness and ethical rationale: "social needs are constructed and can be deliberated on, negotiated, regulated or limited" (Kallis 2019: 270). In this way degrowth blurs and reshapes cultural norms and values into forms that are more relevant and appropriate for addressing our environmental crisis (Perkins 2019). If we cast aside economic growth and hyper-individualism (which promotes excessive personal consumption and fuels economic growth), then sharing material resources, housing, and spaces allows for reducing environmental impacts and increasing social connectedness. Jarvis (2019: 257) states that sharing in line with degrowth principles involves prioritizing "intentional 'we' thinking and ethical purpose" instead of "cultural norms… such as hyper-individual dwelling and conspicuous consumption." As Paulson (2017) explains, degrowth call us to shift value and desire away from productivist achievements and consumption-based identities toward visions of good life variously characterized by health, harmony, pleasure and vitality among humans and ecosystems.

Yet degrowth is not merely another call for changes in values and culture, but also refers to an array of policy strategies at multiple scales that, together, offer a pathway to stay within climate targets *and* increase wellbeing.

It should be emphasized that degrowth scholars agree that production and consumption should not be reduced in places where many people's needs are still not being met. For example, Demaria et al. (2019) argue that in cases where people are living with less than enough, there is clearly a need to increase production and consumption. In other words, degrowth is "not a material process of lowering consumption, an irrelevant demand for those who live within conditions of poverty" (Demaira et al. 2019: 439). The authors also argue that poverty and "underdevelopment" are not necessarily a consequence of the absence of economic growth. In fact, in many cases, poverty is the consequence of economic growth and development interventions. In contrast to growth being seen as alleviating poverty, it should be recognized that growth can result in poverty. Recent analyses suggest that developing countries have been net-creditors to the Global North, sending money out at a rate well beyond the "aid" received from the developed world (GFI 2016). As Demaria et al. (2019: 439) argue:

> The ideology of growth disguises continued colonial relations with a pretense of generalized betterment, while securing the unequal exchanges and the access by capital to cheap raw materials and human labour that is necessary for sustaining growth for some at the expense of others.

Meeting the needs of people in the Global South is critical, but the goal should not simply be economic growth, which Hickel (2017) illustrates goes largely to the wealthy few or is exported. A more appropriate goal is *meeting the needs of people* and supporting health and wellbeing. Growth to meet those needs could be done with the goal of sufficiency in mind, rather than never-ending economic growth and wealth accumulation for the elite. In other words, we must refocus and improve "the development model to make it more efficient at converting resources into well-being" (Hickel 2019). Some degrowth scholars argue that degrowth can open alternative pathways for development in the Global South that could result in more beneficial outcomes for all. As Kallis (2015) explains, degrowth can liberate "conceptual space" for countries to identify their own ideas of wellbeing and "can provide space for the flourishing of alternative cosmovisions and practices in the South, such as *buen vivir* in Latin America or *ubuntu* in Africa." In these ways, it may open pathways for countries in the Global South to achieve high(er) levels of wellbeing on a different path that does not simply prioritize growth.

The term degrowth was specifically chosen by activists and scholars because it is a negative word or "missile word" that directly confronts and challenges the hegemony of growth (Kallis 2015, Liegy and Nelson 2020). As argued by Kallis (2019: 273),

> [c]apitalism and its institutions are legitimated and reproduced in the name of growth. The imaginary and pursuit of growth survived even communist states' attack on capitalist relations. Unless we start changing the words we use and the images that come with them, we will remain stuck in the capitalist imaginary of growth.

Drews and Antal's (2016) study on the use of the term illustrates that the word "degrowth" does have a downward connotation that fosters negative feelings, including fears of having less or forced austerity. They also found that the term in some cases "backfires" because it misleadingly suggests a recession, which is different than a planned economic contraction. However, others argue that the movement must be explicitly against growth and that the term "degrowth" is much less likely to be coopted than more positive terms (Kallis 2018). Despite criticisms, many scholars and activists continue to support the use of the term degrowth for these reasons (Liegy and Nelson 2020).

Addressing inequality while reducing overconsumption and mitigating environmental harm are key goals of degrowth and involve the redistribution of wealth and resources (Hickel 2019). This would reduce environmental harm, as wealthy individuals have a much higher environmental impact. For example, according to Chancel and Piketty (2015) those in the top 1% income bracket in the US emit over 300 metric tons of carbon dioxide equivalent per capita compared to 20 metric tons for the average North American and well above the 6.2 global average. Due to the extreme level of current inequality, ensuring that human needs and social goals can be met without growth will require that wealth is more fairly distributed (Hickel 2019). Therefore, a wealth tax, income cap, or other redistributive reform is critical (see Buch-Hansen and Koch 2019). Other policy proposals associated with degrowth—including work time reduction, advertising restrictions, economic democracy, energy democracy, and nationalizing fossil fuels—that have significant mitigation potential will be discussed in the next chapter focused on specific strategies to minimize global warming.

Synergies Between Ecosocialism and Degrowth

Ecosocialism and degrowth have overlapping yet distinct intellectual and political histories. However, they both aim to subordinate the economy to social and ecological goals. As noted long ago by Karl Polanyi (2001), capitalism attempts to embed social relations in the economic system even though the economy should be "embedded in social relations" (2001: 60). Kaup (2015) extends this notion, arguing that the economy needs to be re-embedded in both the social and natural spheres. Rather than society and nature being subject to a growth-dependent and relatively autonomous economic system, we must make economic goals subordinate to ecological limits and social wellbeing if we are to avoid social-ecological collapse.

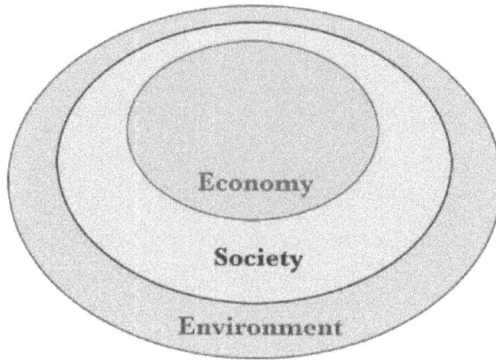

Figure 1: A nested depiction of sustainability from ecological economics that illustrates the economy embedded within society and the environment. https://en.wikipedia.org/wiki/File:Nested_sustainability-v2.gif

This is also supported by the popular concept of doughnut economics, where the economy must fit inside the boundaries (doughnut) of the ecological and biophysical world (Raworth 2017). However, in contrast to degrowth, doughnut economics is described as being "growth agnostic" (Spash 2021). In other words, the concept is not explicitly against growth and does not specifically call for a reduction in overall production and consumption. In contrast, both ecosocialism and degrowth specify the need to reduce production and consumption in wealthy countries to stay within ecological limits.

There has been a vibrant discussion between ecosocialists and degrowth thinkers for around a decade (Andreucci and Engel-Di Mauro 2019). A common criticism of degrowth from a Marxist perspective is that degrowth has not developed a coherent theory of capitalism and, thus, cannot develop an adequate political response to its inherent growth engine (e.g., Foster 2011). Some ecosocialists want to preserve concepts like "growth" and "development," arguing that the meaning of these terms would qualitatively transform in an ecosocialist society (e.g., Vergara-Camus 2019, cf. Löwy 2007). Kallis (2019) argues that degrowth is inherently incompatible with capitalism and that any true socialist alternative should seek to simmer rather than fuel productivism. In *Minima Moralia*, Theodor Adorno argues that socialist productivism, with its calls for boundless production and consumption, is a byproduct of, rather than an alternative to, a society dominated by commodity production. He asks us to imagine an achieved utopia as one of peace and rest rather than more "frantic bustle" and unbridled production:

> If we imagine emancipated society as emancipation from precisely such totality, then vanishing-lines come into view that have little in common with increased production and its human reflections… [A] society rid of its fetters might take thought that even the forces of production are not the deepest substratum of man, but represent his historical form adapted to the production of commodities. Perhaps the true society will grow tired of development and, out of freedom, leave possibilities unused, instead of storming under a confused compulsion to the conquest of strange stars. A mankind which no longer knows want will begin to have an inkling of the delusory, futile nature of all the arrangements hitherto made in order to escape want, which used wealth to produce want on a larger scale… *Rien faire comme une bête* [Doing nothing, like an animal], lying on water and looking peacefully at the sky, 'being, nothing else, without any further definition and fulfilment', might take the place of process, act, satisfaction, and so truly keep the promise of dialectical logic that it would culminate in its origin. None of the abstract concepts comes closer to fulfilled utopia than that of eternal peace. (Adorno 1978: 156-57)

Much of the debates over possible conflicts between ecosocialist and degrowth thinking stems from different interpretations, especially of degrowth. While degrowth indeed celebrates pluralism, most degrowth proponents and scholars now agree that degrowth is clearly an anti-capitalist position (Schmelzer et al. 2022). The

Eco-Marxist Foster (2021) explains, that, if interpreted as focusing only on an anti-growth position, degrowth falls short as it fails to capture the scope of the problem. However, if degrowth is an acknowledgement of the inherent relationship between capitalism and economic growth, then any notions of degrowth being compatible with capitalism ends. It is not a matter of shrinking the scale of production and consumption, but a matter of reconfiguring social relations completely. As Foster (2021) warns, it is not enough to turn the concept of growth upside down, we need a new system of production and consumption all together, with different goals and different ends.

Like many others increasingly interested in these topics, we believe ecosocialist and degrowth thinking provide critical insights necessary for creating a livable future and offer the best possible path forward to create a more just and sustainable world. Despite some misconceptions and different interpretations, especially regarding what degrowth means, we agree with Andreucci and Engel-Di Mauro (2019) that there are important and fertile overlaps between degrowth and ecosocialism. In fact, as mentioned above, the term "degrowth" (*décroissance*) itself was first discussed by the proto-ecosocialist Gorz (Kallis et al. 2015) and, for Kallis (2019), degrowth *is* "socialism without growth" (Andreucci and Engel-Di Mauro 2019). Further, a fundamental ecosocialist argument is that the unsustainability of capitalism is due to its inherent growth engine and, thus, either explicitly or implicitly agree with degrowth's premise that overall production and consumption must decline to meet ecological targets.

In addition, Saito's (2022) overwhelmingly popular book, titled *Marx in the Anthropocene: Towards the Idea of Degrowth Communism*, represents an important connection between Marxism and degrowth. Saito makes a compelling argument that, in his later work, Marx supports a form of degrowth communism. Drawing from overlooked manuscripts, Saito (2022) reveals how Marx's vision of post-capitalism evolved since he wrote *Capital*. His views had shifted to focus more on the natural environment and cyclical relationships, supporting the idea of a *"stationary and circular economy without economic growth"* (Saito 2022: 170 emphases in original). Through illustrating Marx's likely support for degrowth thinking, Saito (2022) effectively opens the door for increased dialogue and collaboration between Marxists and degrowth thinkers. This reinforces the positions of those who already connecting these ideas, such as Latouch who "accepted the idea of ecosocialism as a basis for degrowth" (Saito 2002: 217). While many academics may have once viewed degrowth as a third option, an alternative to both capitalism and socialism, degrowth scholars have become increasingly anti-capitalist, revealing clearer synergies between ecosocialism and degrowth.

Based on the principles and theories that guide ecosocialist and degrowth thinking, we will next examine what specific strategies and programs could be adopted to transition to a new society, a new order that is capable of minimizing global warming. Rather than calling for system changes and a generic transition, we draw from a growing body of literature pointing us in specific directions based on convincing evidence. While specific strategies and policies have been outlined in diverse contexts, they will need to be pushed forward collectively and simultaneously to have the most potential. Thus, the need for a new comprehensive, theoretically informed and empirically supported, climate agenda for system change.

Chapter 3:
A Climate Agenda for System Change

[P]olicy should be made on the basis of robust empirical evidence, rather than on the basis of speculative theoretical possibilities, particularly given the severity of the crisis that is at stake.

– Jason Hickel and Giorgos Kallis (2019)

We believe the climate movement needs to solidify a clear agenda to commence "system change" and that this would serve to strengthen the movement's ability to influence effective and just climate policy. Ecosocialism and degrowth, as examined in the previous chapter, represent a fruitful guide to create a new climate agenda. Here we examine how ideas and proposals from ecosocialist and degrowth scholars can inform concrete agenda items to help support the goal of justly minimizing global warming. Scholars in these areas have not only developed policy and program proposals based on the theoretical foundations of ecosocialism and degrowth, many have also illustrated through evidence that these pathways will likely be a successful way to justly mitigate climate change. While many such examples exist, we highlight a selection of proposals that we feel are both grounded in theory and well-supported by empirical evidence. Here we share the policies and programs that other scholars have evaluated and convincingly illustrated would be effective and just pathways not only to address the climate crisis, but also to foster system change towards a more egalitarian and sustainable world.

Before describing policy applications in detail, it is helpful to illustrate the symbioses between ecosocialism and degrowth by comparing two concrete political proposals: Richard Smith's (2019) ecosocialist plan to avoid catastrophic warming and James G. Speth's (2015; Speth et al. 2018) proposals to address the ecological crisis by reaching a "new political economy." The proposals are helpful illustrations here as one uses the terms "ecosocialism" and "degrowth" (Smith) while the other avoids using either term despite supporting democratic control of the economy and reductions in total throughput (Speth). Smith (2019) proposes an "Emergency Plan," designed for the US, to stay with 1.5°C warming. The plan consists of four proposals: (1) phase out fossil fuels by nationalizing the fossil fuel industry as well as "downstream" industries and those whose entire existence is dependent on fossil fuels (e.g., airlines), (2) a guaranteed jobs program for those who are put out of work, (3) a large-scale and rapid national development of renewables, and (4) a phase-out of ecologically destructive industries (e.g., arms production, single-use plastics, factory farming, etc.). Smith sees capitalist growth dependency as the primary obstacle to avoiding catastrophic warming and defends socializing massive corporations as opposed to small businesses and family farms. Speth et al. (2018: 2) argue, like Smith, that we need "system change" to transition out of "our current system of political economy." They promote three strategies to begin transitioning out of current power structures that block climate action, all of which overlap with Smith's Emergency Plan: (1) buying out fossil fuel companies and phasing out fossil fuel production, (2) transferring energy utilities to public ownership and control, and (3) partnering with "anchor institutions" (public or nonprofit institutions who have a long-term stake in communities, such as universities and hospitals) to fortify democratically controlled energy grids. While these visions provide the beginning of a "system changing" climate agenda, there are additional strategies that we believe are key to justly minimizing global warming.

Upon reviewing the degrowth and ecosocialist literature relevant to climate change, we find at least six policies and programs that many degrowth and ecosocialist thinkers support as part of a solution pathway to address the climate crisis while increasing human wellbeing. We propose that a *climate agenda for system change* should include:

1) Economic democracy

2) Energy democracy and energy cooperatives

3) Work time reduction

4) Advertising restrictions and sufficiency measures

5) Reallocating excess wealth

6) Nationalizing and phasing out fossil fuel companies

Below, we describe each of these strategies and explain why they represent key levers and programs for effective and just climate mitigation. We agree with Hickel and Kallis (2019: 15) that "[p]olicy should be made on the basis of robust empirical evidence, rather than on the basis of speculative theoretical possibilities." Compared to theoretical and hypothetical green growth strategies (given the lack of empirical evidence of absolute, permanent, and global decoupling of growth and GHG emissions – see the introduction), the strategies described below break away from the paradigm of growth and offer well supported and less risky mitigation pathways that also provide the co-benefit of improving equity, justice, and wellbeing. These strategies are also grounded in the theories, principles, and goals associated with ecosocialism and degrowth – namely to increase equity, justice, and human security while staying within ecological thresholds. In other words, they prioritize human wellbeing and ecological sustainability over economic growth and profit accumulation. While some of these strategies can be pursued individually, we will highlight the relationships between specific agenda items and why they would be most effective if implemented together.

1. Economic Democracy

Economic democracy refers to "a system of governing firms in which direct control is redistributed... out of the hands of the capitalists and into the hands of their workers" (Archer 1995: 69). The democratic control of firms allows for the possibility of addressing environment problems: "If work were under the control of workers, human work would be much more likely to be environmentally friendly, since under capitalism's property rules and the imperative of growth, labor is forced to be environmentally harmful" (Bayon 2015: 191, see also Boillat et al. 2012, Johanisova and Wolf 2012, Wolff 2012: 133-134, Gunderson 2019). Democracy in the workplace or "economic democracy" is critical for addressing worker alienation and opening opportunities to use productivity gains in ways other than expansion and increasing levels of production.

Models of economic democracy already exist and vary in degree of worker control and ownership, including worker control of privately-owned firms, worker control of publicly owned firms, and worker control of worker-owned firms (e.g., worker-owned cooperatives). Worker decision-making power ranges from workers receiving a notification that a decision is being made to a majority representation in the forum or body that makes decisions (Archer 1995, Schweickart 1992, Boillat et al. 2012). There are also hybrid models, such as requiring worker representation on a firm's board of directors (Gorton and Schmid 2004). In a democratic system, workers would directly participate in decision-making or have elected representatives participate in all decisions that have impacts on workers and the future of the firm. This includes schedules, work speed, allocation of work duties, technologies and tools used, hiring and firing employees, product quality and quantity, profit-distribution, and investment (Schweickart 1992).

It is important to note that the structure of economic democracy does not necessitate climate mitigation. For example, one of the long-known limitations of worker cooperatives is that they must, if operating in a larger capitalist system, conform to this system's pseudo-natural laws (e.g., Marx 1981: 571). However, democracy in the workplace is a prerequisite to opening more opportunities for changes in production systems. It can create conditions favorable to new priorities that allow for the shrinking of throughput in a socially just way (e.g., Boillat et al. 2012, Johanisova and Wolf 2012). As Bayon (2015: 191) argues, "[i]f work were under the control of workers, human work would be much more likely to be environmentally friendly."

Economic democracy would *allow* for reduced environmental impacts by allowing more goals beyond private gain to be considered in investment decisions, moving beyond the requirement to advertise and sell more products, and by permitting people to be involved in decisions that impact their lives and the environment (Boillat et al. 2012). Therefore, it represents a strategic pre-condition to allow for alternative goals to guide production systems. Increasing economic democracy within production systems can be seen as an interstitial strategy occurring in the cracks of the dominant capitalist system (Wright 2010) or as grassroots action towards ecosocialism or degrowth from below; however, it can also be directed by policy interventions that support organizations pursuing economic democracy.

2. Energy Democracy and Energy Cooperatives

Energy democracy is a three-prong project centered around popular sovereignty over, participatory governance of, and civic ownership of energy systems (Szulecki 2018). Most fundamentally, energy democracy is a movement to reformulate social structures and consciousness in ways that allow energy to be treated as a commons instead of a commodity (Martinez 2017). The Mercator Research Institute on Global Commons (2017) argues that energy should be a common good as it is essential for human wellbeing and is often underprovided. Energy use affects the global commons through carbon emissions and climate change. Treating energy as a commons could help facilitate a transition to renewable energy and also to reduce overall energy consumption through just and democratic means. We agree with Byrne and others (2009: 90) that:

> [A]lthough commons institutions do not in and of themselves guarantee eradication of environmentally exploitive practices, they do offer elements for recovery of political agency in the formation of choices regarding energy and environmental futures and the foundation for a normative reconstitution of the good life.

Energy democracy initiatives challenge capitalism and particularly fossil capitalism. As explained by Carrol (2020: 18), energy democracy

> can open space for democratization and decolonization of economic, political and cultural life. In such a transformation, corporate power would give way to popular power and participatory planning in production and allocation, to environmental stewardship and authentic reconciliation, to a revitalized public sphere and inclusive community development.

A centerpiece in this challenge to capitalist models of energy production and distribution is the expansion of renewable energy cooperatives or community energy projects, like those growing primarily in the EU (e.g., Kunze and Becker 2015). Existing energy cooperatives and related community energy projects have been shown to allow for carbon emissions reductions while meeting social needs (Kunze and Becker 2015). However, like economic democracy (see above) and fossil fuel nationalization (see below), the collective ownership of energy systems does not guarantee reductions in carbon emissions. As Kunze and Becker (2015) explain, "[i]n contrast to conventional private corporate ownership, public and collective ownership opens up possibilities for the social and ecological transformation that degrowth is calling for, though it does in no way automatically guarantee the implementation of such goals" (Kunze and Becker 2015: 427). Like economic democracy, energy democracy, precisely because it is collectively governed, is more adaptable to goals beyond constant energy increases (Byrne et al. 2009) and therefore is another strategic pre-condition to open pathways for systemic change.

Although community energy projects are often implemented at the local level, they can be scaled up to at least the city level through municipal funding and support for energy cooperatives, city-level educational programs, energy sharing programs, whereby profits made through renewable cooperatives are donated to energy funds for the "energy poor," municipalization of energy systems, and related programs. For example, Seoul, South Korea, launched a relatively successful city-wide energy reduction program in 2012, alongside grassroots environmental movements, that implemented a number of programs consistent with energy democracy, including support for energy cooperatives and programs to help communities become energy self-sufficient through renewables development and energy use reduction (Yun 2018, Gunderson and Yun 2021). Although still restricted to local- and city-levels, energy-democratic models of ownership and decision-making provide the blueprints for how to meet energy needs justly and effectively in a future society in which fossil fuels are almost wholly absent (Gunderson et al. 2018).

3. Work Time Reduction

Both Marcuse and Gorz were strong proponents of changing work in society. Marcuse (1955) argues that while humans historically may have needed to work many hours each day to fulfil human needs, due to technology and increased productivity, humans no longer need to work so much to survive. In many cases, unnecessary work is also demeaning and repressive, leaving little time or energy for creative activities. Thus, excess productivity becomes "oppressive productivity" (Marcuse 1964: 17). In agreement with Marcuse, Gorz (1973) states: "[w]e could live better producing less." Gorz (1976) further identifies that excess production becomes "destructive production" as "the disutilities and costs of a productive act exceed the useful effects" and we "wreak ever more destruction to combat the destructive effects of their production." Thus, excess work not only leads to human repression but also to destruction. These arguments lay a strong foundation for more recent calls for reducing worktime.

Work time reduction (WTR) is associated with significant reductions in GHG emissions, ecological footprints, and resource use (e.g., Rosnick and Weisbrot 2006, Knight et al. 2013, Fitzgerald et al. 2015, Fitzgerald et al. 2018). Additionally, WTR has numerous social benefits such as increased autonomy and lower structural unemployment (see LaJeunesse 2009, Gunderson 2019). By using productivity gains to increase social and ecological wellbeing rather than increase production, WTR may help address the underlying problem of climate change: capitalism's inherent growth engine (Stoner 2021).

WTR would involve reducing annual working hours to a new standard, without decreases in pay or loss of benefits, and would likely also involve work sharing models. Work sharing allows less hours worked while avoiding unemployment (Schor 2015). As explained by Pullinger (2014: 14), there are multiple avenues for WTR including limiting the number of working hours per week, increasing holidays each year, increasing time for maternity and paternity leave, increasing sick leave, and offering pre-retirement transitions. Examples of WTR already exist. Most examples have been temporary policies during economic downturns, but increasingly WTR is occurring in European countries (LaJeunesse 2009). There are both social and environmental benefits associated with WTR.

WTR has been shown to reduce carbon emissions (Knight et al.

2013, Fitzgerald et al. 2018). Shorter working hours involve lower rates of production and reduce pressure on resource and energy use. WTR can result in reduced total energy use, as working hours are associated with energy consumption (Fitzgerald et al. 2015). Rosnick and Weisbrot (2006) estimate that if working hours were reduced instead of using productivity gains for increased production, the US would consume 20% less energy. Rosnick (2013: 124) also posits that if we reduce working hours 0.5 % annually over the next century we can "eliminate about one-quarter to one-half, if not more, of any warming that is not already locked in."

In general, because longer working hours are associated with increased carbon emissions, ecological footprints, and energy use, WTR represents a potentially powerful climate change mitigation strategy. Fitzgerald et al. (2018: 1851) examined correlations between carbon emissions and working hours among US states and found a strong positive relationship, concluding that WTR is a "key policy lever to reduce emissions as well as protect employment." In addition, Fitzgerald et al. (2022) find that the influence of working hours on emissions in US states increases in magnitude when there are higher levels of economic inequality. Therefore, policies aimed at reducing inequality could increase emissions reductions along with WTR.

WTR can also offer a range of social benefits including helping to increase levels of full employment, address alienated labor, improve quality of life, and enhance human flourishing (Heikkurinen et al. 2019). As Hickel (2019) explains, WTR would enhance wellbeing:

> [W]ith more free time people would be able to have fun, enjoy conviviality with loved ones, cooperate with neighbors, care for friends and relatives, cook healthy food, exercise and enjoy nature, thus rendering unnecessary the patterns of consumption that are driven by time scarcity.

Other social benefits include time to do creative work, gardening, and self-provisioning including canning and processing home-grown foods, sewing, knitting, art, and pottery. Lastly, as explained by Heikkurinen et al. (2019), there are clear benefits related to increased employment and addressing alienated labor:

> The generalized reduction of working time amounts to a choice as to the kind of society we wish to live in. This can be seen from its two inseparable objectives: (a) that everyone should work less, so that everyone may work and may also develop outside their working lives the personal potential which cannot find expression in their work; (b) that a much greater proportion of the population should be able to have access to skilled, complex, creative and responsible occupational activities which allow them continually to develop and grow.

It is important to recognize that WTR does not necessary guarantee reduced carbon emissions because leisure could conceivably be spent doing more environmentally harmful activities like shopping or travel (Knight et al. 2013, Gunderson 2019). Advertising restrictions (see below) are one way to counteract this possibility and to help encourage low-impact activities. However, with widespread economic democracy and WTR, there would likely be more diverse goals, less marketing and advertising, and less pressure on individuals to consume unnecessary goods. More free time also allows for the self-provisioning activities mentioned above that are low-impact but do take more time.

Stoner (2021) discusses WTR in the context of a Green New Deal to address the climate crisis. In the US, a Green New Deal (GND) resolution was introduced in the House of Representatives by Alexandria Ocasio-Cortez in 2019. While the goals of the resolution included reducing emissions to net-zero by 2050 while increasing jobs, it did not include any mention of WTR which would likely be highly effective to address both. This absence and other features of the GND indicates a failure "to grasp the dynamic of capital as a primary driver of contemporary social change" (Stoner 2021: 14). WTR would represent a "concrete step towards overcoming capitalism" (Stoner 2021: 15). To address these shortcomings, Mastini et al. (2021) discuss what a GND without growth might entail and in terms of work, explain that the job guarantee mentioned in the GND Resolution could be key to the implementation of WTR, and propose that the state could initiate WTR through shorter working weeks or fewer working hours per year, which would then pressure private employers to do the same. Samper et al. (2021), point out that the European Green Deal (2019) fails even to mention work or guaranteed employment, let alone WTR or worker-controlled production systems – all key elements of a GND without growth.

4. Advertising Restrictions and Sufficiency Measures

Advertising restrictions are critical for reducing carbon emissions driven by overproduction and overconsumption. In fact, research has found that social norms to encourage low-carbon choices for individuals were effective but only in the absence of advertising: Castro-Santa (2022) found that "advertising dominated choice and counteracted the positive effects of the social norm," meaning that "low-carbon norms have a limited effectiveness in changing consumer preferences in a world dominated by advertising." In other words, efforts to change consumption and overconsumption remain counteracted by advertising, which continues to strongly influence choices. Advertising restrictions can include banning advertisements for high-carbon products or activities, status goods, goods targeting children, luxury goods – as well as bans on false or misleading labels and restrictions placed on certain media outlets (Nyfors et al. 2020).

Marketing not only restricts human freedom by controlling and stupefying consciousness (e.g., Marcuse 1964), it also contributes to ecological destruction by greasing capitalism's need to produce for the sake of producing (e.g., Löwy 2007: 303f). Galbraith (1958) long ago identified how advertising plays a key role in creating the desires that fuel consumption. Advertising and the media are used to create "false needs" through manipulation (Marcuse 1964). Debord (1983) calls them "pseudo-needs" created specifically to maintain the growing economy. Advertising influences individuals' perceptions of themselves and their social status, compelling them to buy products to address manufactured dissatisfaction (Horkheimer and Adorno 1969). Buying alternatives and "voting with your dollar" supports a belief that through different purchasing one can alleviate negative impacts, yet still fuels overconsumption. We return to this relation between production, consumption, and advertising in chapter 5.

While restricting advertising seems "un-American," even in the US, advertisements aimed at children were heavily regulated until 1984 (Molotsky 1988). Banning advertising for harmful or status commodities and commodities for children could significantly help reduce overconsumption. Other restrictions could include banning advertising in public spaces (Hickel 2019). Advertising restrictions complement other proposals discussed above: democracy in the workplace would likely reduce the imperative to advertise, and reduced advertising would help ensure that increased free-time due to WTR did not result in increased levels of consumption.

Advertising regulation may also be a vehicle for undermining capitalist realism. As Serge Latouche (2015: 120) argues, "denouncing the aggression of advertising" is a "starting point" for stepping out of the restricted imaginary of late capitalist societies. Marcuse ([1964] 2013: 245–246) similarly states that "the mere absence of all advertising and of all indoctrinating media of information and entertainment would plunge the individual into a traumatic void where he would have the chance to wonder and to think, to know himself... and his society."

Parrique et al. (2019) and Nyfors et al. (2020) argue that, in addition to efficiency gains, effective climate policy must include an array of *sufficiency* measures to curb consumption and counteract rebound effects. In addition to advertising restrictions, sufficiency policies can include banning planned obsolesce (Hickel 2021): the act of purposefully manufacturing short-lived products so that they need to be replaced, maintaining higher levels of sales. For example, due to planned obsolescence, Apple's AirPods are designed to last only 18-36 months of daily use before they are no longer effective (Taffel 2022). Also, carbon taxes, subsidizing low-impact goods and activities, as well as information campaigns and "nudging" can be used. Nudging "includes making low-carbon choices more easily accessible or default; framing; consumption monitoring; social comparison; and personalised sufficiency advice" (Nyfors et al. 2020: 14). Phasing out animal agriculture would be an especially impactful sufficiency measure. Eisen and Brown (2022) estimate that phasing out livestock production has the potential to provide "half of the net emissions reductions necessary to limit warming to 2°C by the end of the century." These policy changes combined have the potential to curb unnecessary overconsumption in wealthy countries, a necessary step to effectively and justly reduce GHG emissions. In addition to policy changes, in chapter 5 we will also discuss ways to counter the ideology of overconsumption that is so widespread in wealthy or overdeveloped countries.

5. Reallocation of Excess Wealth

Excess wealth is a key driver of GHG emissions that must also be addressed through policy change. Evidence consistently shows that GHG emissions in all countries increase with income (Hubacek et al. 2017). Inequality in terms of both income and wealth are consistently positively associated with GHG emissions and are especially concentrated at the top of the income and wealth distribution, with global elites having a carbon footprint approximately 14 times that of the lowest global income group (Jorgenson et al. 2018). There is no question that excess wealth increases GHG emissions and specific mechanisms are likely associated with increased access to frequent and private forms of travel (cars, jets, and yachts), owning/building multiple and larger homes, and increased material purchasing and consumption.

As explained by Green and Healy (2022: 1), because the wealthy are disproportionately contributing to the climate crisis, any effective climate policy must not be carbon-centric, but also address wealth inequality and associated political influence:

> [S]ocioeconomic inequalities drive emissions-intensive consumption and production, facilitate the obstruction of climate policies by wealthy elites, undermine public support for climate policy, and weaken the social foundations of collective action.

Policies must be implemented that reduce the extent of excess wealth and also help those whose needs are not being met. Both degrowth and ecosocialist thinkers have proposed a range of means to curb excess wealth and redistribute it to increase necessary social protections. Wealth redistribution can take place in various forms, including a progressive tax, wealth tax, income cap, carbon tax and dividend program (where tax money is redistributed to low-income households), luxury taxes, and other mechanisms. The most appropriate mechanism can be chosen based on the specific social context, yet the primary goal should focus on curbing excess wealth. Reducing excess wealth would represent an effective climate mitigation strategy in itself, as the wealthiest individuals remain the largest GHG emitters and also set a standard for others to pursue affluent livelihoods that involve much higher GHG emissions.

In addition to curbing excess wealth associated with GHG emissions, the surplus can be redistributed to address climate change and increase average wellbeing. While some funds from wealth reallocation should be used for climate mitigation and adaptation programs, it can also be used for increasing social protections, such as providing universal basic income (UBI) or universal basic services. UBI is a very prominent policy proposal within the degrowth literature (Fitzpatrick et al. 2022) and many ecosocialists argue that UBI could be an effective means to reduce environmental harms in certain social conditions. It should be noted that UBI can and has been coopted by conservative thinkers and political parties, who propose replacing other social safety nets with a low UBI and using UBI to suffocate demands for a fair wage (Zamora 2017). However, UBI could be paid for through some of the mechanisms of curbing excess wealth mentioned above and without replacing any social services or involving reducing any social protections. Mulvale (2019) explains how UBI is in line with both degrowth and ecosocialist thinking yet underscores the importance of other policies to ensure high quality housing, health care, food security, and education. As explained by Lawhon and McCreary (2021), evidence suggests that the overall benefits of UBI are most realized when the state also provides a high standard of public services: thus, progressive support for UBI (in contrast to conservative support) is often contingent on the continuation or enhancement of public services or the provision of universal basic services.

Lawhon and McCreary (2020) make a compelling argument that UBI represents a strategic lever to bring about a social-ecological transition in line with both ecosocialism and degrowth. They envision a long-term strategy for UBI that serves as a mechanism to redistribute wealth globally, across national borders. In terms of socialism and ecosocialism, Lawhon and McCreary (2021) argue that UBI can be a key strategy to move beyond capitalism and, drawing from the work of Erik Olin Wright, they explain the possible role of UBI in decommodification. They also explain how "in redistributing wealth, a UBI provides access to capital for alternative, worker-owned facilities" (Lawhon and McCreary 2021: 465). Regarding degrowth, the authors discuss how UBI not only helps to reduce economic inequality but, depending on its design, can also support reduced working hours and reduced ecological impacts. Lastly, Gorz supported UBI, specifically calling for a move away from focusing on the salaried worker as the agent of change for the transition out of capitalism and the need to accept the possibilities of work automation, the phasing out of undesirable and demeaning work, and simultaneously using basic income as a means of increasing social support (Lawhon and McCreary 2021).

6. Nationalizing and Phasing Out Fossil Fuel Companies

Despite all that is known and all that is at stake, fossil fuel companies continue to plan to extract and sell fossil fuel reserves, plans that would eliminate any chance of staying within global climate targets. They are beholden to shareholders and will continue to squeeze every last cent possible out of fossil fuel extraction (Paul et al. 2020). Because fossil fuel companies are not going to stop extracting on their own, nationalizing and phasing out oil, gas, and coal companies is one route to keeping fossil fuels in the ground (e.g., Gowan 2018, Aronoff 2020). We stress the *phasing out* part of this agenda item, as nationalization to accelerate fossil fuel extraction would obviously worsen the climate crisis. This approach also allows for a just transition of workers to new forms of employment in, for example, renewable energy. In addition to fossil fuel companies, nationalization may be a potential strategy for phasing out other carbon-intensive industries in a way that reduces harm to workers and more justly transitions them to other industries (Smith 2019).

Alperovitz and others (2017) detail a policy proposal similar to the 2008 financial crisis response: creating new money ("quantitative easing"), but instead of bailing out banks, using the money to buy out fossil fuel companies. They argue that government buyouts are not uncommon and have occurred throughout US history, including the buyout of tobacco companies between 2004 and 2014. Gowan (2018) also proposes nationalizing fossil fuel companies, which has already been proposed in the United Kingdom and is taking place in Norway. According to US takings laws, governments can purchase fossil fuel companies at market value. Gowan (2018) states that purchasing 51% of fossil fuel shares (a majority stake) would cost about $410 billion and argues that this cost is small compared to the long-term costs of the climate crisis.

Similar to the qualifiers above about collective control and ownership, nationalizing fossil fuels only creates social conditions that open up the potential to reduce carbon emissions and, alone, is not a solution (Paul et al. 2020). Nationalized fossil fuel firms could just as easily be used to increase fossil fuel production and distribution. Indeed, many of the largest fossil fuel firms in the world are state-owned or majority state-owned (e.g., in China). Although nationalization is an insufficient condition to phase out fossil fuel companies, it is likely a necessary condition because the social relations that underlie the growth imperative driving emissions are bolstered by the legal institution of private property (Gunderson and Fyock 2022). Any successful fossil fuel phase-out via nationalization would require a political movement and party committed to this goal and a large-scale transition to renewables.

Why a New Climate Agenda?

We believe the climate movement would be better positioned to gain power if leaders identified and promoted clear policies and programs aimed to effectively and justly address climate change. While they are certainly raising awareness, concern, and participation in activism, even the most well-known leaders in the climate movement too often forgo proposing concrete and transformative alternatives. This failure takes at least two forms. First there are calls for system change coupled with strategies that maintain rather than transform the system driving climate change. For example, strategies like divestment represent symbolic and financial nudges to reduce fossil fuel use but do little to change the system that continues to increase production, consumption, and energy use. System change rhetoric, however, remains a key part of these efforts. For example, Bill McKibben (2019) stated "while I don't know how to change the 'system,' the urgent nature of the climate crisis doesn't let us simply put off action." Without a clear idea of what system change would entail, many environmentalists focus on strategies like divestment and increasing renewable energy sources – representing partial solutions that maintain a system of increasing production, consumption, and energy use. We do not aim here to criticize environmental leaders, but instead call for all environmentalists to give increased attention to specific pathways to achieve the "system change" they call for, the system change truly required to effectively and justly address the climate crisis.

A second way the climate movement has failed to push forward transformative alternatives involves calls for system change without describing how the system should and could change *at all* – calls for system change with no direction as to what to do (cf. Kenis and Mathijs 2014). System change is a key demand in the climate movement, yet most people are uncertain or vague about what is to be done. Greta Thunberg told the United Nations that "if solutions within the system are so impossible to find, then maybe we should change the system itself." In addition, climate protest signs commonly call for "system change." Yet, there is a strategic flaw in demanding system change without at least a rough conception of a desired destination and concrete roadmap to begin the journey. Further articulation is essential to describe what particular changes are necessary. While system change rhetoric is gaining ground in the heart of the climate movement, calls for system change must become much more specific.

One goal of this chapter is to close the gap between demanding that the system must change and identifying strategies to achieve this aim. The six strategies outlined above, grounded in both ecosocialist and degrowth thinking, are a beginning. They are concrete demands and policies currently absent among general calls for system change. While there are clearly stigmatisms and issues associated with using the terms ecosocialism and degrowth, the six strategies outlined in this chapter can be pursued and promoted without using these terms. What is of increasing importance is to share that other strategies, pathways, and systems are possible. Advancing alternatives and being able to articulate what a new system would look like remains critical to minimizing global warming. Based on the evidence, we urge the climate movement—its leaders and activists— to consider this climate agenda and to begin to demand the specific policies and programs necessary for system change.

In addition to the strategies summarized above, The Next System

Project and The Great Transition Initiative are two online sources with many compelling cases for system change as well as specific policy proposals and structural changes to create a new system. As Speth (2015: 11), one of the co-founders of The Next System Project, clearly explains:

> The current system is simply not programmed to secure the well-being of people, place, and planet... If we are to escape the crises now unfolding all around us, we must create a new system of political economy where outcomes that are truly sustainable, equitable, and democratic are commonplace. This is certainly one of the most important tasks any of us can engage in at this moment in history... and system change is not starry-eyed but the only practical way forward.

However, Speth (2015) also explains that when events open pathways for addressing these crises, system-changing strategies must already be designed and ready to be pushed forward by a large and vocal group of supporters.

While these strategies may seem politically unfeasible, planting seeds of possibility today is a prerequisite for consideration, deliberation, and adoption. Many politicians remain tied to vested interests and therefore promote small reforms to a broken system. This power has yet to be meaningfully challenged, as the climate movement continues to lack the power necessary. Changing the system requires taking power, as it is unlikely that politicians who aggressively defend the status quo are going to install a serious mitigation program. An important step in gaining power is articulating clearer and concrete "first steps" through which a systemic transition can occur. Given what is at stake, there is no time to waste and calls for system change must continue to be urgent but, at the same time, more exact in terms of proposed policies and programs. The climate movement needs to propose concrete steps with clear benefits. On this last point, strategy remains crucial to realizing these policies. Although many have proposed policies, the recommendations often lack precision or fail to consider the interactions across proposals (WTR linked with economic democracy, for example). We propose the above interventions, in part, to call into question the current approach to climate change but also acknowledge that reaching these goals requires concrete strategy and specificity around these proposals (Fitzpatrick et al. 2022).

Despite the current inhospitable political context and massive obstacles, which we examine in forthcoming chapters, further developing and articulating these strategies and working to connect them to the climate movement is a worthy endeavor. It is important to remember that many social struggles throughout history at first seemed unfeasible and impossible to overcome. As Marcuse (1967: 3) explains,

> unfeasibility shows itself only after the fact. And it is not surprising that a project for social transformation is designated unfeasible because it has shown itself unrealized in history... the criterion of unfeasibility in this sense is inadequate because it may very well be the case that the realization of a revolutionary project is hindered by counterforces and countertendencies that can be and are overcome...

As mentioned before, we consider the climate agenda described above to be a suite of "non-reformist reforms," as described by Gorz (1976). They represent bold policies to catalyze a transformative pathway out of capitalism. Non-reformist reforms differ from "normal" reforms, because they create structural changes that open up many more possibilities for transformative change. As stated by Kallis (2018: 136), these are

> reforms that, if they were to be implemented, would require the very contours of the system to change radically to accommodate them. And reforms that, simple and commonsensical as they are, expose the irrationality of the system that makes them seem impossible.

We believe that if carefully crafted and implemented in concert, these agenda items would serve to catalyze a social transition to a radically different social order. This order, based on the principles of ecosocialism and degrowth, would curtail overproduction and consumption for the sake of profit maximization and open pathways for democratic decision-making based on new priorities. Thus, implementing this suite of reforms would not only serve to directly mitigate the climate crisis, but would also transform the larger social context and introduce new possibilities for more effective and just climate mitigation options.

Chapter 4:
Mitigation Tools in a
New Social Order

[I]n order to become vehicles of freedom, science and technology would have to change their present direction and goals.

– Herbert Marcuse (1969: 19)

In chapter 1, we criticized some of the tools promoted by techno-capitalists as inherently dangerous and unjust, such as solar geoengineering, when compared to less risky and more equitable alternatives. Other mitigation tools promoted by techno-capitalists are not inordinately risky or inherently ineffective, but simply insufficient without concurrent social changes. In this chapter, we explain how technology-based mitigation strategies, including energy efficiency, renewable energy, and certain approaches to carbon dioxide removal, could be much more effective in a system based on the principles and goals of ecosocialism and degrowth. For simplicity, we will call this new system based on ecosocialism and degrowth (and spurred by the climate agenda in the last chapter) "the new social order" moving forward.

Drawing from critical theorists, we first explain how the social context of technological use and design matters. While we critique blind techno-optimism, we argue that certain technologies have an important role to play in mitigation and could be utilized to meet their full potential in a new social order. Yet, in the current system, they remain constrained and undermined by the ever-growing levels of material production and energy use. Indeed, scientists are increasingly calling for reducing GPD growth in order to harness the full potential of climate mitigation technologies and assert that these degrowth pathways have the lowest risks moving forward (e.g., see Keyßer and Lenzen 2021).

In this chapter, we begin by discussing how technology is neither a savior nor a force of destruction, as its development and implementation is conditioned by the social relations and priorities determining how technology is designed and used. While some scholars and environmentalists enthusiastically adhere to techno-optimism and the view that technology is the solution to environment problems, others associate technology with environmental destruction and social harm. We draw from the work of critical theorists to examine a more nuanced understanding of science and technology in society – as neither a predetermined solution nor an agent of harm. Scientific advances and technologies can be used to achieve different ends depending on their design and use, which is determined by social context. We then apply these ideas to examine the potential of technologies to mitigate climate change in the new social order, where production and consumption levels in wealthy countries are decreasing. We argue that in this new social order technologies can be used differently and to different ends, guided by the central goals of enhancing human wellbeing and staying within ecological limits.

Science and Technology in Social Context

While there are a range of different public attitudes about technology (e.g., see Kerscher and Ehlers 2016), dominant positions on the relationship between science and technology and environmental outcomes can be simplified and divided into two primary camps. First, there are those who claim science and technology will fundamentally improve society's relationship with the biophysical environment and solve problems. In contrast, there are those who argue science and technology are foundational to human attempts to dominate and control nature and represent the ecological destructiveness of modern societies. Here, we briefly explore these positions and examine a more nuanced position on technology as proposed by Herbert Marcuse.

Techno-optimists believe "technological breakthroughs will serve as the means to address each and every environmental problem that arises, allowing society to overcome natural limits and all socio-ecological challenges" (York and Clark 2010: 481). Within social theory, ecological modernization theory (EMT), an influential normative and theoretical assessment of environmental reform, is perhaps the quintessential example of the techno-optimistic camp. EMT proposes that greener technologies, in concert with economic reforms, are the principle means for securing sustainability (e.g. Mol 1995; 1997, Mol and Sonnenfeld 2000). EMT maintains that technological innovation and reforms within contemporary social formations will fundamentally improve society's relationship with nature (e.g. Mol 1997, Mol and Sonnenfeld 2000). Indeed, technological innovation is the "linchpin" of EMT (York and Clark 2010: 483). As Mol (2001: 58) explains, "environmental deterioration is conceived of as a challenge for socio-technical and economic reform, rather than the inevitable consequence of the current institutional structure."

York and Clark (2010) identify three fundamental problems with the techno-optimist position. First, techno-optimists frame environmental problems as purely technical problems that demand purely technical solutions. This overlooks a vast body of research from the environmental social sciences that shows that environmental problems are not only mediated by social influences but are further directly caused by the structure of socio-economic systems. Second, technical fixes often cause unintended consequences and additional problems. Third, as we explained in the introduction of this book, advances in technical efficiency can paradoxically increase consumption and resource use (the Jevons Paradox and rebound effects).

In opposition to the techno-optimists, others argue that science and technology are the principal culprits of environmental harm (Yearley 1997). They argue that science and technology reduce the natural world to a passive object to be dominated by the active subject; there is a moral and epistemological distancing between scientific-technological thought and the environment, thereby reifying the active subject/passive object distinction; and science and technology are reductionistic in a way that breaks apart the real interrelations of ecological systems. There are also empirical and practical arguments: science often serves the society in which it operates (e.g., for economic gains) and scientific and technological innovation is primarily concerned with exploiting rather than benefiting the natural environment.

We draw from the theories of the first-generation Frankfurt School, particularly from Marcuse, who we believe not only largely transcended this debate, but still offers applicable theories, especially for understanding the relations between science, technology, and the environment. Our goal is to further projects that bridge the debate between techno-enthusiasts and -skeptics (Kerschner et al. 2018), as we believe that pathways to most effectively address the climate crisis will need to embrace technology, yet in a new social context and with new end goals. Members of the Frankfurt School argued that science and technology in capitalist societies—as embedded social projects—are largely utilized to dominate and exploit the environment and human beings; however, they maintained that these institutions have the potential to be reformed in a more rational society. In a new social order, science and technology can be used for different ends. As stated by Marcuse (1967), "I believe that the potential liberating blessings of technology and industrialization will not even begin to be real and visible until capitalist industrialization and capitalist technology have been done away with."

In Horkheimer and Adorno's well-known *Dialectic of Enlightenment* (1969), they argue that the historical project of using reason to dominate nature and free humanity from the binds of nature's authority, a project rooted in antiquity but taking full form in the modern era, had paradoxically resulted in the enslavement of human beings along with nature (or the rest of nature). What is considered progress in Western civilization "runs in a single strand, on the rails of the mere domination of nature" (Adorno 1998: 212), an instrumental rationality "reproduced" in society and the self. With the spread and domination of instrumental reason, incapable of formulating substantively rational ends, we see the development and spread of capitalism, unreflective technical progress, and a context where reason has lost its aim resulting in the domination of humans and nature as an end in itself. Reason remains irrational when it endures as "frantic development of productivity, conquest of nature, [and] enlargement of the mass of goods" (Marcuse 1968: 207). The development of modern science was theorized as a significant development in the project of domination. As Horkheimer (1993: 314-15) states,

> [t]he foundation of modern natural science was established during the Renaissance. The aim of this science is to identify, with the support of systematically employed empirical knowledge, regularities in nature's course, by means of which one can then either effect or hinder certain effects as are required – in other words, to dominate nature to the greatest extent possible.

Marcuse (1989: 123) argues that viewing the development of modern science and technology as a process that was separate from the development of capitalism was naïve, as in both developments everything that exists must be reduced into something that is measurable, calculable, and quantifiable so that it can be mastered in terms of efficiency and productivity. Marcuse (2011: 154) explains that modern science, even "pure" science, is always "potentially applied science [technology]" because the potential of using and shaping nature is inherent in the structure of modern scientific method, where nature is one-sidedly regarded as "stuff" to be manipulated for human ends.

Science and technology are organized within capitalist societies—their pregiven reality—as a medium for the domination of humans and nature. Therefore, they are far from being autonomous or independent forces. Technological use and its outcomes are determined by the "pregiven empirical reality" (Marcuse 2011: 152), or, "in line with the prevalent interests in the respective society" (Marcuse 2001: 44). Thus, in a society organized around mastery and domination, humans use technology to further the domination of both nature and other humans. Also, in a society organized to assure capital accumulation for the ruling class, technology will often be used in ways to increase profits for those in power, even if this entails hampering its ability to achieve other goals. As explained by Marcuse (1968: 223-24), "[t]echnology is always a historical-social project: in it is projected what a society and its ruling interests intend to do with men and things." Stated differently in *An Essay on Liberation*: there is nothing inherently repressive about technologies, but only due to the "presence" of ruling interests "in" them, determining "their number, their life span, their power, their place in life, and the need for them" (Marcuse 1969: 12).

However, Marcuse is also aware that the creation and adaptation of new productive forces can radically transform social relations. He argues that technical achievements reinforced and altered the way in which domination took place in social relations and between society and nature. In short, "the technological power of the apparatus affects the entire rationality of those whom it serves" (Marcuse 1978: 141). While critical of technology used to further domination in capitalist societies, Marcuse sees the liberatory potential of technology that remained stymied and obstructed in capitalist societies. He believes the "ultimate purpose" of technology was to free humans from excess toil, yet this could not be realized in the current social order. Indeed, Marcuse's earliest essays argues that technology ought to be utilized to increase human happiness and one of the deepest contradictions of capitalism is that it is used, instead, to increase unhappiness (see Kellner 1984: 120).

Marcuse states that to fully utilize the potential liberatory potential of technology, humanity must develop a very different relationship with the natural world, or what he calls an "aesthetic ethos" or "the new sensibility" (Marcuse 1969, 1972). Drawing from Marx (1964: 181), Marcuse argues that this new ethos would attend to the aesthetic qualities of nature, an attention that could help alter human-nature interactions: the "human appropriation" of nature "would be nonviolent, nondestructive: oriented on the life-enhancing, sensuous, aesthetic qualities inherent in nature" (Marcuse 1972: 67). He hopes for a new "liberating" form of mastery that "involves the reduction of misery, violence, and cruelty" (Marcuse 1964: 236). For example,

> [c]ultivation of the soil is qualitatively different from destruction of the soil, extraction of natural resources from wasteful exploitation, clearing forests from wholesale deforestation. Poverty, disease, and cancerous growth are natural as well as human ills – their reduction and removal is liberation of life. (Marcuse 1964: 240)

As a social-historical human activity, Marcuse explains that the aesthetic attitude toward nature would foster a new science and technology that could be used to preserve, support, and enhance life rather than dominate, exploit, and destroy it. Marcuse (1969: 19) states: "in order to become vehicles of freedom, science and technology would have to change their present direction and goals; they would have to be reconstructed in accord with a new sensibility." Thus, any radical change in values, science, and technology was dependent upon a radically different social order, a non-capitalist order based on a new aesthetic attitude.

Having examined the overlapping principles, goals, and agendas associated with ecosocialism and degrowth in the previous chapters, we argue that under the new social order—guided by these principles, goals and agendas—technologies could be used for different purposes and result in different ends. In other words, not for the purpose of domination and mastery over nature, nor the purpose of capital accumulation for those in power, but to most effectively and justly minimize global warming and to protect human wellbeing and ecological integrity.

In this radically different social order, technologies would no longer be undermined by the economic growth imperative and would have the potential to more effectively and rapidly mitigate climate change. Freed from the profit imperative and the goals of ruling interests, technologies could be designed as vehicles to prioritize social wellbeing and ecological sustainability and could be harnessed to the greatest extent possible for the ends of justly minimizing global warming. In this new social order, technologies would have much greater potential to result in sustainable, just, equitable outcomes, especially when compared to the techno-capitalist agenda.

In the following sections, we examine the potential of technological advancements and tools already being used and developed to more effectively mitigate climate change in a new social order. This includes energy efficiency, yet in a social context where sufficiency efforts are reducing total energy use (Parrique et al. 2019). This also entails a true renewable energy transition, in a system where fossil fuels are being rapidly phased out and collective ownership and management of new renewable energy systems allows for reduced energy use and just access to energy governance. Lastly, this includes the use of certain "negative emissions technologies" designed and used to maximize carbon capture and permanent storage rather than remaining limited and constrained by the profit imperative and market conditions.

Efficiency *and* Sufficiency

In their report *Decoupling Debunked*, Parrique et al. (2019: 3) explain that decoupling based on green technology and efficiency gains is not enough to stay within ecological limits because it ignores the effects of increasing levels of production and consumption:

> Existing policy strategies aiming to increase efficiency have to be complemented by the pursuit of sufficiency, that is the direct downscaling of economic production in many sectors and parallel reduction of consumption that together will enable the good life within the planet's ecological limits.

They explain that, while many policies already focus on efficiency, they should focus on sufficiency as well, because reducing overall production and consumption is *even more important* than efficiency gains. Sufficiency requires producing and consuming what we need, not infinitely more and more simply for the sake of economic growth and profit accumulation.

In the introductory chapter, we briefly discussed the limitations of green technology as a solution to the climate crisis and the role of the Jevons Paradox and the rebound effect. The Jevons Paradox was named after the economist William Stanley Jevons for his finding that improved efficiency of steam engines increased total coal consumption (Clark and Foster 2001). It refers to the commonly found association between increased resource use despite improved efficiency. It is called a paradox as a reasonable assumption in that improvements in efficiency will decrease total resource use because fewer resources are used per economic unit. The adjoining concept of a "rebound effect" refers to when the benefits of efficiency gains are partially consumed by increases in resource use due to improvements in efficiency (Santarius 2012). A full realization of the environmental gains of improved efficiency means that there is no rebound effect (a 0% rebound effect). Rebound effects above 100% are termed "backfire effects" or "backfires." This means that total resource use is higher after the improved efficiency was implemented due to improvements in efficiency. Some use the term the Jevons Paradox to refer strictly to backfires while others use the term to refer to any paradoxical association between increases in resource use despite efficiency improvements. The underlying quandary of the Jevons Paradox is that total resource use increases despite efficiency gains.

Scholars have put forth a number of possible direct and indirect causes and pathways that may explain the Jevons Paradox. York and McGee (2015) summarize the most common hypotheses (cf. Sorrel 2007, Santarius 2012):

- *Direct association explanations:* The most common explanation of a rebound effect is that improved efficiency reduces the price per unit of production and/or consumption, thereby stimulating production and/or consumption and, thus, resource use.

- *Indirect association explanations:* The most commonly theorized indirect explanation is when the money saved by producers and/or consumers due to efficiency gains is spent on other forms of resource use. Another proposed indirect association points to new high-resource use pathways following structural transformations in production and consumption due to efficiency improvements.

- *Structural explanation:* Capitalist societies aim to maximize profits through two routes: (1) reduce costs of production and (2) produce/sell more, requiring resource use. Improvements in efficiency reduce costs, thereby increasing profits, which are reinvested to expand production, requiring higher rates of resource use.

We agree with others that it is important to place the Jevons Paradox in social-structural context (e.g., Foster 2000, York et al. 2011, Foster et al. 2010, Freeman et al. 2015, York and McGee 2016). Economic growth as a necessary condition of the Jevons Paradox is emphasized in York and McGee's (2015: 85) theory that improved efficiency may form and/or strengthen "developmental pathways that over time lead to rising resource consumption." For example, resource efficiency is a cost-reduction strategy that, by increasing profits, increases production. That is, rebound effects may operate through an indirect structural mechanism, which partially explains the common association between economic growth and environmental stress despite higher levels of efficiency, especially at the national level (e.g., York et al. 2011, Jorgenson and Clark 2012). Indeed, nations with higher levels of efficiency generally have higher rates of carbon emissions, electricity consumption, and energy use (York and McGee 2015). Although the causes of the Jevons Paradox are likely diverse and multi-layered, it is significant that all explanations presuppose the existence of continued economic growth.

We argue that policies and strategies associated with degrowth and ecosocialism are central to minimizing the Jevons Paradox/rebound effects. However, simply having a non-growing economy may not be enough to maximize the climate mitigation potential of efficiency improvements, as additional social context matters. Drawing from neo-classical economic assumptions, Saunders (2014) develops a model to illustrates that in a zero-growth market economy, when efficiency gains in technology are introduced, rebounds persist in full force. However, Saunders' (2014) model assumes an unchanging labor force and unchanging household preferences. In this case, efficient technologies in a zero-growth economy increase salaries and translate into increased household consumption. However, if implementing the climate agenda outlined in the previous chapter, especially work time reduction (WTR) and interventions to discourage consumption (e.g., advertising restrictions), the results would change. Saunders (2014) argues against Herman Daly's (2005, 2008) view that technology gains can be used while resource use remains at a steady state. However, in a different social context, we agree with Daly that it is possible for a steady state economy and efficiency gains to exist concurrently, and that this would be a desirable pathway to address the climate crisis. Policy interventions and social changes related to production and consumption, as outlined in chapter 3, could alter how efficiency gains and technological development can translate into effective climate mitigation.

Others agree that the Jevons Paradox/rebound effects could be minimized or even eliminated through policy interventions. According to York and McGee (2015: 4),

> [i]t is important to emphasize that there is no necessary reason that the Jevons/rebound effect must occur. In principle, policies can be designed to ensure that efficiency gains are converted into lower resource consumption rather than higher levels of production.

WTR plays a key role in harnessing the benefits of technological efficiency gains. As York and McGee (2015: 4) explain, "since worker productivity is a measure of labour efficiency, and it seems intuitive that if workers are becoming more efficient they should need to work less." Yet in a capitalist system this has not been the case as increased efficiency leads to the expansion of production. In contrast, in a new social order, efficiency gains could result in fewer working hours. Reducing the time dedicated to production, production infrastructure, and the private ownership of resources would all help to address rebound effects (Gunderson and Yun 2017).

In addition, reducing consumption and consumption-encouraging infrastructure is also key to reducing the Jevons Paradox and rebound effects (Gunderson and Yun 2017). Policy interventions can be used to direct these changes including advertising restrictions and bans, luxury taxes, wealth taxes, carbon taxes, and promoting a culture of sufficiency and simple living. As Freire-Gonzalez (2021: 3) explains, the "economic perspective is the assumption that human wants are essentially infinite, and the desire for commodities in general is taken to be insatiable." Yet, the assumption of human insatiability undermines human wellbeing. Capitalism drives what Freire-Gonzalez (2021) calls "systemic insatiability" and, thus, increased resource use and ecological destruction. To enhance human wellbeing and stay within ecological limits, a new system of sufficiency is required, as well as a system that addresses inequality. As greater wealth is associated with higher GHG emissions and resource use, addressing inequality through income caps or wealth taxes would serve to reduce emissions while also curbing consumption and reducing rebound effects. Therefore, interventions to reduce both production and consumption are necessary to minimize rebound effects.

To illustrate this point further, we extend York and McGee's (2015: 82-83) fruitful thought experiment meant to clarify the social drivers of the Jevons Paradox and rebound effects. They ask us to imagine two worlds akin to contemporary society, one in which people drive extremely efficient personal vehicles (50 kilometers per one liter of fuel) and the other in which people drive extremely inefficient personal vehicles (one kilometer per 50 liters of fuel). Other forms of transportation would also have similar disparities in fuel efficiency. One may initially assume that less fuel would be consumed in the extremely efficient world (hereafter, World 1). However, if one considers human behavioral adjustments to social structure, they argue that in the extremely low-efficiency world (hereafter, World 2) more people would walk and ride bikes and very few people would drive due to the high financial expense and how immobile engines would become (cf. Owens 2011). More importantly, World 2 would also likely look significantly different:

> In the low-efficiency world, it is possible that there would be no sprawling suburbs, innumerable roads, and expectations that people travel far for work, entertainment, or shopping. In the world with high fuel efficiency, there would likely be very little constraint on driving, so that the infrastructure much like our own world but more so, would be designed around cars and innovation would be directed to further develop car-centric technologies. (York and McGee 2015: 83)

Their point is not to make a case for fuel inefficiency, but to illustrate the social drivers of the Jevons Paradox. They do not make a case for fuel inefficiency as Owens (2011) does due to an important qualifier: these are not inevitable outcomes and would change in different conditions. Applying the principles of degrowth and ecosocialism (see chapter 2) to guide our economy would be such a condition.

In addition to imagining the very high-efficiency (World 1) and very low-efficiency (World 2) hypothetical worlds, in which a growing economy is assumed, we ask the reader to imagine two more hypothetical worlds: a very high-efficiency world *with a degrowing economy* (hereafter, World 3) and a very low-efficiency world *with a degrowing economy* (hereafter, World 4). Of these four worlds—(1) efficient-growing (World 1), (2) inefficient-growing (World 2), (3) efficient-degrowing (World 3), and (4) inefficient-degrowing (World 4)—which would consume the lowest total amount of fuel? We agree with York and McGee that it is very probable that World 2 would consume less fuel than World 1. However, if one compares World 2 to a high-efficiency world in the new social order (World 3), the outcome changes.

In the new social order guided by degrowth and ecosocialist strategies (World 3), production and consumption standards and behaviors can address many rebound effects. People travel to work fewer times per week, share and/or publicly own far fewer personal vehicles (those used would be highly efficient), rely much more on walking, biking, and highly efficient public transportation, restrict long-distance travel, place a high value on local enjoyments, prioritizing local production and consumption of agricultural and other goods (i.e., less distance between production and consumption), producing fewer total products, etc. In this scenario, it seems reasonable to assume that not only would World 3 (efficient-degrowing) consume less fuel than World 2 (inefficient-growing), but would almost certainly experience a much lower intensity of rebound effects than World 1 (efficient-growing) *because the reduced consumption of resources is an organizing societal principle.* While the example here is transportation, this argument holds for other forms of resource use, such as electricity production.

One could make a reasonable case that World 4 (inefficient-degrowing) would consume fewer resources than World 3 (efficient-degrowing). While this may be valid, we assume that even in a shrinking economy many modern uses of energy would, while used less, perform functions that a degrowing society would likely desire to maintain for social development. For example, in the case of transportation, if a degrowing society desires to continue using less environmentally harmful forms of transportation, such as light rails, street cars, and railways, as well as more environmentally harmful forms, such as planes and personal vehicles (even if total use is significantly reduced), it would be more desirable to use more efficient energy conversion technologies because the environmental gains of efficiency can be realized in a the new social order. Thus, the Jevons Paradox would disappear, or at least lessen.

Supporting a Genuine Renewable Energy Transition

A new social order based on ecosocialism and degrowth would also be much better positioned to realize the potential environmental gains of renewable/alternative energy. This is because the energy boomerang effect, discussed in our introductory chapter, is predicated on the imperative to increase energy throughput using money saved through the reduced costs of energy. Due to this effect, we have not seen a true *transition* to renewable energy but instead an overall increase in total energy use with renewables slowly taking up a larger slice of an ever-growing energy pie (York and Bell 2019). In contrast, what is necessary to mitigate climate change is a rapid and genuine transition to renewable energy sources with a deliberative and fast strategy to reduce fossil fuel extraction and use.

An ecosocialist/degrowing economy would have the potential to contain the energy boomerang effect for two reasons. First, this new social order supports the absolute reduction of carbon energy, e.g., through a progressively tightening carbon cap (Lorek 2015). This means that society would avoid scenarios in which fossil-fuel based energy expands despite the expansion in renewable energy (e.g., Ernsting 2015). In other words, alternative energy development would have the opportunity to expand without a simultaneous expansion in carbon energy. Diverse measures could be adopted to progressively reduce fossil fuel use, including ending fossil fuel subsidies, taxing carbon emissions, introducing public education programs concerning carbon budgets, adopting the use of "post-growth" indicators instead of GDP, and redirecting public spending from high- to low-carbon infrastructure.

The second reason this new social order would mitigate the energy boomerang effect is because it involves reductions in total energy use. As Trainer (2012: 591) argues, "[renewables] cannot fuel a consumer society for all" (cf. Alexander 2014: 13–14, Trainer 2010). In other words, using less energy in wealthy countries must be part of the energy transition. Shorter working hours is one way to reduce total energy use as working time increases energy consumption and this relationship has intensified over time (Fitzgerald et al. 2015). However, this potential depends on what activities people engage in during their expanded free time (Knight et al. 2013). In the new social order, low-energy/carbon activities would be encouraged and incentivized as well as lifestyle changes that reduce total energy use.

Examining the potential of lifestyle changes to reduce household energy use, Alexander and Yacoumis (2016) identify a diversity of behavioral changes including: increasing walking and biking, using solar shower bags for hot water, insulating housing, dressing appropriately to reduce heater use, using clotheslines rather than dryers, and shifting toward non-electronic based entertainment. They estimate that these changes can reduce total household energy consumption by 49% and are easy ways households can support an overall energy descent. However, significant and widespread behavioral changes often presuppose structural changes. This system would not only limit how much electricity can be produced through fossil fuel sources via appropriate ownership and governance structures, but would result in less total residential electricity, including alternative energy-generated electricity (Lietaert 2010).

In addition, we agree that many "problems of technology can be overcome through open access and elimination of undemocratic control by corporations and elites" (Kerschner et al. 2015: 31). Because growth-dependency is predicated on the private ownership and control of productive technologies, addressing the issue of ownership and control is especially important to begin intentionally contracting total energy use. Collective ownership usually refers to two different models: (1) worker and/or cooperative ownership (i.e., ownership and democratic control directly in worker/public hands) and (2) state ownership (i.e., nationalization and bureaucratic state control). However, Kunze and Becker (2015) argue that ownership of energy infrastructures need not be limited to the state vs. cooperative dichotomy, and it is more important to explore how ownership structures achieve wider social and environmental goals (cf. Thombs 2019). For example, the nationalization of fossil fuel companies may be the best form of collective ownership for shrinking fossil fuel production and use (e.g., Gowan 2018).

Collective ownership, on its own, is not a sufficient condition to resolve the energy boomerang effect. However, collective ownership is likely (1) a necessary condition to intentionally and sustainably degrow an economy (and reduce total energy use) and (2) a condition conducive to passing policies that limit the use of fossil fuel-based energy. Byrne et al. (2009: 90) discuss reframing energy as a collectively owned commons, explaining that

> although commons institutions do not in and of themselves guarantee eradication of environmentally exploitive practices, they do offer elements for recovery of political agency in the formation of choices regarding energy and environmental futures and the foundation for a normative reconstitution of the good life.

In the new social order, specific social and environmental goals would govern energy systems that are local and democratic (Tsagkari et al. 2021). The goals of local energy systems can go beyond a commitment to reducing fossil fuel-based energy and increasing the production of electricity from alternative energy sources to include specific goals and strategies for positive social change and environmental and social justice (Kunze & Becker 2015).

"Community energy" (also called "community renewable energy" or "community owned renewable energy") represents an emergent means to foster local decision-making and guide genuine energy transitions. This entails "projects where communities (of place of interest) exhibit a high degree of ownership and control, as well as benefiting collectively from the outcomes" (Seyfang et al. 2013: 978). Such initiatives have proliferated in the past few decades with examples across the globe, and some have chosen goals and strategies in line with ecosocialism and degrowth (Rommel et al. 2018). Whether explicitly oriented with these agendas or not, these energy initiatives have the potential to choose pathways to transition to renewables in a decentralized, democratic, and collective way while also reducing total energy consumption. Byrne et al. (2009: 91) state that with community energy, "we have the chance to do something impossible in the era of energy obesity: relocate energy-ecology-society relations in a commons space." More than simply providing energy from a different source, viewing energy from a collective ownership or a commons perspective focuses attention on sovereignty and empowerment for communities who can direct their own energy transitions.

In summary, the energy boomerang effect could be contained given measures to progressively reduce carbon energy use, reductions in total energy use, and if there was no imperative to increase total energy throughput using money saved through alternative energy development. The energy boomerang effect is not an outcome of alternative energy development per se, but only of alternative energy development in a particular kind of society. In the new social order, one that promotes and funds community energy development, it is possible to have a *genuine* renewable energy transition.

Negative Emissions Technologies

Lastly, we examine the potential for atmospheric carbon removal and storage to serve as a mitigation tool in a new social order. In contrast to some techno-optimists, we do not believe carbon removal is *the* solution to the climate crisis (see chapter 1). However, in a new social order, grounded in the goals of ecosocialism and degrowth, carbon removal strategies could be used more effectively and could be one tool among many used to minimize global warming. As discussed in chapter 1, technologies to capture and store carbon are widely supported by the fossil fuel industry as a way to address climate change while continuing to use fossil fuels. However, in the new social order, rapidly phasing out fossil fuels would be a priority and capturing and storing carbon (known as negative emissions) could be used in conjunction with other mitigation strategies. Here we focus on Direct Air Capture (DAC) as a negative emissions technology, as it is being increasingly called essential to meet the terms of the Paris Agreement and new sources of funding continue to expand research and development (Verma 2022).

Before we discuss the mitigation potential of DAC, it is important to note that there are less technologically sophisticated ways to remove carbon from the atmosphere. These are often referred to as "nature-based" or "natural" climate solutions (NCSs). NCSs increase carbon storage "naturally" through reforestation, forest conservation, fire management, cropland and grazing management, and coastal and peat restoration. NCSs also have the added co-benefit of protecting and enhancing biodiversity (Griscom et al. 2017, Mori et al. 2021). However, as with many other climate mitigation strategies, NCSs alone are not sufficient to keep temperature within global targets and should not be used as justification to delay cutting energy and industry emissions. NCSs, like tree planting, are widely supported by the public yet also have certain limitations, uncertainties, and risks (Bellamy and Osaka 2020). Some studies indicate NCSs can tackle up to 30% of mitigation needs while others argue that competition for land will significantly constrain this potential (Griscom et al. 2019).

While there are many reasons to support NCS, here we focus on how technology is being used to remove carbon, performing the work of trees with much lower land requirements.

As discussed in chapter 1, DAC has, in principle, the potential to result in negative emissions, reducing atmospheric concentrations of carbon. Total negative emissions, however, depend on the source of energy used to power DAC. A DAC facility would need to be powered by renewable energy (e.g., solar or wind) to maximize negative emissions. Currently, DAC remains largely under-developed due to the high costs and limited profitable products for sale (Stone 2018). Investment from government and private funders continues to increase and many hope that as carbon prices increase DAC will become a profitable enterprise (Verma 2022). Most operations today must create a usable product for sale in order to make the operation financially sustainable. For example, some companies with DAC facilities have focused on converting CO_2 into a liquid fuel, which results in a carbon neutral rather than a carbon negative operation. In the current social order, for most companies, DAC is not a rational investment without a profitable product to sell.

However, in the new social order, where a central goal is to stay within ecological limits, we can imagine extensive public investments in DAC and state-owned and even community-run DAC facilities as a part of a diverse mitigation plan. Increasing evidence suggests that DAC implemented widely and powered by solar or wind energy for long-term storage could result in meaningful carbon sequestration. Wohland et al. (2018) find that DAC powered by variable renewables is a promising approach that can result in negative emissions of up to 500 Mt CO_2/year in Europe, using excess renewable energy only. Breyer et al. (2019) examine a regional model for DAC fully powered by wind and solar and conclude that possibilities for implementation and the benefits of these systems have been widely overlooked.

Widespread implementation of DAC powered by wind or solar energy could contribute to carbon removal; however, there are two current obstacles. The first is political-economic: extensive government intervention would be necessary to make this possible, as current market conditions constrain this possibility. Incentivizing negative emissions projects through the right carrots and sticks could make conditions more favorable (Bellamy and Osaka 2020). In a different social order moving beyond the profit imperative and market-based approaches, more direct and effective policies could be implemented. For example, following a model of public ownership over energy systems (see Gunderson et al. 2018), DAC could be designed in conjunction with solar and wind projects to support a negative emissions network. In the immediate future, a conceivable option is a national program that hires scientists to research and develop wind- and solar-powered DAC technology with participatory democratic decision-making.

Freed from the growth and profit imperatives, DAC could be used in a way that maximizes carbon removal. In other words, with publicly funded programs free from current market constraints, DAC could be used in ways that contributes to meaningful negative emissions. While we do not believe DAC is a "silver-bullet" or *the* solution to the climate crisis, in the new social order it could be used (along with reductions in totally energy use) as part of a diverse portfolio of mitigation strategies.

Technology for Different Ends

A critique of widespread techno-optimism should not spill over into a rejection of the potential positive employment of modern technology for contributing to the creation of an ecological society. Otherwise, one falls prey to the same ideological assumptions as the techno-optimists who presuppose that technology is an entirely autonomous force, unconditioned by social context. While we agree with the sound reasons that we ought to be skeptical of quick technological fixes to environmental problems (e.g., Dentzman et al. 2016, Foster et al. 2010, Gunderson et al. 2018, York & Clark 2010), there are also good reasons to predict that altering social conditions would change the kinds and range of harmful or helpful environmental effects of already-existing technologies as well as open new possibilities for technology design.

Technology in general *can* be specifically used for protecting nature and society, yet this requires liberation from the profit motive and use based on new substantive goals (Marcuse 1964). Whether a technology could be used for more rational ends in different social conditions requires an analysis of the given technology, an approach to technology assessment that is neither Promethean nor technophobic (Gunderson et al. 2019). As awareness of these social relations and constraints increases, so do calls for social-structural transformation, for shifting priorities to put social and ecological wellbeing before profit, and for reducing total material and energy throughput to stay within ecological limits (Foster 2010, Kallis 2018, Kallis et al. 2012). In a society that no longer operates under the logic of profit maximization, the full potential of technological solutions to climate change may be realized. In concert with the policies and programs outlined in the previous chapter, we believe technological investments in efficiency, renewable energy, and DAC could all be harnessed to their full potential in terms of reducing atmospheric carbon concentrations. None of these technological strategies alone is sufficient to address the climate crisis, yet with no time to waste there are many mitigation tools that we can use in new ways that will make them much more effective.

Chapter 5:
Confronting
Overconsumption

The point is not to refrain from consuming more and more, but to consume less and less - there is no other way of conserving the available reserves for future generations. This is what ecological realism is about.

– André Gorz (1980: 13)

Overconsumption by affluent individuals is a significant driver of GHG emissions (Jorgenson et al. 2018, Wiedmann et al. 2020). We believe this can only be partially addressed by policies related to advertising restrictions and wealth redistribution in the new climate agenda. In this chapter, we acknowledge that more lies beneath the surface. There are key ideological elements of widespread overconsumption in wealthy countries as well as structural drivers. Both structural and ideological aspects of overconsumption must be addressed. First, adopting the "non-reformist reforms" discussed in chapter 3 would shift the social context. The resulting new social order would then open possibilities for the ideological transformation necessary to transition to a culture of sufficiency rather than ever-increasing levels of consumption.

We do not conceive of overconsumption as a blanket problem, seeing as much of the world is in dire need of *more* consumption.

We acknowledge that there are many people globally whose needs are not being met and who require higher levels of consumption. It is those who are most affluent who are most responsible for consumption-based GHG emissions. However, we do not blame individuals for overconsumption. In this chapter, we examine the underlying causes of overconsumption related to both structural drivers as well as the ideologies of overconsumption that reinforce individual consumptive behavior.

Overconsumption can be understood as excess purchasing of non-necessary, positional, or luxury goods that increase GHG emissions and contribute to other harmful environmental and social impacts. A good portion of these impacts come from the wealthiest individuals (Jorgenson et al. 2018). As mentioned before, those in the top 1% income bracket in the US emit over 300 metric tons of carbon dioxide equivalent per capita, compared to 20 metric tons for the average North American and well above the 6.2 global average (Chancel and Picketty 2015). While our discussion in this chapter applies to people and governments across the globe, we use the US as a primary example to better understand the drivers of overconsumption. The US represents a highly consumptive country. For example, the US has less than 5% of the global population but uses a quarter of global fossil fuels (Worldwatch 2018). As other countries increasingly attempt to emulate the "American lifestyle," these trends in production, consumption, and GHG emissions continue to spread globally.

What does overconsumption look like? Over the 20th century, American families spent a larger share of their income on luxury goods and what Brown (1995) calls positional goods: those material items purchased to mimic the spending of wealthier families. The US now has more cars than licensed drivers (Worldwatch 2018), and, since 1973, US homes have increased in size from 1660 to 2740 square feet on average (US Department of Housing and Urban Development 2015), despite having fewer people per household. However, material wealth has not necessarily increased wellbeing.

After a certain level, studies have shown a negative correlation between consumption and wellbeing (Lee and Anh 2016). Despite widespread "moderate" levels of overconsumption in many wealthy countries, it is the wealthiest individuals that contribute the greatest GHG emissions through extravagant high-carbon lifestyles (Green and Heely 2022). The wealthy global elite tend to have much higher levels of overconsumption including multiple large homes, multiple cars, and private transportation means such as private airplanes and yachts. As stated in Jorgenson et al.'s (2019: 5) review of drivers of climate change:

> Globally, households with incomes in the top 10% are responsible for 36% of carbon emissions, while those in the bottom 50% are responsible for only 15% of emissions. The average annual carbon footprint of global elites is about 14 times that of the lowest income group.

Thus, overconsumption generally, but especially among the wealthiest, is critical to address.

In the previous chapter, we identified technologies that could be harnessed to mitigate climate change; however, gains from these technologies continue to be "diminished or cancelled out" by growing levels of overconsumption globally (Wiedmann et al. 2020). As supported by ecosocialism and degrowth, production and consumption must be reduced below current levels to address the climate crisis. Without this contraction, the economy will, in the long run, likely collapse due to the contradiction of continually increasing production on a finite planet (Schmelzer 2016). Based on the biophysical limitations of the Earth, Jackson (2009) argues it is not a matter of *if* the economy will contract but *when*. We agree that to effectively and justly mitigate climate change the underlying drivers of overconsumption must be identified and addressed (Wiedmann et al. 2020). In this chapter, we explain why this must involve moving beyond a focus on individuals as the cause of overconsumption and instead must simultaneously address both the structural as well as the ideological drivers of overconsumption.

Beyond Individual Consumer Change

It is not surprising that many people continue to focus on what individuals can do to reduce their personal GHG emissions. Fossil fuel companies have spent millions of dollars on promoting individual behavioral changes as the solution to climate change to insulate their own actions from regulation (McFell-Johnsen 2021). This focus on individual actions is not surprising for several reasons: it is used to shift blame away from industries and governments and it is in line with neoliberal ideologies that continue to shape how the climate crisis is perceived as a problem and the identification of appropriate solutions.

If we live in a world where outcomes are determined by aggregate freely-made individual decisions, then solutions to problems should focus on these individual decisions. Neoliberal ideology and the sanctity of individualism have become naturalized in capitalist societies over the past several decades. For many people these notions are now commonsense, as neoliberalism has become the dominant "hegemonic" ideology (Gramsci 1971). Individual choice is sacred and emphasized through a focus on entrepreneurship and consumerism (Harvey 2007). The neoliberal project has also socialized the individualization of subjects in ways that undermine collective action and organized efforts to improve societal wellbeing. Lastly, neoliberal ideology continues to promote skepticism about government programs and policies or other collective endeavors to address social problems.

Green consumerism emerged as the ultimate neoliberal solution to climate change. As explained by Swafield and Bell (2012: 258), this creates a "neoliberal environmental citizen" who... "promote pro-environmental behavior but only in ways that were consistent with a neoliberal account of how social or behavioral change can be and should be achieved." The underling belief is that individuals can solve the climate crisis through making different consumption choices that reduce GHG emissions. This involves buying items such as energy efficient appliances and lightbulbs, hybrid cars, and solar panels. In media responses to the IPCC special report (IPCC 2018), reporters focused on changes people can make in their individual behaviors and personal consumption. For example, a CNN article highlighted "what consumers can do," listing changes in personal transportation (e.g., buy a hybrid car) and housing (e.g., buy a more efficient air conditioner), among others (Mackintosh 2018). This solution approach supports increasing consumption and profits but in a way that is supposedly environmentally sustainable ("green" growth).

In addition to green consumption, many environmentalists consume less or change lifestyle behaviors to reduce personal GHG emissions. This includes buying fewer material goods or no new material goods – what Greta Thunberg calls "shop-stop" and others call "buycott." This also includes driving less or not at all, limiting or refraining from air travel, and reducing or eliminating the consumption of animal products. According to a study by Doherty and others (2020), the vast majority of Extinction Rebellion activists surveyed had adopted a range of pro-environmental behaviors including: buycotting, changing their diet, consuming less, reusing products, reducing energy use, and buying used or second-hand goods.

Yet, those who live a low-carbon lifestyle do so with difficulty, as their lifestyle goes against the dominant economic and cultural tide, and they must carefully maneuver against the forceful current. In addition to the personal challenges involved in changing one's lifestyle to reduce GHG emission, evidence indicates that individual changes will not be sufficient to address the climate crisis (see the introduction). It is not that these actions would not be beneficial and contribute towards emissions reductions, but they will not be enough to keep warming within 1.5°C or 2°C. Even coordinated individual actions at a massive scale would leave the industries, infrastructures, and production processes that create the majority of emission intact.

As illustrated with evidence in the introduction of this book, individual behavior and lifestyle changes alone will not come close to reducing emissions at the rate and scale necessary to keep emissions within 1.5°C or even 2°C. While individual consumption and behavioral changes are insufficient, this does not mean that they should not be pursued, only that they are far from a panacea. In addition, evidence suggests that in some cases adopting personal and household actions to reduce carbon emissions can result in reduced support for climate policies (Werfel 2017). Lastly, individual lifestyle and behavior changes are not occurring at the scale and pace necessary to achieve the full potential of these estimates.

Despite these realities, there are clear ethical reasons for individuals to seek to reduce their personal carbon footprints. Even if individual actions are not enough to address the climate crisis (and in some cases may serve as a distraction from systemic change), many individuals believe that low-carbon living is the right thing to do. One justification is articulated by Knights (2019: 529), who argues that even though individual actions are relatively "inconsequential," that personal GHG emissions reduction is still "morally obligatory" based on the following argument:

A. To remain a member of a harming group is a moral wrongdoing;

B. The performance of consumption actions constitutes remaining a member of a harming group;

C. Therefore, the performance of consumption actions is a moral wrongdoing.

In other words, by living a high-consumptive and carbon-intensive lifestyle, individuals are members of a harming group, and a "virtue-based" perspective illustrates the "moral wrong-doing of remaining a member of such a group" (Knights 2019: 544). Baatz and Voget-Kleschin (2019) develop a different justification for individual actions to reduce emissions (even when "inconsequential") based on a notion of moral equity and not exceeding an individual's "fair share" of GHG emissions entitlements. Baatz and Voget-Kleschin (2019: 577) argue that an individual's (e.g., A's) GHG emissions are morally wrong if: "1. A exceeds her fair share of emissions entitlements, and 2. By emitting, A contributes to a harmful activity." Indeed, there are clear moral justifications for personally pursuing a low carbon footprint. However, in addition to low-carbon living, it remains critical that activists demand the systemic changes that are required to address the majority of emissions driving the climate crisis.

The only way to limit global warming to 2°C or below is to implement systemic changes. Because efforts focused solely on individual-level changes often represent pseudo-action (Gunderson 2021), where actions "contribute to the stabilization of the order which they intend to attack" (Blühdorn 2017), we focus here on the need to address the structural drivers of overconsumption as well as the ideologies (largely promoted by producers and the state) that drive individual consumptive behavior.

The Structural Drivers of Overconsumption

A key relationship that undermines the effectiveness of green consumerism is that, in many cases, production and marketing drive consumption. In other words, consumer choices rarely reshape production and therefore "buying green" or "voting with your dollar" is far from an effective mechanism of social change. As Galbraith (1958: 136) explains, there is a "dependence effect," where consumption is driven by desires created by producers through advertising: "wants thus come to depend on output." In this section, we emphasize that overconsumption is a necessary product of an expanding, growth-dependent capitalist system.

Neoclassical economics portrays production as responding to consumer demand. However, this is not always the case. Evidence contradicts this relationship and supports the Marxist notion of structured consumption where worker-consumers play a key role in keeping aggregate consumption high to maintain the growth of the economic system. For example, Schnaiberg (1980) explains that consumption "cannot be treated as independent of the changing structure of producer power and producer technology" and therefore there are "limits to a consumption oriented environmental reform policy" (Schnaiberg 1980: 161). Schnaiberg (1980: 192) concludes his analysis by stating that "consumption cannot be the leading factor in the expansion of production. Increased consumption may permit expanded production, but it does not generally cause it."

Scholars before Schnaiberg (1980) reach the same conclusion. Contradicting the economic theory that "it is the marginal *consumer* who determines the direction of production," Max Weber (1978: 92) argues that, "given the actual distribution of power, this is only true in a limited sense for the modern situation. To a large degree, even though the consumer has to be in a position to buy, his wants are 'awakened' and 'directed' by the entrepreneur." This relationship between capitalist production and consumption is also described well by the Marxist phenomenologist Enzo Paci (1972: 436-437):

> [I]n an affluent society... men become consuming animals or a *commodity which consumes* those commodities that abstract capitalism needs to have consumed. From the very beginning, capitalism has put aside use-value in order to produce commodities need not by consumers but by exchange-value. … The [consumer of the affluent society] is forced to become a machine for preestablished consumption. Eventually, he spontaneously desires what capital wants him to desire, even alienation, on every level of life.

Members of the Frankfurt School also describe how capitalist production requires and therefore creates increasing rates of excess consumption. While the standard explanation is that production increases to meet the needs of consumers, "[i]n reality, a cycle of manipulation and retroactive need is unifying the system ever more tightly" (Horkheimer and Adorno 1969: 95). Without increasing levels of consumption, "the established mode of production could not be sustained" (Marcuse 1964: 246). To support capitalist production, the individual must become a consumer who buys more and more, "redefined by the rationality of the given system" (Marcuse 1964: 12). As explained by Horkheimer and Adorno (1969: 106):

> The consumers are the workers and salaried employees, the farmers and the petty bourgeois. Capitalist production hems them in so tightly, in body and soul, that they unresistingly succumb to whatever is proffered to them.

In this way, the individual is transformed into a consumer who helps to perpetuate the capitalist system.

To increase rates of consumption, media is harnessed to advertise goods and create false needs. Through advertising, individuals are subjected to the "manipulation of needs by vested interests" and instructed "to behave and consume in accordance with the advertisements, to love and hate what others love and hate" and to fulfill "false needs" (Marcuse 1964: 3,5). Similar to Marcuse's description of false needs, the French Marxist and Situationist Guy Debord (1983: §51) discusses the propagation of "pseudo-needs" which serve to increase wealth for the ruling class:

> The satisfaction of primary human needs is replaced by an uninterrupted fabrication of pseudo-needs which are reduced to the single pseudo-need of maintaining the reign of the autonomous economy.

Advertising changes individuals' perceptions of themselves and their status, compelling them to buy products to address their dissatisfaction. Even when individuals know they will not be fulfilled, they still consume: "The triumph of advertising in the culture industry is that consumers feel compelled to buy and use its products even though they see through them" (Horkheimer and Adorno 1969: 167). In the US, total expenditures on advertising have risen to over $205 billion annually (Griner 2017). Not only has advertising greatly increased in recent decades but public policies have shifted, enabling greater advertising reach (Schor 2014).

As described by Western Marxists, the structure of the capitalist system compels ongoing expansion in production and economic growth and requires increasing levels of excess consumption. Yet, this is not sustainable in a finite world with biophysical limits. Increasingly, scientists are concluding the entire economic system and the way it is organized must change. For example, as Wiedmann and others (2020: 7-8) explain, "the profit-driven mechanism of prevailing economic systems prevents the necessary reduction of impacts" and we must "replace GDP as a measure of prosperity" and "[e]xpect likely shrinking of GDP if sufficient environmental policies are enacted." More and more scientists agree, economic growth must be curtailed. This means abandoning capitalism, which is inherently growth-dependent, and considering the strategies and programs described in this book from proponents of ecosocialism and degrowth. In other words, addressing overconsumption requires a structural change to a new social order. However, we also acknowledge that in order to gain the support for structural changes and a transition to a more sustainable social order, we must also identify and confront the ideology of overconsumption that remains a barrier to change.

Overconsumption as Ideology

Confronting overconsumption requires recognizing the powerful role of ideology (see the introduction). The creation and internalization of ideologies was essential to create the worker-consumer of monopoly capitalism, who has become essential for sustaining high rates of production and economic growth. Martinez (2017) describes strategic decisions aimed to create worker-consumers. For example, following industrial disputes in 1919 and a surge in socialist and anarchist supporters, US industry leaders decided to reduce the chances of a worker rebellion by giving workers increased wages, bank credit, and more leisure time – all for the purpose of encouraging increased rates of consumption. They believed increased consumption would more than offset increased wages and would serve to pacify workers, distracting them with material pursuits and deterring labor rebellions. In this way, workers are made into "a commodity that consumes" – a key cog keeping the treadmill of production increasing in scale and speed (Schnaiberg 1980).

Ideology conceals the role of the consumer and the drivers of overconsumption. Producers rely on consumers for increasing economic growth and use ideology, primarily communicated in the form of advertising, to create willing subjects. These subjects keep consuming because they believe that increasing consumption results in increased happiness, consumption is part of the "good life," consumption relates to their identity and status, and they "need" certain commodities to address dissatisfaction. In addition, the message that consumers have total freedom and power in their consumption choices supports the notion of "voting with your dollar" and addressing problems through changing consumption patterns. Thus, consumption becomes the answer to many social issues and a convenient answer for those profiting from increased consumption. This relates to environmental issues including climate change, where consumer-oriented approaches do little to address the ongoing production driving us toward ecological collapse. These messages continue to conceal that capital is perpetuating overconsumption for the irrational end of self-accumulation, keeping consumers on the treadmill of consumption to reap increasing profits.

These ideologies were recognized long ago, and their prevalence have only increased over time. The transformation of consumption, in relation to larger changes in the structure of capitalism, was a central concern of the Frankfurt School and Debord. To illustrate overconsumerism as a form of ideology in wider social-structure context, we draw on two concepts from this line of thought: Marcuse's "false needs" and Debord's "spectacle" to better understand how ideology has and continues to promote overconsumption through promoting specific false messages and narratives.

Marcuse's (1964: 5) "false needs" refers to needs "which are superimposed upon the individual by particular social interests in his repression" (Marcuse 1964: 5). Although the notion of false needs, because it is contrasted with "true needs," has been criticized for its elitism and universalism (for review, see Fitzgerald 1985), the concept sheds light on the external, manipulative, and structurally necessary expansion of desires characteristic of monopoly capitalism, a form of social control that perpetuates growth and the existing social order. Marcuse argues that the vast majority of modern consumption takes place to satisfy manufactured false needs. Critical to this argument is how the expansion of needs "perpetuate a system whose continuation impedes the fulfillment of individual and social needs and potentials" (Kellner 1983: 68).

The deceptions of false needs also relate to false notions of freedom and attaining "the good life" (Marcuse 1964: 49). While "the good life" is about freedoms, these are "deceptive liberties [such] as free competition at administered prices, a free press which censors itself, free choice between brands and gadgets" (Marcuse 1964: 7). This false liberty hides the repressive domination of the ruling class. Debord (1983: §§47, 48, 56) describes this deceit as the "consumer illusion," living a "counterfeit life," and a "spectacular sham." Freedom is an illusion and "false choice is in spectacular abundance" (Debord 1983: §62). Buying more or different things also offers "false models of revolution to local revolutionaries" who believe that through their purchasing choices they can change the world. The lie that consumers are free and can attain "the good life" results in false notions of satisfaction and a "pacified existence" (Marcuse 1964: 242). However, "the good life" always remains out of reach, as "[t]he culture industry endlessly cheats its consumers out of what it endlessly promises" (Horkheimer and Adorno 1969: 111). Unnecessarily high levels of both work and consumption only serve to alienate and repress worker-consumers. As Gorz (1988: 22) explains:

The economic rationalization of work will thus sweep away the ancient idea of freedom and existential autonomy. It produces individuals who, being alienated in their work, will, necessarily, be alienated in their consumption as well and, eventually, in their needs. Since there is no limit to the quantity of money that can be earned and spent, there will no longer be any limit to the needs that money allows them to have or to the need for money itself. These needs increase in line with social wealth.

Thus, a progression of ever-increasing work, production, wealth, and consumption traps individuals in this cycle, stifling a fulfilling life (and emitting ever more GHGs).

While this deception goes unnoticed by the majority of people, they unknowingly feel its impact. Most people "cling to the myth of success" and "insist unwaveringly on the ideology by which they are enslaved" (Horkheimer and Adorno 1969: 106). As Marcuse (1964) explains, overconsumption becomes a way of life, a part of personal identity, and a sign of success. It is no longer questioned and "the result is the atrophy of the mental organs for grasping the contradictions and the alternatives" (Marcuse 1964: 79). Unfortunately, Marcuse explains, the nourishment from increasing unnecessary consumption is not the same nourishment required by the human soul. This results in what Debord (1983: §42) similarly calls, "alienated consumption." Living for consumption, as opposed to consume in order to live, degrades our lives and produces isolation- imprisoned by what he calls "the spectacle."

Debord's "spectacle" refers "to the vast institutional and technical apparatus of contemporary capitalism, to all the methods power employs, outside direct force, to relegate subjects to passivity and to obscure the nature and effects of capitalism's power and deprivations" (Best and Kellner 1999: 132). The two arenas commonly associated with the spectacle are mass consumption and mass media. It is difficult to disentangle the media from "consumer culture," as images are usually commodities and commodities are peddled through images. For example, the distinction between news and entertainment is indistinguishable or, at best, fuzzy in an "infotainment" society (Kellner 2003). Further, the effects of the spectacle in these two arenas are interrelated:

> The spectacle is the notion that all human relations are mediated by images from advertising, film and other sections of the mass media, driven towards controlling people's activities and consciousness. The need for the production and consumption of commodities (both material and cultural) is ensured by the reign of the spectacle, which is the enemy of a directly-lived and fully human life. (Barnard, 2004: 106-107)

Indeed, Debord (1983) describes the spectacle as "the moment when the commodity has attained the *total occupation* of social life" and a "permanent opium war which aims to make people identify goods with commodities" (§§42, 44, see also §§65-69).

In these ways and others, ideology promotes overconsumption while masking the irrationality of the capitalist system of never-ending production, consumption, and destruction. Gorz (1980: 23) echoes these sentiments stating that the goal is growth, at the expense of human well-being and ecological degradation:

> This is the nature of consumption in affluent societies: it ensures the growth of capital without increasing either the level of general satisfaction or the number of genuinely useful goods... Production becomes more and more destructive and wasteful; the destruction or obsolescence of products is built into them – their rapid deterioration is programmed.

In his essay titled *A Sick Planet*, Debord (1971) also specifically addresses the environmental impacts of this irrational system. Years before climate change became a prominent environmental issue, Debord (1971: 85) claims that capitalist production is now in "its final stage" and "what is now produced, directly, is death." As global temperatures increase and conditions near tipping points, the expanding capitalist economy continues to produce more and more, yet what many fail to see is that it is now increasingly producing death and destruction.

Dismantling the Drivers of Overconsumption

Examining the structural and ideological drivers of overconsumption reveals the fallacy in placing the onus of change on individual "consumers" who will force producers to follow their lead. These strategies will not be effective, as those benefiting from increasing levels of production continue to encourage and promote overconsumption. In other words, whenever one rhetorically asks, "Do we really 'need' all of this?" in reference to a megamall or consumerist lifestyles, the answer is "Yes," so long as capitalism lumbers on. Overconsumption is a necessary and secondary byproduct of capitalist production. Specific to climate change, continued widespread support for increasing levels of production and economic growth will undermine efforts to reduce GHG emissions and limit catastrophic warming. Given the relationships between production and GHG emissions, effective mitigation efforts will require significant systemic changes in work, production, consumption, advertising, and social norms.

Ending overconsumption requires both unmasking the underlying ideologies that are guiding the masses on a path towards destruction and also implementing the structural changes necessary to curtail endless growth and live safely within ecological limits. The structural changes outlined in chapter 3 (including WTR, job sharing, income caps, wealth taxes, and banning planned obsolescence) would all contribute towards reducing unnecessary production and consumption. Advertising restrictions and "simple living" campaigns could play a key role in curtailing the ideology of overconsumption, or the ongoing systemic propagation of false needs and illusionary spectacles of material satisfaction. Instead of promoting materialism, cultural norms could shift to support sufficiency and living with enough rather than always more.

Any impactful and socially desirable changes would require interrelated changes in production, consumption, and consciousness. Thus, worker cooperatives, WTR, and advertising limits, among other parts of the climate agenda outline in chapter 3, should be pursued together. For example, one reason Boillat et al. (2012: 602) support economic democracy on environmental grounds is there would be no structural imperative to advertise to meet manufactured "needs." Excess wealth is a key driver of overconsumption that must also be addressed through multiple policy changes. As inequality of both income and wealth are positively associated with GHG emissions both income caps and wealth taxes could be effective means to reduce excess wealth. Policies must be implemented that reduce the extent of excess wealth, curbing overconsumption and associated GHG emissions. This can also help ideological transformation. Addressing excess wealth and overconsumption at the top can set an example for the majority, who often are convinced by the spectacle of affluence and manipulative advertising to seek out more and more wealth and material accumulation. As Gorz (1980: 27) put it, anticipating Jason Hickel's (2021) degrowth book *Less is More*:

> the link between "more" and "better" has now been broken. "Better" may now mean "less": creating as few needs as possible, satisfying them with the smallest possible expenditure of materials, energy, and work, and imposing the least burden on the environment.

While Western Marxists were generally pessimistic about the possibilities for social transformation to liberate the "advanced" capitalist countries from useless toil, on the one hand, and overconsumption during "free time," on the other, Marcuse offers some affirmative guidance for moving forward, supporting prescriptions that are in line with degrowth and ecosocialism. Marcuse (1964) argues that we need new institutions that let "individuals work for themselves and speak for themselves" and that society requires a "redefinition of needs" to identify and put aside false needs as well as freedom from repressive advertising (Marcuse 1964: 206, 245). Marcuse (1964: 4) states that "[t]he unrealistic sound of these propositions is indicative, not of their utopian character, but the strength of the forces that prevent their realization."

As powerful forces protect and maintain capitalist interests and the growth imperative, the destructive impacts of this system are becoming ever clearer to an increasing number of individuals. Addressing overconsumption must be a part of any ethical response to climate change. Gorz (1980) was among the first wave of people arguing for intergenerational justice and this, for him, involves changing the way we consume today so that those in the future will have what they need to live. To counter the structural and ideological drivers of overconsumption (and climate change), individuals must reclaim their status as *citizens*, not simply *consumers* being strategically used to keep the growth-dependent capitalist system lumbering along. These *citizens* must recognize the ideologies for what they are, identify and promote systemic alternatives, and organize enough political power to implement change.

Chapter 6:
Pathways for
Transformation

Who are the realists and who are the dreamers?

– André Gorz (1980: 86)

As it is increasingly clear that society cannot carry on with the status quo, there are a growing number of scholars and activists calling for social transformation beyond capitalism. While there are differences between degrowth and ecosocialist thinking, we have explored both areas of scholarship and have identified a synergistic agenda to prioritize ecological and social wellbeing. We acknowledge there are stigmas associated with terms like "ecosocialism" and "degrowth." However, the specific policies and programs can be pursued without using these terms. While we join a large group of scholars now calling for a shift to a post-capitalist system, we also join a smaller group who have gone further through articulating specific policies and programs to be pursued. Yet, in many of these cases what is often still lacking is a thoughtful exploration or even some general ideas as to how these desired changes might become a reality. What pathways for change should be pursued? What *are* the possible pathways for change? In this chapter we examine these critical questions.

As explained by Gorz (1967) and others (Foster 2019, Kallis 2020), revolutionary reforms, like those described in chapter 3, can advance radical social change, and may act as part of a "transitional program" (Löwy 2015: 37) out of capitalism. In this way, bold policy responses to climate change could in fact "change everything" about society (Klein 2014). However, Gorz (1967: 6 emphasis added) also makes clear that while much thought is put into the question of what to do "[w]hen we are in power... *the whole question is precisely to get there, to create the means and will to get there.*" This remains a tremendous challenge as powerful actors and institutions continue to use ample resources to maintain the status quo. However, we know that social transformation has happened in the past. Indeed, unexpected events can occur that ultimately catalyze positive change. We also recognize that the fact that environmental and social conditions are worsening does not necessary mean that things will start to get better. As Beck (2016: 47) explains, we cannot assume that "the positive side effects of negative side effects automatically create a better world." A better world *has to be made.* Despite the paramount challenges ahead, we believe it is useful and necessary to explore the possible pathways and routes for positive change that exist, even if they seem unlikely. Context also matters. We are three scholars from the US, where aspects of this agenda would face far more opposition than in other regions of the Global North, especially in some European countries. Still, we find it a critical part of the conversation to begin to examine how this agenda could become a reality through specific pathways for change.

We also must acknowledge that, in contrast to other crises that might trigger radical social change, the time lag between GHG emissions and global warming presents a clear predicament in terms of implementing an effective and just response. Social change often occurs when people's needs are not being met to a degree that is drastically inconsistent with expectations, and it is becomes clear that society must be radically transformed. As Foster (2018) explains, if climate change continues unmitigated the impacts could trigger a large-scale revolution, yet "[t]he worry is that by the time the catastrophic conditions are felt on a wide enough scale, and by the time people mobilize, the situation may be immeasurably worse, with much of it out of our control. That is of course our greatest fear." Waiting for impacts to trigger a social response leaves us locked into significant warming. By the time there is a social revolution in response to climate impacts we may have already reached critical tipping points altering ecological systems in irreversible ways.

While there may be critical thresholds that should be avoided, we do not know exactly what these are and when they will occur. As David Wallace-Wells (2019) explains,

> global warming is not binary. It is not a matter of "yes" or "no," not a question of "fucked" or "not." Instead, it is a problem that gets worse over time the longer we produce greenhouse gas, and can be made better if we choose to stop. Which means that no matter how hot it gets, no matter how fully climate change transforms the planet and the way we live on it, it will always be the case that the next decade could contain more warming, and more suffering, or less warming and less suffering. Just how much is up to us, and always will be.

There is still a possibility for a less bad future, with less loss and suffering, that is worth pursuing. This future requires a new climate agenda for system change. Thinking through this agenda, discussing it with others, and demanding it politically serves to increase the chances of it becoming a reality. Despite our pessimism that these reforms will be adopted anytime soon (especially in the US), we find it worthy to articulate why they should be pursued and also to explore *how this level of social change might be achieved.*

As those in power are very unlikely to cede that power, more is required of civil society to demand change through encouraging or forcing federal governments and international organizations to take bold action. We agree with Kallis (2018: 141) that "expecting that the dominant classes will somehow release their power and forgo their immediate interests in the name of a broader common good is unrealistic." Collective actions from civil society can have a range of possible impacts, from very little to triggering radical change. Social movements have the potential to address global crisis through pressuring governments, elites, and international governing bodies to adopt new policy platforms and goals (Almeida and Chase-Dunn 2018).

We now have a global "climate movement" or "climate justice movement" which has emerged in response to the increasing threats of global warming (Almeida 2019). While the climate movement remained marginal and ephemeral over the last few decades, starting in 2018 and 2019, we saw the initiation of a more visible and permanent climate movement emerge globally. Galvanized by the IPCC's special report on 1.5°C (2018), groups already in existence became more active, with Extinction Rebellion (XR) and Fridays for Future (FFF) emerging first in Europe and then globally and the Sunrise Movement pushing for a Green New Deal to be a top priority in the US. Swedish teen Greta Thunberg became a spokesperson for ·climate action uniting young activists across the globe. In September 2019, youth-led organizations coordinated the largest climate strike in world history (with at least 4 million participants) and the "Global Week for Future" involved between 7 and 8 million participants (Fisher 2022). This wave of new action and momentum led Foster (2019) to state:

> We are seeing today what appear to be the beginnings of an ecological revolution, a new historical moment unlike any humanity has experienced... The meteoric rise of Thunberg and the student climate strike movement, the Sunrise Movement, Extinction Rebellion, and the Green New Deal, all within the brief span of a year, coupled with the actual protests and strikes of millions of climate change activists, the vast majority of them young, has meant a massive transformation of the environmental struggle in the advanced capitalist states.

Despite the stagnation in climate activism caused by the global Covid-19 pandemic, climate activist groups continue to organize direct actions, demanding bold climate responses from world leaders. XR and FFF continue to hold seasonal rebellions and school strikes on Fridays, respectively. Other groups have increased direct actions, such as Ende Gelande blocking coal mines in Germany and Just Stop Oil delaying the transport of fossil fuels in the United Kingdom. There is no doubt that a climate movement has emerged that is larger, more diverse, and growing more rapidly than ever. Yet it is still *so far* from what is necessary to challenge power and push forward an effective and just climate agenda. How can this movement become large enough and strong enough to bring about positive social change? While we do not presume to have all the answers, we find this question worth examining.

In this chapter we start with a short overview of different theories of social transformation that inform our understanding of how social change occurs and what is possible moving forward. Other authors have more deeply examined these theories elsewhere and we will include key citations that can help the reader learn more regarding the origins and specifics of each perspective. Here, we aim only to illustrate a few key concepts, some old and some new, that guide our understanding of what pathways can be pursued to catalyze and guide positive social transformation. We then focus specifically on: (1) the importance of identifying and confronting forces of social reproduction, (2) eroding the legitimacy of current powers, and (3) specific strategies that could be adopted by a larger and more unified social movement.

What Can We Learn from Theory?

Specific to the climate crisis, and more generally in terms achieving a post-capitalist future, scholars have turned to specific theories of social transformation to guide their understandings of possible paths forward. While Marcuse and Gorz offer helpful critiques of the capitalist system as well as insightful programs for a new social order, many questions remain regarding *how* this transformation might be achieved. Gorz (1967) argues that being specific about programs and policies is essential and focuses on non-reformist reforms – yet how do concerned citizens effectively challenge power to make these reforms possible? Many theories of change stem from Marx's portrayal of the capitalist system as inherently contradictory, leading to crises and, ultimately, a transformation from capitalist modes of production to socialism or barbarism (Foster 2019). Others, including Gramsci, Polanyi, and Wright, have elaborated upon this model of system change and routes for positive transformation. In addition, more recently scholars have focused specifically on social change in the context of the climate crisis to understand how it presents new challenges in terms of triggering effective and just social responses. Here, we briefly summarize some key concepts related to several different theories of transformation, as they will inform our discussion of barriers and opportunities throughout the rest of this chapter.

Gramsci (1971) built on Marx's conception of ideology to show how culture can increase the social acceptance of ideas that can prevent social change. Beliefs can become "hegemonic" or accepted norms that shape society and what is possible. From a Gramscian perspective, social change involves countering and challenging hegemonic beliefs that are reinforced in political and civil society. Gramsci distinguished between the "political society," or coercive power centers, including police, military, government institutions, and "civil society," non-coercive actors across society, including families and workers (D'Alisa and Kallis 2016). This bifurcation in society creates power differentials enabling those in power to create "common senses," which "are articulated, embodied and performed every day in practice" (D'Alisa and Kallis 2020). Civil society can organize to strategically counter hegemonic beliefs that stymie positive social change. However, Gramsci also warned of "passive revolution," in which social actors seek change in ways that actually maintain and extend existing political and economic powers (Trantas

2021). This process defuses the potential for transformative change. This diffusion emerges through cooptation from elite political actors and institutions, not through coercion but through discourses that privileges elite interests. Although the policies and practices emanating from these discourses do not benefit them, civil society takes them on as their own, which can undermine positive social change. *What this means for a new climate agenda*: (1) a climate agenda will require countering hegemonic beliefs about economic growth and neoliberal governance, and (2) the climate movement must identify and resist passive revolutionary pathways that serve to maintain the status quo and current power relations.

Polanyi's seminal book, *The Great Transformation* (2001), reflects upon two historical waves of market expansion and the counter-movements that emerged to protect society from the negative impacts of commodification. As explained by Burawoy (2015), we now find ourselves amid yet another wave of market expansion that entails the commodification of nature, with the climate crisis representing the ultimate negative impact to society. In response, a double-movement emerges including a countermovement calling for social protections from climate change and the ecological crisis. In contrast to market-based solutions to the climate crisis that serve to further commodify nature, a true countermovement to the climate crisis would involve less commodification or, in other words, solutions discussed in this book related to collective ownership and cooperative governance (Stuart et al. 2019). The climate movement must demand actions that make the economy embedded within (or subservient to) ecological and social goals, where social priorities for sustainability and wellbeing dictate economic relations. In comparison to the double-movements that Polanyi wrote about, the current struggle differs in the increased temporal delay in the development of social harms from global warming. It remains unclear whether a sufficiently powerful countermovement can mobilize to address the climate crisis and transform society before we pass a threshold towards uncontrollable and irreversible warming.

A bold climate movement could represent part of a Polanyian countermovement, yet inclusion and expansion to include other movements experiencing broader yet related social harms associated with inequality, race, and health would increase the power of this countermovement (Fraser 2014). *What this means for a new climate agenda*: effective responses to the social harms of climate change will need to go much further than market-based mechanisms and must include making economic relations serve the greater goals of ecological sustainability and social wellbeing (a countermovement must be system changing).

An increasing number of scholars and activists have drawn from the work of Wright (2010) to understand how social change occurs. In *Envisioning Real Utopias* (2010), Wright uses historical patterns to articulate a theory of social transformation that includes: (1) identifying and challenging forces of social reproduction that maintain the status quo, (2) creating and politicizing problems with the current social order (eroding its legitimacy), (3) taking advantage of unintended consequences and unexpected events, and (4) simultaneously adopting multiple transformational strategies that involve creating alternatives/"building the new" as well as eroding the old through a series of reforms (Wright 2010, 2019). While Wright (2010) called the latter "synergistic" strategies, which are based on class compromise and incremental policy changes, the temporal characteristics of climate change leave little time for compromise and incremental change. In this case, Wright's (2010) ideas on the "logic of rupture" would support using strategic disruption to pressure the state to adopt more rapid and bold policy changes. Wright does not support violent uprisings based on the negative historical outcomes, but does support using disruptive logic. *What this means for a new climate agenda*: (1) powerful actors and vested interests continue to maintain current relations and must be identified and overcome, (2) efforts must focus on undermining the legitimacy of ruling actors and institutions, (3) recent climate policies that infuse money into building up low-carbon alternatives but must do more to erode the current fossil fuel infrastructure protected by vested interests, and (4) the logic of disruption or non-violent disruptive strategies may be necessary to pressure bold climate action.

More recently, Fisher and Jorgenson (2019) articulate the idea of an AnthroShift triggered by the increasing risks of global warming. Drawing from Ulrich Beck's (1992, 1999) concepts of risk society and reflexive modernization, they explain how social change and radical transformation is often driven by responses to crisis, war, or economic depression. Like these other threats, global warming can also trigger a societal response. Yet, to instigate the radical response to climate change necessary, a mass mobilization from civil society is likely necessary using either nonviolent or confrontational strategies (Fisher 2022). As explained by Fisher and Jorgenson (2019: 50), "risk drives a reconfiguration among social actors that in turn leads to a different relationship between society and the natural environment." However, they explain that risk motivated societal pivots may not necessarily lead to improved conditions as portrayed by more optimistic ecological modernization and reflexive modernization theorists. In fact, increasing risks to society can result in multi-direction rather than unidirectional shifts in society-environment relations. For example, rather than directly responding to global warming threats through effective and just mitigation, other responses (e.g., geoengineering) could make things worse for the majority of people. Just because risks are increasing and threats are widely perceived does not mean unidirectional efforts will emerge that effectively address these risks. Indeed, we see the possibility of risks increasing even more if solutions are in line with the techno-capitalist climate agenda. There is also the possibility of directions shifting in a "pendulum of society-environmental relationships" brought about by changes in leadership or other conditions – moving towards protection or further harm and back again (Fisher and Jorgenson 2019: 343). *What this means for a new climate agenda*: (1) just increasing awareness about risks is not enough, (2) we need a carefully directed response to risk led by mass mobilizations in civil society, and (3) one step forward may be followed by two steps back.

Guided by the insights and concepts highlighted here, the following section discusses three dimensions of social transformation that might be the most useful to the climate movement. First, we explore overcoming ongoing forces of social reproduction – or the vested interests that maintain the status quo and reinforce hegemonic beliefs about what our system can and should be. Second, we discuss already emerging pathways to challenge the legitimacy of these powers and how this might be further pursued to enlarge cracks and fissures in current power structures. This could result in a much larger and cohesive movement demanding change. Lastly, we examine what kinds of direct action and specific strategies for change could be employed and discuss differing views on these strategies and their possible effectiveness.

Countering Forces of Social Reproduction

As Wright (2010: 276) explains, "social structures and institutions that systematically impose harms on people require vigorous mechanisms of active social reproduction in order to be sustained over time." Therefore, social change requires identifying the forces of social reproduction maintaining the status quo and countering these forces. Many discussions about forces of social reproduction and the climate crisis refer to these forces as "vested interests." Vested interests typically include the fossil fuel industry, but also actors in transportation, energy, development, finance, or politics currently benefiting from maintaining a fossil-fuel-based infrastructure and a neoliberal capitalist economy. As Wright (2010) points out, identifying and countering forces of social reproduction is a prerequisite to social transformation.

Vested interests maintain the current fossil-fuel-based and profit-oriented system through various means, including think tanks that create policy, funding corporate-friendly political campaigns as well as campaigns against left-wing politicians, and entering politics.

There are also more subtle strategies, such as greenwashing. Some of these strategies take place secretly and behind closed doors, such as the removal of any references to "vested interests" and the redaction of other portions of recent IPCC reports. As Foster and Clark (2022) explain, a scientific-consensus version of the "Summary for Policymakers" of Working Group III in the IPCC's AR6 report on mitigation was leaked to the media in the summer of 2021. Comparing this version to the officially released version approved by governments illustrates how all criticisms of vested interests including the term "vested interests" were deleted from the report. In addition, missing was a statement about the radical nature of change necessary: "We need transformational change operating on processes and behaviours at all levels: individual, communities, business, institutions and governments. We must redefine our way of life and consumption." Foster and Clark (2022) list other statements also removed from the IPCC report including the need to:

(1) eliminate all coal-fired plants worldwide this decade, in order to avoid greatly surpassing the 1.5°C target;

(2) carry out immediate, rapid transformational change in the political-economic regime affecting production, consumption, and energy use;

(3) shift to low-energy solutions;

(4) implement plans for "accelerated mitigation"; and

(5) support mass social movements against climate change rooted in the most vulnerable sectors of society, advancing a radical just transition

They add that "the redacted governmental-consensus report went so far as to claim that the number of coal-fired plants could be increased due to the promise of carbon capture and sequestration – a view that the scientists had rejected" (Foster and Clark 2022).

As this illustrates, vested interests are very real and are actively coopting and taking over the scientific and political processes that have been created to inform the public about climate change and protect people from climate catastrophe. Actors with vested interests in maintaining the system driving climate change have been dubbed the *climate change countermovement* (CCCM) (Brulle 2022). As described by Srivstav and Raferty (2021), "members of the CCCM may include industry associations, carbon-exposed firms, utilities, workers, unions, corporate-funded think tanks, state-owned enterprises and, government ministries with strong incentives to protect carbon-intensive interests," and these actors engage in "tactics to *prevent, repeal, weaken or delay* existing and proposed climate policies." Resources in the CCCM greatly overshadow those available to the climate movement (Brulle 2018). The CCCM has successfully delayed climate action, including the widely supported (low-hanging fruit) act of ending fossil fuel subsidies.

Much of what the CCCM does falls under what Wright (2010) calls *active* forms of social reproduction – actively reproducing the current social order through specific tactics and strategies that maintain structures and power relations. Brulle (2018) found that between 2000 and 2016 over $2 billion were spent on lobbying over US climate policy, the vast majority from corporations in the utility, transportation, and fossil fuel industries. This also occurs at the state level in the US. For example, a ballot initiative in Washington state to institute a carbon tax failed to get enough votes in 2018 after the fossil fuel industry spent a record $30 million to defeat it (Groom 2018). Representatives in the US Congress receive massive sums of money from fossil fuel companies, some more than others. In the Senate, those who do not support a GND have received, on average, seven times more money from the fossil fuel industry compared to those who publicly support the resolution (Kauffman 2019). Active social reproduction also includes agency and regulatory capture and misinformation campaigns to confuse the public about specific policies (Fisher 2022).

Fossil fuel companies, especially those identified as the "carbon majors," are spending an increasing amount of money to block climate policy while misleading the public. A 2019 report found that fossil fuel companies spend around $200 million each year to block meaningful climate policy through lobbying and an additional $195 million each year on advertising campaigns that falsely suggest they are devoting significant funds to green initiatives (Laville 2019). Others have found that fossil fuel companies will publicly support alternative energy and efforts to reduce GHG emissions while simultaneously lobbying to undermine climate legislation (Grumbach 2015 – in Brulle 2018, Laville 2019) and that, based on scientific reviews of financial data, claims of fossil fuel companies "going green" are completely false (Li et al. 2022).

There are also more *passive* forms of social reproduction that reinforce social norms and dampen motivation for collective action. High carbon consumption levels in everyday life have been normalized in wealthy countries with few people demanding alternatives in transportation and energy. Another key form of passive reproduction is the reinforcement of neoliberal notions that individuals are responsible for climate change. This notion is spread through beliefs about green consumerism, "doing one's part," and minimizing personal carbon footprints. In 2020, a subsidiary of British Petroleum introduced the personal carbon tracker app VYVE so that individuals could do their part to reduce emissions. This was met with scathing responses from climate scientists and activists, who called attention to BP's massive contributions to the climate crisis and lack of responsibility. A focus on individual actions is not surprising for several reasons: it shifts blame away from industries and governments and it is in line with hegemonic neoliberal ideologies that continue to shape how the climate crisis is perceived as a problem as well as the identification of solutions. While passive reproduction plays an important role in the climate crisis and the perpetuation of the system driving the crisis, this form of reproduction is in many cases driven by producers' efforts to increase consumption and profit, a structural byproduct of expanding capitalist production.

Lastly, as the climate movement gains more support, which we expect with increasing climate-related disasters, we will likely see increased efforts from vested interests to further coopt and transform the movement. The environmental movement has already been largely coopted, conforming with capitalism by supporting market-based solutions and green growth. As described in this book, green growth remains an illusion that undermines any possibility of minimizing global warming. The radical environmental movement, which emerged in the 1960s, was critical of capitalism but was largely coopted by ideas of a pro-capitalist environmental state using market-mechanisms to solve environmental problems (Foster and Clark 2022). Thus, the climate movement is already starting from a compromised and false environmental position that must be rectified. Any surge in the climate movement is likely to be met with additional efforts from the CCCM to neutralize anti-capitalist ideas and infiltrate goals, in line with Gramsci's concept of a passive revolution (Spash and Guisan 2021, Spash 2021). Attempts to maintain the status quo through influencing social movements will continue and climate movement organizations must be vigilant and ready to push back against these influences.

It is critical to identify the forces of social reproduction so that social movements can map out ways to overcome these forces (Wright 2010). In recent years, even more scholars and journalists are revealing these forces, exposing obvious greenwashing, outright lies, and false PR campaigns from fossil fuel companies as well as the extensive amounts of money the CCCM spends on lobbying and campaign contributions to elected officials. The Climate Social Science Network represents a collective of social scientists studying climate change and much of their research focuses on the obstruction efforts of the CCCM. Members of this group's work have been featured in *The New York Times* and other large media outlets exposing key financial relationships and levers of influence (e.g., Robert Brulle, the Network's research director). Scholars in this network have also become the focus of lawsuits initiated by firms that represent vested interests, as their work is deemed an increasing threat. Despite efforts to deter this work, even more effort is necessary to further reveal forces of social reproduction to the general public. Media outlets and academics must bravely stand up to powerful actors and expose the ways that they continue to knowingly push society further into climate catastrophe. Work exposing these forces is critical to discredit and erode the legitimacy of key actors and institutions.

Eroding Legitimacy

Eroding the legitimacy of the actors and institutions that actively maintain the status quo is essential to open pathways for change. Part of fostering social transformation involves overcoming hegemonic beliefs as well as casting doubt on the actors and institutions who have been upholding those beliefs for their own benefit. Social reproduction serves to maintain the current social order, yet social transformation can occur due to the formation of "cracks and openings in the system of reproduction" often based on the "exposed limits and contradictions of reproduction" (Wright 2010: 291, 297). Gaps and contradictions are important to identify and politicize because they can "open up spaces for transformative strategies" (Wright 2010: 290). In other words, exposing and politicizing gaps and contradictions can make meaningful social transformation possible. When cracks and crises occur, effort must focus on *delegitimizing* hegemonic actors and institutions, illustrating how the system they benefit from no longer works and is causing widespread social harm.

Srivatav and Rafaty (2021) analyze the political strategies available to the climate movement and discuss specific "antagonistic" actions to delegitimize vested interests. Civil society, especially activists, can use various means to erode confidence and respect. This can include directed protests, sit-ins, naming and shaming tactics, consumer boycotts, divestment campaigns, and other mass mobilizations and acts of civil disobedience. This can influence consumption and voting behavior, but more importantly it can be used as part of a narrative, along with the politicization of specific events, to cast doubt on leaders. Lawsuits are also a mechanism to publicly blame and shame companies and force government action. For example, in 2019 the Dutch supreme court ruled that the government must act to protect its citizens from climate change and, according to a UN official, this represents "the most important climate change court decision in the world so far, confirming that human rights are jeopardized by the climate emergency" (Kaminksi 2019). As Srivtav and Rafaty (2021) explain, "the antagonist mantra can be summarized by: name, shame, boycott, and sue."

Concerned citizens and activists are also increasingly framing the climate crisis as a moral issue. Poll after poll illustrates that the majority of people (even in the US) are concerned about climate change. Framing climate change as a moral issue centered on intergenerational injustice may be a key leverage point to help the climate movement gain more support and to delegitimize those who maintain the status quo. Wright (2019) argues that most people are motivated by moral concerns rather than class or economic concerns. As youth activists increasingly demand that world leaders protect their future, they draw attention to the immorality of continuing with business as usual. This contributes to the shaming of leaders and delegitimizing those who seem not to care about intergenerational justice (Srivtav and Rafaty 2021). In other words, inaction knowingly leaves children exposed to a catastrophic future. The fact that the system, as currently configured, is unable to respond to a moral imperative that resonates with nearly all humans may help to delegitimize the system as a whole.

An increased focus on the moral imperative to protect all children on Earth may be a way to catalyze support for a new climate agenda that acts boldly and rapidly. This strategy is based on an understanding of core values. Values relate to the "beliefs people hold about what is good, both in terms of how people should behave in the world and how our social institutions should function" (Wright 2019, 131; for review in environmental context, see Dietz 2015). Climate change threatens some core values held by many people, including *equality* (framed as climate justice, intergenerational justice, and climate apartheid) and *freedom*, as in freedom to a life not impaired by the climate crisis. Lawsuits such as *Juliana vs. US* and *La Rose v. Her Majesty the Queen* (Canada) from youth activists continue to bring attention to the question of a constitutional right to life and freedom from climate change impacts. An international group of youth have also formally filed a human rights complaint with the United Nations, stating that under the UN Convention of The Rights of the Child, world leaders must protect all children from the catastrophic impacts of climate change. A powerful moral frame could help shift the climate crisis from the confines of left-wing politics to become a universal issue of justice, equality, and freedom. This is a fruitful development, and the climate movement should take advantage of unexpected events to further the delegitimization process. The system itself is doing much of the heavy lifting for activists, engaging in continual self-delegitimization by eroding possibilities for a livable future. The importance of moral framing is also recognized by Marcuse (1969), who states that for liberation to be successful, "the sociological and political vocabulary must be radically reshaped: it must be stripped of its false neutrality; it must be methodically and provocatively 'moralized.'"

Challenging Power

As forces of social reproduction are weakened, organized social movements must emerge to deliberately shape positive social change. Schweickart (2016) states that, beyond a legitimation crisis, social transformation requires a mass movement that is sustained over time. Similarly, Kallis (2018) explains that: "political institutional changes will not come without a critical mass of people involved." In line with Polanyi's "double movement," Gorz (1967) discussed the importance of "counter-powers" and Reich (2016) the importance "countervailing powers" mobilized for social transformation. In other words, radical action to minimize global warming is unlikely to occur without a meaningful social movement demanding change.

Transformation scholars argue that rapid and radical social change will necessitate not only a large social movement, but one that can effectively challenge power. As explained by Han and Barrnet-Loro (2018), "movements focus on power. Instead of focusing only on individual action, they focus on collective action. To become a source of power, collective action must be transformative." Within the climate movement and the scholar-activist communities, disagreements and debates remain about *how* the movement should effectively challenge power. In addition, the state (federal governments across the globe) continues to subsidize fossil fuels and privilege their interests, working with them to maintain and continue fossil fuel-based infrastructure and investments (Coady et al. 2017). Therefore, actions that pressure governments to switch their alliances are necessary – actions that challenge power.

Frances Fox Piven (2008) provides some relevant insights on challenging power. Drawing from classic scholarship on social movements, Piven (2008: 20) examines how power can be challenged by the masses and from below:

> Unlike wealth and force, which are concentrated at the top of social hierarchies, the leverage inherent in interdependencies is potentially widespread, especially in a densely interconnected society where the division of labor is far advanced. This leverage can in principle be activated by all parties to social relations, and it can also be activated from below, by the withdrawal of contributions to social cooperation by people at the lower end of hierarchical social relations.

Through withdrawing cooperation and disrupting normal social relations, power at the top can be challenged from below. Piven (2008: 21, 23) describes disruption as "the leverage that results from the breakdown of institutionally regulated cooperation" and states that disruption is "a power strategy that rests on withdrawing cooperation in social relations." However, an important distinction exists between disruptions that serve to communicate ideas versus disruptions that challenge power. A climate protest, such as the People's Climate March in 2014, communicates to others the increasing concern people have about climate change and increases awareness about climate change as a serious issue. However, a pre-planned and approved protest march does little to disrupt social relations in ways that bring the system to a halt. These actions may have more to do with performance and spectacle than education and disruption.

XR uses disruption as a key tactic, but is it challenging power? XR aims to use non-violent acts of civil disobedience to disrupt the system and make governments cave to their demands. This includes longer-term targeted rebellions in London that shut down major areas of commerce and government, resulting in thousands of arrests. XR focuses on bringing "the government to a grinding halt" and taking a "hatchet" to the extractivist capitalist system (Boyer 2019). As quoted in Boyer (2019), XR leaders state they "refuse to participate in the system" and instead focus pressuring government through a "massive upheaval." With much larger and more sustained rebellions, XR would be much more disruptive. Even so, the rebellions have been communicative. Evidence suggests that XR actions have effectively influenced the way those in the United Kingdom think about climate change, increasing public concern and support for government action (Carbon Brief 2019, Smith 2021, Kountouris and Williams 2022). But has it encouraged bold and effective government action? Some claim that government actions in response to XR have been largely symbolic: declaring a climate emergency and holding a citizen's assembly have both been done, but not in a way that has resulted in bold climate action. Has XR challenged power or merely increased awareness through spectacle, causing a temporary inconvenience for those who need to work or travel through key locations in London?

Additional groups in the climate movement have adopted disruptive strategies including Ende Gelande, blocking coal mines and extractive sites in Germany, and Just Stop Oil, delaying the transport of fossil fuels in the United Kingdom. Is power being challenged in these cases? Or do these disruptions simply represent theatrics and minor annoyances and delays to fossil interest? Again, Piven (2008: 24) offers some insights on what it means to challenge power:

> Protest movements do try to communicate their grievances, of course, with slogans, banners, antics, rallies, marches, and so on. They do this partly to build the movement and its morale, and partly to appeal for allies. The reverberations of disruptive actions, the shut-downs or highway blockages or property destruction, are inevitably also communicative. But while disruption thus usually gives the protestors voice, voice alone does not give the protesters much power.

What then challenges power? Piven (2008) argues that effectively challenging power requires developing networks of *solidarity* that make collective action a meaningful leverage point. Challenging power depends on organized masses of people ceasing to cooperate and withdrawing participation in the system. Thus, the legendary influence of organized labor unions and strikes as well as the strategic and forceful responses from global elites to breakdown all forms of organizing from below that might challenge their power.

Many scholars and activists cite the work or Chenoweth and Stephan (2011), who claim that when a critical mass of 3.5% of the population participates in sustained non-violent disruption it can trigger large-scale social transformation. This indeed is one of XR's primary goals, yet XR participation remains far from 3.5% of the population. At this level of engagement, there are few examples of sustained activism beyond movements in response to repressive and autocratic leadership (Fisher 2022). Climate change has yet to galvanize that level of response, yet evidence suggests that even smaller levels of activism can make an impact. While causation is difficult to establish, a 2018 study shows that GHG emissions have been declining in US states where there have been more pro-environmental protests (Muñoz et al. 2018). To pressure governments to adopt a *radical and bold* climate agenda, it is widely agreed that a much larger and sustained mass mobilization is required. These actions meet Wright's (2019) description of "resisting" strategies. Wright (2019: 49) explains that resistance is a "ubiquitous response to the harms of the system." While we have seen smaller acts of temporary resistance, such as Occupy Wall Street, the climate movement has now reached an unprecedented size and level of persistence. However, it is still much smaller than is necessary. A critical mass of people acting in solidarity continues to be lacking and significantly limits the climate movement's impact.

Foster (2022) calls for the rise of the environmental proletariat to challenge power through an eco-revolutionary wave and cites the rise of a diversity of groups globally who may foreshadow a larger eco-revolutionary struggle:

(1) [T]he Landless Workers' Movement (MST) in Brazil;

(2) the international peasants alliance La Via Campesina;

(3) Venezuela's nascent, if besieged, communal state;

(4) Cuba's revolutionary ecology and epidemiology;

(5) the natural-resource nationalist, anti-extractivist, and postcolonial movements in Africa;

(6) the Farmer's Revolt in India;

(7) China's goal of a socialist-based ecological civilization;

(8) the student-led climate strikes in Europe;

(9) the Green New Deal, Red New Deal, just transition, environmental justice, and Black Lives Matter struggles in the United States and Canada; and

(10) the revival on every inhabited continent of Indigenous environmental struggles

A "planetary revolt of humanity," Foster (2022) argues, will only succeed in challenging power if it can form a "more unified, revolutionary human subject." This, Foster (2019) explains, is more likely to emerge from the Global South, where we see the most rapid growth in environmental proletariat actions and where people increasingly face degraded environmental conditions. Through solidarity, this is envisioned to take place globally with an environmental proletariat that includes "millions, even billions, of people" taking part (Foster and Clark 2022).

Yet, as we head deeper into the climate crisis, we have yet to see large-enough numbers of people ready to join a mass solidarity movement. Wright (2019: 119, 121) calls this "the most vexing problem" and "the biggest puzzle" for emancipatory transformation: the creation of collective agency and solidarity to drive forward change. The question remains: "who is going to participate in such struggles? Where is the collective agent capable of sustaining struggles to erode capitalism?" (Wright 2019: 117). Among activists and social scientists there are increasing calls for the emergence of a "movement of movements," or a mass movement that unites causes and can effectively challenge power. For example, to address ongoing climate delay and inaction, Stoddart et al. (2021) call for "the building of common causes across social movements and intersectional interests, linking climate justice with, for example, gender justice and racial justice, and learning from the experiences and knowledge of indigenous communities." We and many others fear that by the time a critical mass of people is impacted by climate change to the degree that they mobilize to demand that their needs be met, we will already be on a course for irreversible and catastrophic warming. *How do you mobilize a mass movement in advance of the worst impacts and social harms?*

Still, the climate impacts witnessed thus far (as well as future projections) have already catalyzed several large climate protests and other more continuous, yet smaller, actions from specific groups. For example, as of 2023, Extinction Rebellion and Just Stop Oil activist groups in the United Kingdom are planning to continue and ramp up their efforts to demand climate action. While we still do not see a critical mass of people revolting against climate inaction, it is possible that once a larger climate movement emerges, and climate impacts continue to worsen, more people will join. As Marcuse (1967) states in *The End of Utopia*,

> [t]he social agents of revolution—and this is orthodox Marx— are formed only in the process of the transformation itself, and one cannot count on a situation in which the revolutionary forces are there ready-made, so to speak, when the revolutionary movement begins.

It may be that the climate movement must become a stronger more prominent collective force, or join up with other social movements, before the social agents of transformation emerge.

In the absence of a mass social movement to demand radical climate action, other strategies are being pursued. For example, the Sunrise Movement works through the channels of US electoral politics to strategically get people elected who will support climate action, even if it is reformist action rather than revolutionary. They have, by most accounts, changed the climate discussion in the US and helped to push forward the first piece of national climate legislation in the nation's history. While hailed by some as a victory, as it provides $369 billion for energy and climate change related projects, the 2022 Inflation Reduction Act was a clear compromise that fails to even end fossil fuel subsidies. Injecting money into energy and climate-related development does nothing to directly reduce fossil fuel extraction and use, and again will likely result in increased total energy use without any additional policy measures. While many agree it is better than nothing and the Sunrise Movement has received widespread accolades for its "success," the act does little to direct a rapid and *radical* transition to a low-carbon society and does not address increasing levels of production and consumption that continue to undermine all efforts to mitigate climate change.

Despite this disappointing compromise, the Sunrise Movement has taken a step in the right direction. If the climate movement is going to successfully challenge power and implement an effective and just transition program, it will also need to embrace mass politics. Sunrise has effectively raised public awareness *and* increased political support for climate action. In contrast, XR has attempted to remain "beyond politics" with demands that have failed to be translated into specific climate policies. Politics is key to a social transformation and the climate movement will need to be increasingly specific about what policies should be supported. As we argue throughout this book, demanding "system change" broadly fails to engage the politics necessary. The climate movement will not create any level of measurable change if it sticks to "movementism" – protests, disruptions, demonstrations, "naming and shaming," etc. while avoiding taking or directing state power (Heideman 2020). Movementism has defined left-wing politics for decades, especially in the US, with very little to show for it. To have a consequential impact on emissions and adaptation measures, the climate movement will have to enter the frustrating and disappointing world of formal politics. In chapter 6, we will return to the ambiguities and difficulties presented by state politics.

The Sunrise Movement's approach largely matches Wright's (2010) depiction of synergistic transformation strategies that are often incremental reforms and class compromises. However, with climate change we do not have time for an incremental and compromised approach, as scientists continue to call for immediate changes in all aspects of society. Without a mass social movement to drive radical change forward, it is hard to see how we will get transformative policies that could most effectively and justly minimize global warming. Without a mass movement to galvanize direct and effective climate action at the national level, others have started to encourage more localized participation and political tactics.

One way to increase impact is to shepherd forward specific policy changes at different scales of governance. Harvey and Gillis (2022) call for increased and widespread public participation demanding that local and state governments take actions to mitigate climate change. This means citizens must be informed about the specifics of land use, zoning, housing codes, and transportation laws. It also means showing up at meetings and where decisions are made to demand that infrastructure and planning is heading towards a low-carbon future. While it is much more likely that people will show up to protest against something (e.g., a coal mine), what would it look like if critical masses of people showed up to demand specific changes in planning? Harvey and Gillis (2022) argue that if many people (a participatory solidarity movement) in many locations across the world all took local action it could have widespread impacts. In other words, collective action could be oriented towards more localized strategic decision-making. While these efforts can be important and can add up, a system prioritizing profit and economic growth will continue to limit and undermine local mitigation efforts. These efforts would be more meaningful if done in combination with a bold climate agenda that slows production and consumption, deliberately phases out fossil fuels, and increases opportunities for direct democratic decision-making in energy, transportation, and planning. In the current social context and without a mass solidarity movement, decentralized actions will likely not add up and could distract people from challenging the powers necessary for social transformation. Given the many obstacles involved in influencing politics, other tactics are increasingly being considered and promoted by climate activists and scholars.

In *How to Blow Up a Pipeline*, Malm (2021) argues that property destruction, specifically industrial sabotage and the destruction of new fossil fuel infrastructure, is a key tactic necessary to challenge the power of fossil fuels and pressure governments to adopt bolder climate policies. Referring to the climate movement, Malm (2021: 99) states:

> So here is what this movement of millions should do, for a start: announce and enforce the prohibition. Damage and destroy new CO2-emitting devices. Put them out of commission, pick them apart, demolish them, burn them, blow them up. Let the capitalists who keep on investing in the fire know that their properties will be trashed.

Malm explains how property destruction and violence have been fringe yet key parts of many social movements. Based on the current and future violence and harm related to fossil fuel use, Malm argues that we are morally obligated to act now through acts of sabotage to stop this harm. While property destruction can be considered violence, Malm explains the importance of careful, precise, and skillful acts of strategic property destruction that do not harm individuals. Though bombing buildings and infrastructure without maiming or killing humans is easier said than done (see Sovacool and Dunlap 2022: 12).

Others may increasingly consider acts of violence that do harm people. In the science fiction novel *Ministry for the Future* (2020), Kim Stanley Robinson depicts a possible (near) future where an underground group of militant climate activists use drones, kidnapping, and murder to influence or exterminate actors who continue to pursue fossil fuel development, despite the group's warnings and direct threats. The rationale thus being that violence towards these individuals will save billions of lives in the future. More revolutionary actors in the climate movement may be increasingly drawn towards these tactics, especially because the critical mass of collective actors necessary for effective non-violent action has yet to emerge.

In an interview, Foster (2021) makes arguments for contextualizing the use of sabotage as a means to challenge power. While non-violent protest is still preferred, Foster explains how the capitalist state has a monopoly on the "legitimate use of force," yet this will likely be challenged as climate impacts become more severe. Foster (2021), states:

> Sabotage (which of course derives etymologically from the French *sabot, wooden shoe*, and from workers throwing shoes in machines) will necessarily be part of an ecological revolution, and so will attacks on private property, given that the owners of the means of production (the wealthy and corporations) are destroying the earth itself so as to expand their financial holdings. ...It seems inevitable to me that as the stakes for humanity rise, more and more people will inevitably take this general stance, recognizing that human survival (as well as human freedom) is at issue.

Sabotage, property destruction, or other violent tactics in general may become more prevalent in the future due to the failure of existing institutions to address climate change, widespread despair and helplessness, and the emptiness of most climate politics. While we do not have a unified position on the use of these tactics, we agree that it is important to consider the available evidence and to weigh the possible implications and outcomes.

There are reasons to believe property destruction may be a counterproductive and ineffective way forward (Gunderson and Charles 2023). First, evidence suggests property destruction and violence often reduce public support for social movements (Wang and Piazza 2016, Simpson et al. 2018, Feinberg et al. 2020, Wasow 2020), though this relationship is not always present and is mediated by social factors (Jaeger et al. 2015, Muñoz and Anduiza 2016, Baggetta and Myers 2022). To provide one example, instances of property destruction and violence associated with Civil Rights protests likely tipped the 1968 election for Richard Nixon by increasing support for a "Law and Order" candidate among whites in counties near the violence (Wasow 2020). A successful climate movement depends on mass politics, which requires majority public support. Second, a comparative study of 323 resistance movements between 1900 and 2006 found that nonviolent resistance campaigns were "nearly twice as likely to achieve full or partial success as their violent counterparts" (Chenoweth and Stephan 2011: 7). Note that they conceptualize property destruction and industrial sabotage as forms of violence in their coding. Further, the rate of success by violent movements has *decreased* over time. Third, those who engage in property destruction may be embracing the same tactics promoted by agent provocateurs. Government agents and counter-activists who infiltrate protests and social movements often promote or commit property destruction and violence because they know it will have negative consequences for the movement (Chase 2021). For example, the FBI's program (COINTELPRO) to destroy the Black Liberation Movement and similar movements strategically encouraged Civil Rights activists to abandon nonviolent tactics. The fact that agent provocateurs encourage property destruction and violence to *dismantle* movements may be the most damning case against the sincere activists within a movement who promote property destruction or violence (Chase 2021).

In addition, property destruction could increase the scope and severity of state repression. For example, in a comparative study of state responses to dissent, violent strategies of dissent (a code that includes guerilla warfare and/or riots) did not predict state sanctions, likely because the presence of violent dissent "generally leads to the implementation of other strategies of behavioral control including state-sponsored terrorism, armed attacks and political executions" (Davenport 1995: 701). Indeed, the FBI already considers "eco-terrorists" a "serious terrorist threat" in the US (Watson 2002, see Loadenthal 2013a) and environmental activists who engage in property destruction have faced repression and sanctions (Vanderheiden 2008, Loadenthal 2013b). If "climatage" became a common strategy in the climate movement, one can assume the deployment of counterterrorist measures. Most scholars understand that acts of violence often result in more violence. Property destruction and violence in many historical cases have been met with escalated violence from law enforcement or military responses, as authorities attempt to restore institutional order (Piven 2008, Fisher 2022). This has and can result in tragic outcomes for activists and civilians. Most importantly, it is difficult to imagine how the climate movement could win a fight against the repressive arm of the state, at least in the US (see chapter 7).

While disruption remains a key aspect of social movements, disruption can take many forms. Wright (2010) specifically argues against violent means to systemic change, or "ruptural" transformation strategies, explaining that historically they have not resulted in positive outcomes. Instead, Wright (2010) supports the "logic of rupture" or disruptive tactics to aid in emancipatory transformation – tactics that disrupt or shut down the system. As discussed earlier, Piven (2008) distinguishes between disruptions that communicate concern and discontent and disruptions that actually challenge power, the latter requiring solidarity and a mass movement. One likely reason that property destruction and violent tactics are gaining traction is the lack of a critical mass of mobilized citizens to create the solidarity necessary for a power-challenging disruption. As we will discuss in the next chapter, there are many reasons why the majority of people feel helpless and remain inactive despite their concern about climate change. A lack of solidarity to demand climate action remains a key challenge in the climate movement and it is questionable whether the escalation of property destruction or violence as a tactic will help or hinder the growth of the movement. Within the climate movement and among scholars, disagreement and discussions continue over the use of militant strategies. While it is impossible to predict the outcomes associated these tactics, the potential exists to challenge power but also to alienate those who might otherwise support the climate movement's efforts.

Pursuing the Still-Possible

In the absence of a mass mobilization to demand bold climate action, many people feel desperate. With what is at stake, there is a moral imperative to act—to do something—that many people feel. This feeling will likely grow over time as climate disasters result in more loss and suffering. Will we eventually see a mass mobilization? What would it take to catalyze this mass mobilization? In the absence of a mass mobilization, will we see more militant acts like sabotage? We cannot predict the future and therefore cannot answer these questions. But we have examined some specific pathways for change and possible routes forward to enact an effective and just climate agenda. Much depends on the emergence of widespread solidarity and the growth of a mass movement based on moral imperatives. The path is not clear, and it will definitely not be easy. Yet, there are still possibilities for these transformations to occur and, with everything at stake, these possibilities are worth pursuing.

Positive social transformation requires ongoing processes of deep thought, open communication, democratic decision-making, and collective action. It is critical that we avoid succumbing to defeatism and fatalism so that these processes continue. Defeatism is feeling that we have already lost. Climate change is occurring and will continue to occur, yet we have not lost the battle. Every degree matters and means something in terms of human and ecological impacts. Many battles remain as we work towards a more livable future. Fatalism refers to the feeling that there is no point in acting because it is simply the fate of humans to destroy themselves. In other words, the fate of humanity is already set and we have no agency to change destiny. Both mindsets result in inaction and only ensure that the worst-case scenarios are realized. While we are pessimistic about the outlook for the future (more on this in the next chapter), pessimism does not necessarily result in defeatist or fatalistic thinking. Time is not on our side and there are immense challenges to justly minimizing global warming. But with this awareness of what we are up against, we can move forward with realistic clarity about what is at stake and what is still possible. As Marcuse (1968) explains:

> [A] very real and very pragmatic opposition is required of us if we are to make ourselves and others conscious of these possibilities and the forces that hinder and deny them. An opposition is required that is free of all illusion but also of all defeatism, for through its mere existence defeatism betrays the possibility of freedom to the status quo.

Chapter 7:
Real Helplessness and Authentic Hope

On the one hand we find the absolute necessity of first liberating consciousness, on the other we see ourselves confronted by a concentration of power against which even the freest consciousness appears ridiculous and impotent.

– Herbert Marcuse (1967: 10)

While some people choose to downplay the risks of the climate crisis and play up "progress" towards a "green" transition, evidence suggests that current responses are utterly inadequate for avoiding catastrophic climate change. Many scientists and authors have already detailed how severe the ecological and social consequences will likely be, painting a bleak future plagued with climate-related tragedies. Given the situation, citizens should not only be concerned, they should be outraged. Despite *all that is known*, world leaders are continuing to lead us toward ecological and societal collapse. Some leading drivers of inaction are clearly deliberate (Brulle and Norgaard 2019). We begin with two clear examples of why people should be outraged before we examine why they are not: (1) inadequate global emissions reduction commitments and the failure to meet these inadequate commitments, and (2) industry- and government-backed plans to continue to extract and transport massive fossil fuel reserves that would end any chance of staying within global climate targets.

Many people are unaware of what the COP (Conference of the Parties) meetings are and what they have accomplished, despite hearing that they are important for addressing climate change. Often media sources highlight the unprecedented promises to reduce GHG emissions made at these meetings, leaving one feeling that progress is being made. However, by all accounts, the greatest global effort to coordinate emissions reductions has failed. First, the pledges of all 193 parties (192 countries and the EU) associated with the Paris Agreement (2015) are collectively meant to keep global temperatures "well below 2°C above preindustrial levels" while "pursuing efforts to limit the temperature increase to 1.5°C above pre-industrial levels." However, the parties fall short from meeting this goal. Each signing party committed to meet a Nationally Determined Contribution (NDC), but these NDCs fail to add up to the reductions necessary. In other words, these pledges created independently by specific governments do not add up to the reductions to stay within 1.5°C or even 2°C of warming. There remains an *immense gap* between the cumulative NDC commitments and what would be necessary to stay within climate targets. The graphic depictions of this gap are distressing (e.g., see Figure 2). Current pledges as of 2022, if met, would likely result in 2.4°C warming (carbontracker.org).

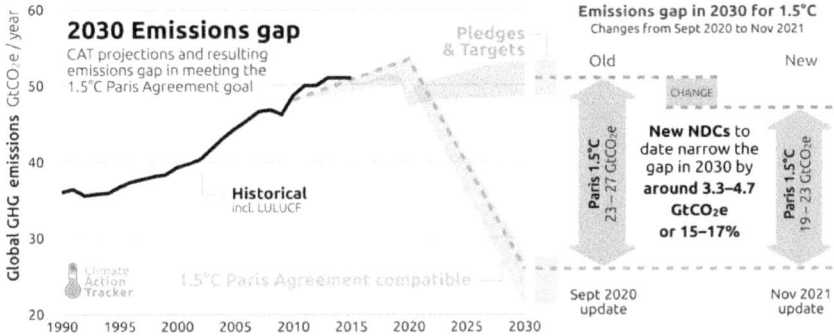

Figure 2: Climate Action Tracker CAT Emissions Gap. climateactiontracker.org

Even with a promise to make these commitments more aggressive over time, the parties have not stepped up. They agreed to "ratchet up" their pledges after the Paris Agreement (2020) and submit even more ambitious commitments. Many countries failed to meet the deadline of submitting new NDCs and some submitted NDCs that did not increase in ambition, including Australia, Brazil, Russia, and Mexico. With changes in the governing political party, Australia has since submitted a new more ambitious NDC. However, even with updated commitments (resulting in 2.4°C), countries still fall short of meeting these commitments. Carbon Action Tracker (CAT) rates each party as highly insufficient, insufficient, almost sufficient, and Paris Agreement compatible. The EU and the US rank as insufficient, with the United Kingdom ranking as almost sufficient along with Norway among highly industrialized nations. No countries have achieved an overall CAT ranking compatible with the Paris Agreement. Another challenge is successfully converting the stated goals and plans into effective policy, action, and results. In other words, GHG emissions reduction has certainly not become a priority for global leaders, despite grand speeches at COP meetings. In contrast, despite a dip in emissions during 2020 due to the Covid-19 pandemic, emissions are still going up.

Another disturbing reality also overlooked by media focused on "progress" to address climate change is that additional funding for solar and wind will not be sufficient to avoid catastrophe if current oil reserves are not *kept in the ground* (as well as reducing overproduction and overconsumption). The carbon budget to stay within 1.5°C is 400–500 billion tons of GHGs and identified fossil fuel reserves would emit approximately 3.5 trillion tons of GHGs, seven times the carbon budget (Milman 2022). The US has the most reserves and alone could extract enough fossil fuels to surpass the carbon budget. In addition, as of fall 2022, new reports indicate that 24,000 km of new oil pipelines are being developed around the world, with 40% already under construction, many backed by national governments (Carrington 2022) and fossil fuel companies have clear plans to exploit new fossil reserves for the next decade (Carrington and Taylor 2022). Despite the talk at COP meetings, governments are not phasing out fossil fuel use and are instead supporting *new development* that will easily surpass the carbon budget to stay within 1.5°C or even 2°C. When world leaders and media outlets highlight how much money is being invested in renewable energy, this overlooks that fossil fuel reserves are still being further developed. Keeping the vast majority of reserves in the ground is essential (hence our support for nationalizing and phasing out fossil fuel companies). The ease at which governments and fossil fuel companies continue to plan and carry out new fossil fuel development is appalling given the climate science, mass public concern about climate change, and pledged reduction commitments.

Inaction is even more appalling, absurd, and outrageous when one begins to consider the projected estimates of climate related mortality. If current emission levels do not change, we are on track to have a 4.4°C warmer future by the end of the century (UN 2023). The UN (2023) explains that meeting the goals of the Paris Agreement would save approximately one million lives per year between 2023 and 2050 through air pollution reductions alone. However, the current trajectory is stark: instead of phasing out fossil fuels, "countries are instead planning and projecting an average annual increase of 2 per cent, which by 2030 would result in more than double the production consistent with the 1.5°C limit" (UN 2023). The World Health Organization (WHO 2023) reports that climate change is currently responsible for at least 150,000 deaths per year and that this rate will double by 2030. In another article titled "The Mortality Cost of Carbon," Bressler (2021) estimates that "[b]elow 2°C, projected yearly excess deaths from climate change are relatively constant at around 100,000 per year" and that "[a]bove 2°C, projected yearly excess deaths from climate change increase at an increasing rate in global average temperatures, rising to over four million excess deaths at 4°C." Bressler (2021) explains that every 4,434 metric tons of carbon added beyond the 2020 rate of emissions kills one person and that at our current trajectory we will see 83 million excess deaths directly related to climate change by 2100. It is impossible to fathom the real-life suffering and loss that will be experienced on this trajectory.

Another reason to be outraged is that the majority of citizens want climate action. National and global polls consistently illustrate that most citizens are concerned about climate change and most also believe that their governments are not doing enough to address it (Funk et al. 2020, IPSOS 2022). With this level of concern, the facts above should enrage global citizens, yet there remains a disconnect between concern about climate change and action. Where is the mass mobilization necessary to pressure governments to prioritize human survival over industry profits and wealth accumulation? Why is there a gulf between concern about climate change and effective strategies to change the system driving climate change (Blühdorn 2007; Gifford 2011; Norgaard 2011; Stoner and Melathopoulos 2015; Ollinaho 2016; Browne 2018)?

One explanation is "real helplessness." Real helplessness refers to a rationally perceived (i.e., actual) inability to effectively reduce the threat of climate change due to political-economic conditions that render individuals powerless, stupefied, and repressed (Gunderson 2022). If there are no functioning organizations through which actors can challenge or transform harmful actors, let alone the social structures that they emerged from, then there is an objective inability to adequately translate climate concern into action. This is true when, "in the case of environmental problems[,] it may be reasonable to ascribe responsibility to institutional actors such as governments or corporations" (Dietz, 2015: 338, see Stern et al. 1986). In the next section, we elaborate on the concept of "real helplessness," how it manifests, and its role in stifling action and a mass climate movement. This helplessness is structural, not merely psychological, and must be acknowledged as many avenues for transformation have been closed off. What pathways are then left to focus on and pursue? Or, are we truly helpless?

In contrast to the majority of citizens who fail to act in response to the climate crisis, we also discuss what drives those who do act in some way despite feelings of helplessness. The few individuals who do devote their time, energy, and, sometimes, careers to climate activism do so with full awareness of the reality of the climate crisis, the direness of the situation, and the bleak outlook for the future. Why do they not succumb to defeatism and fatalism? Why, despite knowing how helpless they really are, do they continue to act? We discuss the personal choice to continue to act, to do something, in response to the climate crisis despite pessimistic/realistic outlooks and feelings of helplessness. This is fueled by *authentic hope*, or a realistic sense of hope emerging from despair. Activists focus on the process of doing what they believe is right, even if they doubt the outcome will be good or successful.

While the last chapter discussed pathways for change that can be pursued (the range of the possible), this chapter focuses on another critical (and very personal) aspect of the climate crisis: the feelings that result in inaction or action, and the social conditions that shape these emotions. Much has been written about the melancholy, anxiety, dread, and related emotions experienced in the face of the environmental crisis, sometimes termed "eco-despair, "environmental grief," "climate anxiety," and "eco-anxiety" (e.g., Li and Monroe 2019, Clayton 2020). Here, we focus on the dialectic of helplessness and hope in social context. Current power structures continue to shape what is possible, our sense of agency, and feelings of helplessness. Those that continue to act may be acting in ways that remains insufficient and ineffective (e.g., theatrics that merely communicate concern). Yet what else can be done without a critical mass of people acting in solidarity to challenge power? Some act hoping that a mass movement will emerge or hoping that their actions will have some impact. Even when they think their actions will come to no ends, some are still compelled to act. These are personal choices that emerge within the historical context of this moment. We examine this context and the related feelings of helplessness about *what can be done* that plague concerned citizens, activists, and scholars.

Real Helplessness

To examine the relationship between helplessness and climate inaction, we discuss three dimensions of real helplessness: (1) powerlessness, (2) stupefaction, and (3) repression. Powerlessness refers to the absence of powerful organizations to challenge the status quo of capitalist social relations driving the climate crisis. Stupefaction occurs through the channels of the culture industry, where entertainment and media industries distract the masses and discourage unity. Lastly, repression involves the increasingly repressive state apparatus that uses surveillance, threats, the criminal justice system, and violence to extinguish oppositional groups and activities. While individuals may feel helpless for various reasons, this context contributes to a crushing sense of defenseless paralysis that challenges the possibility of a mass climate movement. Through identifying these mechanisms, we can also identify levers to possibly change the social-structural context driving real helplessness.

Powerlessness

Powerlessness describes the inability of individuals to exert sufficient control over the law-like structures that condition their own behaviors and thoughts. In capitalist societies, there is a general lack of human control over commodity production. The ability of powerlessness to separate concern about the world, on the one hand, and action, on the other, is explained well by Douglas Rushkoff (2009: xxi):

> [P]eople of all social classes [are] making choices that go against their better judgment because they believe it's really the only sensible way to act under the circumstances...[But these] decisions are not even occurring in the real world. They are the false choices of an artificial landscape – one in which our decision-making is as coerced as that of a person getting mugged. Only we've forgotten that our choices are being made under painstakingly manufactured duress.

In other words, the fracturing of concern (our "better judgement") from right and/or effective action in part stems from the inability of individuals, alone or in small groups, to exert adequate control over the structural processes of this "artificial landscape." One can be aware of, and be concerned about, capitalist contradictions and their negative social impacts, but lack the capacity to take consequential action to alter these conditions. Jäger and Leusder (2020: 42) argue that, "[t]he stability [of modern capitalism] probably owes far more to a mood of resignation, as people make peace with a world that is hostile to their flourishing. They know this world to be a product of human agency, but they cannot control it" (cf. Chibber 2022). The result is atomized individuals facing a system that is literally "out of control," a condition familiar to many of those alarmed by climate change.

In neoliberal capitalist societies, especially the US, two specific political-economic trends have increased powerlessness: (1) the decline of unions and (2) a two-party system. Both heighten powerlessness in climate politics. The argument is not that union decline and the two-party system drive climate change. Instead, the argument is that union decline and the two-party system further undermine the ability to take effective climate action. While no modern society has managed to move beyond capitalism, including state "socialist" countries, it is undeniable that labor movements and left-wing parties, as collective-political projects, have historically reformed capitalism. Powerlessness varies based on the political economy of a country, including its labor laws, union rates and power, levels of economic democracy, and the ability of left-wing parties to influence policy and state machinery. For example, due to high union rates, codetermination laws, a parliamentary system, and other institutions, German steel workers have more power than American Uber drivers to exert influence over capitalist dynamics. In comparison, in neoliberal-capitalist countries organizations that could at least achieve a minimal level of collective control over irrational social processes have waned for decades.

One historical cause of powerlessness in climate politics today is the decline of labor unions since the 1970s. Although labor unions and "trade union consciousness" can, at times, preserve rather than challenge capitalism, unions are a key institution through which people can exert some power over the structural forces that typically operate behind their backs. Unions have the potential to reduce emissions because organized labor can play a role in slowing the treadmill of production that requires increases in throughput and emissions by (1) resisting high-energy labor-saving technology or demanding compensation for technological unemployment; (2) diverting surpluses to non-treadmill activities by supporting social programs like unemployment relief; (3) promoting non-market values and concerns; and (4) advocating for environmental goals (Obach 2004). In fact, Obach (2004) argues that unions have accelerated their treadmill-slowing tactics due to (1) the pro-environmentalism of a bigger service sector; (2) a shrinking industrial sector that feels less threatened by environmentalism than it does by economic liberalization; and (3) new pro-environment union leadership. Two of the most important mitigation strategies that unions can help realize today are: (1) "just transition" projects and transformative "Green New Deal" proposals, when distinct from "green growth" approaches (Gould et al. 2004, Barca 2015), and (2) work time reduction, a policy associated with reductions in emissions in increases in wellbeing (for review, see Gunderson, 2019) (see chapter 3). In short, unions have the potential to play a transformative role in reducing emissions (e.g., Hampton 2018, Tomassetti 2020). However, the *power* to realize any system-level changes presuppose high union densities, which are low and/or declining in many Western countries (Vachon et al. 2016).

Countries with a two-party political system also deepen the gap between concern about climate change and the ability to achieve effective climate action. Fueled by a hegemonic neoliberalism (Antonio & Brulle 2011), views on climate change are starkly polarized along political lines in the US (McCright & Dunlap 2011), with Republican politicians and voters much more likely to deny the existence of climate change and/or its anthropogenic causes. However, the centrists of the Democratic Party engage in their own form of climate denial by criticizing the radical proposals needed to address climate change and even receiving donations from carbon-intensive industries (Marcetic 2019). Consider President Joe Biden's climate change-related appointments, including Rep. Cedric Richmond as leader of the White House Office of Public Engagement, who acts as a liaison to climate activists despite receiving hundreds of thousands of dollars in donations from the fossil fuel industry (Sirota et al., 2020), and John Kerry, "a long-time apologist for fossil fuel fracking, and a reliable promoter of false climate solutions like market-based carbon-trading schemes," as an international climate envoy (Food & Water Watch 2020). Perhaps it is still too early to make a decisive judgement of the Biden administration's approach to climate change. While the Inflation Reduction Act is better than nothing, it is packed with contradictions and built on market-friendly and techno-optimistic assumptions (Jones 2022). Further, in August and September of 2021 alone, the Biden administration released a formal statement encouraging OPEC and its allies to increase oil output (Hunnicutt & Mason 2021), reaffirmed its support expanding offshore drilling (Bragman 2021), and resumed oil and gas leasing on public lands (Corbett 2021), a practice in which he now outpaces Trump despite a campaign promise to ban the practice (Phillips 2022). It is possible that the transition from the Trump administration to the Biden administration is a transition from "literal climate denialism" to "ideological climate denialism," a denialism that acknowledges that climate change is real, driven by humans, and should be acted on, yet misdiagnoses the drivers of climate change, limits effective action, and maintains the underlying drivers of climate change (see the introduction).

Yet the two-party system is a secondary problem. The primary problem is the degree to which corporate interests have captured state power and eroded democratic processes (e.g., Nyberg 2021). Two-party systems merely narrow down the possibility of creating progressive political programs that counter those interests, an issue stacked atop other barriers growing from plutocratic conditions. Although two-party systems are especially inflexible for adequately dealing with the climate crisis, there is a pressing political-strategic contradiction facing attempts to address climate change via state policy, even within multi-party, parliamentary systems. On the one hand, economic criteria remain the foundation of decision making about the design, performance and evaluation of production and consumption, dwarfing any ecological concerns. Further, it is unlikely that the state will take the side of ecological demands if these demands threaten the general accumulation of capital. On the other hand, it is difficult to imagine other institutions with the power to implement the rapid and large-scale collective programs immediately needed to reduce carbon emissions (e.g., see Smith 2019). As O'Connor (1998: 155) explains, "the state is deeply implicated in the crisis of nature. This same state—under the democratic control of civil society—can be the basis for the reconstruction of nature, and our relationships to nature." Yet there is a vast gap between the latter vision of a truly democratic and ecological state—regardless of whether this is a viable vision— and the neoliberal state. Importantly, powerless, atomized, and unorganized actors cannot transform the latter into the former.

Powerlessness in climate politics relates to people's inability to exert control over the elemental processes of capitalism that steadily increase GHG emissions (Brown 2018). Even if one is concerned about climate change, the levers that guide the structural drivers of climate change are far beyond one's atomized grasp. Those that do see and grasp for these levers, will have different levels of success depending on the specific context. For example, countries with long social-democratic traditions, stronger socialist and green parties (as well as red-green coalitions), and higher levels of economic democracy have generally been more successful in reducing GHG emissions. Increasing economic democracy, union organizing, and social-democratic traditions represent possible way to reduce powerlessness. However, in a country like the US, one concerned about climate change is left facing an uncontrollable political-economic system that drives climate change without effective collective-political means to alter its course. In this powerless position, the culture industry offers powerful anesthetics.

Stupefaction

It is impossible to overstate the power of the culture industry over consciousness. The term "culture industry" was introduced by Horkheimer and Adorno in *Dialectic of Enlightenment* (1969), and further elaborated by Adorno (1991), to account for the commodification and standardization of culture and cultural products. The culture industry is "geared to profit-making, controlled by centralized interlocking corporations, and staffed with marketing and financial experts, management and production teams, technicians, 'star' reporters, writers, actors, musicians, and other creative talent" (Cook 1996: x). Socialization has increasingly transferred from the hands of the family to the hands of monopolized firms. Further, "[t]he line between fiction and reality, friend and marketer, community and shopping center, has gotten blurred," and our behaviors and thoughts are so deeply enmeshed in mass marketing, media, and consumption that the latter are taken as pregiven facts (Rushkoff 2008: xxii).

Helplessness in climate politics is deepened through the fundamental stupefying message of the culture industry: things are the way they are, and this is how they ought to be, or things cannot be fundamentally different (Horkheimer and Adorno 1969: 147f; Cook 1996: ch. 4). The culture industry drives the gap between concern and action by "removing the thought that there is any alternative to the status quo" (Bernstein 1991: 9), reinforcing capitalist realism (Fisher 2009) and one-dimensional thinking (Marcuse 1964). Its stupefying fog currently restricts the horizons of climate solutions and climate politics. The culture industry renders people stupefied through at least two processes: (1) the manipulation of attention, interpretation, and imagination, or, "cognitive control," and (2) amusement.

Cognitive control—strategies through which news media, advertising, and the entertainment industry modify attention, interpretation, and imagination—is one route through which the culture industry produces helplessness. In relation to attention and interpretation, a small handful of massive entertainment, news media, and marketing firms spend hundreds of billions of dollars to alter what people think is important enough to attend to and how they interpret what is attended to. Climate change interpretations are modified through at least three strategies: (1) the denial of the problem, or seriousness of the problem, (2) misdiagnosing the causes of the problem, and (3) promoting ineffective solutions to the problem (Gunderson et al. 2020).

Fed talking points and reports from the climate change countermovement—made up of conservative politicians, right-wing think tanks, the fossil fuel industry, and others—the conservative news media often denies the reality of climate change and/or the anthropogenic drivers of climate change (Carmichael et al. 2017) (see above). The culture industry also controls cognition by encouraging ineffective climate solutions and the narrowing of political horizons obstructs the ability to imagine potential alternative social futures. One may learn that climate change is a problem and demands solutions from the news media, but, because the largest news media firms, which reach the largest number of viewers, tend to affirm and defend the system (e.g., Herman & Chomsky 1988), it is rare to find interpretations of climate change as a byproduct of a growth-dependent capitalist economy or promotions of mitigation strategies that push beyond the barriers of what capitalism can deliver. In short, news media is a dominant mechanism through which misdiagnoses of climate change are presented and within-system pseudo-solutions to climate change are sold.

The culture industry is also a dominant site of the cooptation of potentially radical ideas and practices (e.g., Kperogi 2011), including responses to climate change. From advertising campaigns that decontextualize anti-Vietnam War songs from the 1960s to peddle denim jeans to countless corporations "supporting" LGBTQ rights through rainbow-laced advertisements during "Pride Month," the culture industry is skilled in repackaging and selling back anything that mimics or borders on rebellion. It is not that there is a conspiracy among marketing, entertainment, and media firms to coopt potentially revolutionary movements, it is simply profitable to tap into dissatisfaction. In the early 1970s, Marcuse (1994: 53) already recognized how easily environmental politics could be "neutralized" (coopted) through green marketing and reformism. The marketing industry has skillfully tapped into concern about climate change and other kinds of environmental discontent by supplying green commodities to the concerned and ostensibly autonomous ecoconsumers of neoliberal societies (Stoner 2021). For example, if one is concerned about the health consequences of environmental degradation and climate change, one can purchase organic products rather than pursue political changes that alter the social conditions that drive environmental health risks (e.g., Szasz 2007). It is precisely because one is politically helpless that those concerned about climate change wonder "What can *I* do to help?" and look to the market for answers and consolation (Gunderson 2021a).

Along with cognitive-control, amusement is a second route through which the culture industry produces and reinforces helplessness in climate politics. Stupefaction via amusement must be understood in relation to powerlessness (see above). The culture industry is an escape from the nagging feeling that one is unable to control the causes of these discontents.

> Pleasure always means not to think about anything, to forget suffering even where it is shown. *Basically it is helplessness.* It is flight; not, as is asserted, flight from a wretched reality, but from the last remaining thought of resistance. The liberation which amusement promises is freedom from thought and from negation. (Horkheimer and Adorno 1969: 144, emphasis added)

Cultural commodities are anesthetics that numb the likelihood of resistance and reduce the tension between what is and what is possible (Marcuse 1964), fostering the feeling that the promise of happiness has already been realized (see Jameson 1990: 147). Amusement is a clear escape from pressing concerns like climate change. The culture industry, "as a distraction from climate change[,] means that constant attention to media, advertising, and cultural products thematizes topics and events that are often of far less importance than the risk of catastrophic climate change" (Gunderson et al. 2020: 56). Consider how much more time is spent on a typical day gazing at the spectacle—watching a Netflix series, scrolling through social media sites, playing video games, shopping, etc.—than is spent reflecting on the risk of climate catastrophe. This widespread distraction reduces awareness about alternatives and serves to burry any motivation to change the system, giving way to helplessness and inaction.

In summary, stupefaction through cognitive control and amusement is a pillar of real helplessness in climate politics. Yet it is likely impossible for the culture industry to fully penetrate consciousness: "[W]hatever the culture industry sets before people in their free time is indeed consumed and accepted but with a kind of reservation… The real interests of individuals are still strong enough to resist, up to a point, their total appropriation" (Adorno 1998: 175). However, even in the unlikely situation in which the negative effects of climate change cut through the blur of stupefaction, spurring an organized anti-capitalist movement, the next pillar of real helplessness, repression, could barricade the existing social order.

Repression

Repression is the third pillar of real helplessness in climate politics. Althusser (1971) uses the term "repressive state apparatus" (RSA) to refer to the political infrastructure that reproduces existing capitalist social relations through violence, including "symbolic violence" and administrative power. The very aim of the RSA is to render people helpless through force. As a "'machine' of repression," one function of the state is to "ensure their [ruling class] domination over the working class" and it achieves this function through a collection of institutions, including centralized government, state bureaucratic administration, the military, and the criminal justice system (Althusser 1971: 137, 142).

If powerlessness and stupefied people ever organized into a mass movement to alter the current conditions that render them helpless, it is likely that the RSA would respond to this movement with force and violence. From "*preemptory* raids on the homes of protestors before the [2008 Republican National] convention had even started" (Balko 2013: 295) to the violent tactics used to suppress Occupy Wall Street protestors (e.g., Tracey 2011), the police are a visible wing of the RSA. Law enforcement's ability to control individuals, including activists, has expanded in the age of surveillance capitalism, where one can use data scraped from "smart" devices and social media to identify and charge subjects and monitor protestors (Zuboff 2019: 387f). Historically the RSA steps in whenever people challenge the social order that renders them helpless. Due to frustrations with the electoral system's inability to achieve climate action, coupled with the ineffectiveness of mostly performative climate protests, there are calls to "overthrow the elites" (Hedges 2020) or carry out an ecological or climate revolution (Foster 2009, Magdoff and Williams 2017). However, the RSA is a potentially insurmountable barrier to a successful climate revolution, at least in the US context.

Monitoring environmental activists is well underway. For example, emails reveal that the FBI, police, and other law enforcement agencies worked together to monitor Oregon environmental activists (Wilson and Parrish 2019). The NSA's Prism program was "motivated in part by fears that environmentally-linked disasters could spur anti-government activism" (Ahmed 2013). It is difficult to imagine how climate activists could effectively challenge surveillance in the age of digital technology systems controlled by megacorporations and drones. Police already draw on "surveillance-as-a-service" companies to monitor environmental activists (Zuboff 2019: 387f) and drones were used to monitor activists protesting Energy Transfer Partners' Dakota Access Pipeline (DAPL) (Parrish 2019). Surveillance would surely be an obstacle the RSA presents to the unlikely prospect of a climate revolution.

Surveillance is only one means through which environmental protest is criminalized, a growing trend in many countries (Taylor 2021). Another is direct violence. Reports indicate that between 2012 and 2022 over 1,700 environmental activists were murdered by governments, hitmen, or organized crime – mostly in Brazil, Colombia, Mexico, the Philippines and Honduras (Greenfield 2022). While this may seem unimaginable in other contexts, it is likely that incidences of violence will rise as the stakes increase for extractive industries and activists. Along with surveillance and direct violence, Nosek (2020) identifies two other means through which state and corporate actors—often cooperatively—stifle dissent: federal- and state-level legislation and retaliatory lawsuits. The former method increases penalties for participating in environmental protests, particularly against those who act against fossil fuel infrastructure (e.g., pipelines). The latter method, retaliatory lawsuits, are used against climate protestors and supportive organizations. For example, Energy Transfer Partners sued Greenpeace and others for their resistance to DAPL (Nosek, 2020). In some contexts, the courts can also protect the right to protest. When the London Metropolitan Police banned Extinction Rebellion protests in 2019, a High Court ruling deemed the ban unlawful (Dodd and Taylor 2019).

Coupled with the further criminalization of environmental protest, military force is another potential of the RSA to stop a climate revolution. This is especially true in the US, which spends over $700 billion a year on defense. While military force has not been used in the US against climate activists, it is important to note that preparation for responses to catastrophes, including environmental catastrophes, is an underlying motivation for the Department of Defense's forthright statements about the possibility of deploying the military against internal civil unrest and the Pentagon's formation of troops for in-country deployment (Ahmed 2013). However, one need not imagine future military interventions cracking down on climate protests to get a glimpse of what this may look like. Energy Transfer Partners' privatized military response to DAPL protests illustrates clear repression:

> In fall 2016, DAPL security guards attacked water protectors with dogs and pepper spray. Energy Transfer Partners hired TigerSwan, a paramilitary organization, to oversee its security responses to the anti-DAPL movement… TigerSwan proceeded to surveil and harass water protectors, whom it viewed as akin to jihadists. Militarized local police confronted water protectors with sound cannons, fired rubber bullets and water cannons at them in sub-freezing temperatures, and arrested hundreds of them in a manner that drew international condemnation and allegations of unlawful detainment. (Nosek 2020: 74)

In summary, the repression of climate activists through violence, surveillance, legislation, lawsuits, and other means represents another way that climate activists are made helpless. Repression depends on the circumstances of the specific country, powers, and norms. Yet in many cases it remains a very real possibility. Even in the unlikely future scenario of a revolutionary, highly organized, militant, and massive climate movement, in some places the RSA would likely respond with further criminalization and possible military deployment. Coupled with the other two pillars of real helplessness, powerlessness and stupefaction, repression further reduces the ability to effectively challenge the structural drivers of climate change.

The Reality of Helplessness

It is only with this political-economic backdrop that the gap between concern about climate change and effective climate action can be understood. These three pillars of helplessness impact people differently, but cumulatively they have served to reduce action despite concern. They distract a large portion of the population from the severity of the climate crisis and the possible alternatives (stupefaction). For those who want to act, it remains incredibly difficult to find any effective channels to direct systemic change without any existing organizations of resistance or a flexible and responsive political system (powerlessness). Lastly, repression against environmental activism already occurs and will likely increase, with more incidences of surveillance, arrests, lawsuits, and direct violence. Together these represent the range of reasons why an individual may feel, and truly is, helpless to act to address the climate crisis.

We do not aim here to suggest that action is futile, as more action is critically needed. Despite currently limited avenues and possibilities for action, action is still worth pursuing. As we will discuss at the end of this chapter, action can take on many different forms beyond protests or personal consumption changes. Through discussing real helplessness, we aim to identify the very real factors that continue to affect individuals and the possibilities for a mass climate movement. These factors are a result of the current social-economic and historic context. Yet they are not inevitable or immutable (Solnit 2016), as social conditions continue to change, sometimes in surprising ways. Even in the current social context, despite the reality of helplessness, many people still choose to act.

Authentic Hope: To Act, No Matter What

After writing about repression, domination, and the harms of capitalism for decades, in the 1960s Herbert Marcuse became more focused more on liberation and the possibilities for positive social transformation. Part of this quest for liberation is indeed believing it is possible, despite the odds. It is also being aware of the reality and the challenges ahead. Hope plays a key part in the struggle to keep the vision of change in full view, despite the chances of success. As Marcuse (1969) states in *An Essay on Liberation*:

> The proposition is no more—and no less—than a hope. Prior to its realization, it is indeed only the individual, the individuals, who can judge, with no other legitimation than their consciousness and conscience. But these individuals are more and other than private persons with their particular contingent preferences and interests. Their judgment transcends their subjectivity to the degree to which it is based on independent thought and information, on a rational analysis and evaluation of their society. The existence of a majority of individuals capable of such rationality has been the assumption on which democratic theory has been based.

The potential for liberation depends on hope – not a false hope, but an authentic hope where one is aware of the challenges, but knows that pursuing a better society is still possible and worth fighting for. As Rebecca Solnit (2016: 20), explains in her book *Hope in the Dark*, "[a]uthentic hope requires clarity—seeing the troubles in this world—and imagination, seeing what might lie beyond these situations that are perhaps not inevitable and immutable."

Hope exists in the realm of uncertainty. It describes the future, unknown events, and "yet unrealized possibilities" (Kretz 2013: 932). As explained by Rebecca Solnit (2016: xiv), uncertainty and instability are the basis of hope: "Hope is an embrace of the unknown and the unknowable." A sense of the probability or prospects of a desired outcome can range from unlikely to very likely. The only requirement for hope is a "worldview that proposes that development, betterment, and/or change is *possible*" (Courville and Piper 2004: 58, emphasis added).

Hope also requires an honest assessment of real-world conditions and the possibility for actions to successfully achieve one's desired outcome (Lowe 2019). If there is a small possibility of achieving the desired outcome, anything greater than zero, then there are grounds for hope. Based on the sensed likelihood of success, there can be different "gradations in the strength of one's hope, in that one's sense of hope can be strong or weak," but for hope to be justified there must be at least some "probability of realizing the hoped for state of affairs" (Kretz 2013: 932). These gradients or strengths of hope can shift over time along a spectrum. For many climate activists and concerned citizens, hope for effective mitigation has shifted from likely to *merely possible* (Gunderson 2019).

There are gradations of possibility that shed light on gradients of hope. Drawing form Bloch (1986), Gunderson (2019: 8) describes "layers of the possible" and distinguishes between "real" and "mere" possibilities. A *real* possibility involves a clear way to bring about the realization of a desired outcome and in many cases the path is "already underway" (Hudson 1982: 134, cited in Gunderson 2019). In contrast, a *mere* possibility "only dimly illuminates a possible but perhaps unlikely future that is blocked by either a lack of potential (e.g., social organization, technology) or capacity (the right will or revolutionary consciousness)" (Gunderson 2019: 3). Hope can still exist when outcomes are merely possible. As stated by Solnit (2016: 22), "[h]ope is not a door, but a sense that there might be a door at some point, some way out of the present moment even before that way is found or followed." Paying attention to *mere* possibilities can help us identify social futures that at some point may become *real* possibilities when certain constraints are overcome or no longer present (Gunderson 2019).

Given current and projected levels of global warming and the ongoing lack of meaningful political responses, as well as the reality that emissions today will continue to warm the planet for several decades, optimistic accounts of being able to stop any additional warming represents a false or fraudulent hope. The best-case scenario desired by environmentalists a decade ago is no longer possible; therefore, any hope for that scenario is false. Solnit (2016: 19) discusses Bloch's (1986) notion of "fraudulent hope" applying it to the example of President G.W. Bush claiming we would win the Iraq War and make the world safer place, convincing us that "another world is unnecessary, 'that everything is fine – now go back to sleep." False hope is deceptive yet can be very comforting in troubling times.

In terms of climate change, it is this type of fraudulent hope that dominates popular and mainstream discussions about climate change solutions (Gunderson 2019). For example, any belief in renewable energy or carbon storage, without social changes, as silver-bullet solutions lies far outside the realm of reality (see Gunderson et al. 2018, Stuart et al. 2020). As stated by Thompson (2010: 57), "[w]ishing only for an alternative energy solution, instead of making preparations for cultural change" is analogous to "turning away from reality." Thompson (2010) further explains how the focus on an alternative energy solution distracts us and prevents us from other and better possible futures. It is an appealing narrative because it provides the false assurance that there will be a "technological solution to save us all the trouble of significant behavioral and conceptual change" (Thompson 2010: 57).

Given the definition of authentic hope requiring action, passive hope is another form of false or fraudulent hope. Macy and Johnston (2012) explain that passive hope involves waiting for others to bring about a desired outcome. Passive hope has no agency. As Lueck (2007) describes, hoping it will not snow is both passive and false because there are no thoughts or actions that can have a possible effect. Passive hope can also demotivate action based on the assumption that others or something else will act or be the driver of the future. Stating "I hope the climate doesn't get worse" without action, or that, "I hope the government adopts a climate policy" without action, are examples of passive and false hope. They promote "a false sense of security and optimism, thus placating some and leaving them less likely to take action" (Lowe 2019: 482). Environmental activist Jensen (2006: 4) condemns passive hope and argues that only through releasing it can we actively work to address the climate crisis:

> When we stop hoping for external assistance, when we stop hoping that the awful situation we're in will somehow resolve itself, when we stop hoping the situation will somehow not get worse, then we are finally free—truly free—to honestly start working to resolve it. I would say that when hope dies, action begins.

Many activists have given up passive and false hope that someone else will fix the climate crisis, have realized the direness of the situation, and embraced an authentic form of hope that guides continued action, no matter what. A common XR slogan is "hope dies, action begins." Yet, this "death" of hope, as described by Jenson, is the death of passive and false hope. Only through truly seeing the dire state of the world, feeling the despair, and still actively working to create the best possible future, do we find a hope for what is left. Rather than denying loss, Cassegard and Thorn (2018) state that loss and grief need to be expressed by postapocalyptic environmentalists. They state that "the acceptance of loss can be a wellspring of new forms of activism and new forms of struggles, including attempts to salvage what can still be saved" (Cassegard and Thorn 2018: 14). In this way, embracing loss and grief can be a source of new hope, hope from despair: "giving up hope may be a way to gain hope" (Cassegard and Thorn 2018: 14). As explained by Kretz (2013: 936) telling the truth about the reality of the situation and feeling grief and loss does not mean that hope and action is lost, but that activists can adopt a new hope based on what is still possible:

> [O]ne can acknowledge serious, even dire circumstances, without feeling that it necessitates giving up all hope. Even for one convinced that it is too late, that humans have already done too much damage to reverse it quickly enough to afford a long and healthy future, we can be hopeful about stopping humans' contributions to that damage such that we lengthen the period of time both we, and the non-human world as we know it, are around.

While pessimistic (and realistic), this view also highlights that there is still much that can be saved and the value in adopting a sense of authentic hope focusing on what is still possible. Therefore, for many people, action to fight for the best possible future is justified.

Hope is often contrasted with despair, defined widely as the lack of (or loss of) hope: a state of hopelessness. As stated by Lueck (2007: 252-253), "if obstacles are seen as insurmountable or ignored, the agentic power of hope is dissolved and despair arises." Despair emerges when the desired outcome seems impossible and there is no perceived possibility of it becoming a reality (Kretz 2013). Treanor (2010: 26) explains:

> [D]espair is fatal to both environmental progress and individual flourishing, and is therefore a vice. It is fatal to environmental progress because while it is true that we may not be able to adequately respond to certain crises in time to avoid their negative effects, failing to try ensures failure and often exacerbates the situation. Despair is fatal to flourishing because it undermines our belief in the significance of our actions and our lives.

Kretz (2013) agrees that despair demotivates action, as having a vision of positive possibilities is required to motivate action. In these terms, despair is related to defeatism, the notion that there is no way to win so why bother trying, and fatalism: one's actions make no difference in a future that is already determined. All agency to change the situation is lost, as "there is no belief in any action making a difference," and the outcome becomes "a self-fulfilling prophecy" (Lueck 2007: 251). When all possibility seems gone, inaction and despair take over.

Despair, defeatism, and fatalism are increasingly common among environmentalists. As explained by Milbrath (1995: 108), "the very idea of trying to move a society to a sustainable condition seems like such a huge undertaking that many conclude there is no point in trying." The challenge of getting global leaders to quickly and effectively tackle climate change is indeed massive and daunting. As explained by Treanor (2010: 26), "[i]n the face of this complex and daunting constellation of crises it would be easy to despair, to throw in the towel, acknowledge the cause is hopeless, and get what enjoyment we can out of life for as long as we can get it." In his *New Yorker* article, titled "What if We Stopped Pretending?," Jonathan Franzen (2019) writes: "All-out war on climate change made sense only as long as it was winnable. Once you accept that we've lost it, other kinds of action take on greater meaning." He then argues we should devote more attention to adaptation and enjoying what we personally value (a privileged position as many will not be able to avoid the worst impacts of climate change). While in many ways Franzen is telling the truth about the dire climate reality, the idea that continuing to demand a large global response is futile represents a fatalistic position. It is a position based on a false notion of global warming as an "all or nothing" situation. This perception is not only inaccurate, but also demotivates action. In contrast, Wallace-Wells (2019) argues: "no matter how hot it gets, no matter how fully climate change transforms the planet and the way we live on it, it will always be the case that the next decade could contain more warming, and more suffering, or less warming and less suffering." In other words, there is still a possibility for a less bad future that is worth fighting for. This requires a new kind of hope that is not blind, but fully aware of reality and the *mere* possibility of paths that would effectively mitigate global warming. As Marcuse (1967) stresses: "[a]n opposition is required that is free of all illusion but also of all defeatism, for through its mere existence defeatism betrays the possibility of freedom to the status quo."

It is possible to have a pessimistic view that is still not defeatist or fatalistic. We are already experiencing global warming and a non-warming future is no longer possible. One could also fully accept the very low chances of the widely desired "World War II level mobilization" to prevent as much future warming as possible. Yet, this does not have to result in inaction. Authentic hope is based on telling the truth about actual possibilities (Lowe 2019). One can be pessimistic, yet still actively working for a less bad future. While pessimism need not be fatalistic, it is important that "a pessimistic perspective ought to avoid the dusk of fatalism through a persistent search for alternatives" (Gunderson 2019: 6). By being realistic about the dialectic of actuality and possibility, one can be pessimistic, and even in a state of despair, but not fall into fatalism and inaction.

Despair may even create new forms of hope, driving action to save what is left (Cassegard and Thorn 2018). This emergent hope is authentic because it recognizes the truth, rejects false hope, and focuses on what is still possible to save or salvage. This authentic hope is often seen among climate activists along with a virtue ethics approach. As summarized well by Lowe (2019: 481-482), Williston (2015) argues:

> A major advantage to promoting a virtue ethics approach for dealing with climate change is that virtues are "agent-focused" and not as tied to consequences or outcomes... In other words, they enable moral agents to do what is right even when the results are not likely to be particularly effective or rewarding. Thus, they are more dependent on our character than on our perceived prospects for success.

This approach is not focused on outcomes, but on a *commitment* to action "regardless of the outcomes" (Lowe 2019: 482). This virtue of commitment (despite the unknown outcome) is a characteristic that fuels authentic hope for what is still possible.

Action Beyond Activism

The imagination, unifying sensibility and reason, becomes "productive" as it becomes practical: a guiding force in the reconstruction of reality.

— Herbert Marcuse (1969: 6)

Many people feel helpless and indeed in many ways *are* helpless, as many avenues to direct a system-changing response to the climate crisis have been closed off. While the context is different between nations, in many cases powerlessness, stupefaction, and repression co-exist in ways that reinforce helplessness and inaction. As described in this chapter, these forces maintain the great disparity between those who are concerned about the climate crisis and those who are doing something about it. These remain major impediments to a mass social movement demanding system change, including the climate agenda outlined in this book. This does not mean those in the climate movement should give up, as we do not know what the future holds, and what unexpected events might trigger a large mobilization. This is still possible, and it is worth identifying the factors reinforcing helplessness and how they might be overcome.

While our discussion on authentic hope referred mostly to what motivates climate activists, we want to acknowledge that there are myriad ways to *act* beyond activism. Not everyone is an activist. It especially takes certain skills and characteristics to be an effective organizer. Many people can act in other ways that include learning about alternatives and communicating them to others. This can also include the work of imagining solution pathways and thinking through possibilities for system change. Any work that goes against the notion that "there is no alternative" increases the possibilities for emancipatory transformation. Countering capitalist realism (Fisher 2009) and one-dimensional thinking (Marcuse 1964) is critical to push forward the transformations necessary to justly respond to the climate crisis. Through identifying, examining, and evaluating pathways for a systemic alternative, we support "alternative realism" (Bonneuil and Fressoz 2017) and the notion that alternatives to the current system not only exist but are still possible to achieve. While not immediately likely, this pathway is still possible and therefore worth pursuing. More action on these fronts is critically needed.

However, in some cases action without design can be counterproductive, therefore much thought is necessary to craft more emancipatory futures. Adorno (1968) argues that action not guided by thought will result in "pseudo-action," which draws a lot of attention and publicity but will likely not result in the desired emancipatory ends. In response to critiques of being resigned and inactive in the practical processes of social transformation, Adorno explains that thinking is part of the process. It is, in fact, one of the most important parts.

> People locked in desperately want to get out. In such situations one doesn't think anymore, or does so only under fictive premises. Within absolutized praxis only reaction is possible and therefore false. Only thinking could find an exit, and moreover a thinking whose results are not stipulated, as is so often the case in discussions in which it is already settled who should be right, discussions that do not advance the cause but rather inevitably degenerate into tactics. If the doors are barricaded, then thought more than ever should not stop short. It should analyze the reasons and subsequently draw the conclusions. It is up to thought not to accept the situation as final. (Adorno 1968: 291)

> Thinking is not the intellectual reproduction of what already exists anyway. As long as it doesn't break off, thinking has a secure hold on possibility. (Adorno 1968: 292)

In writing this book, we agree that thinking about a systemic alternative to minimize global warming is worth doing, and that imagining how we might design and achieve a system-changing climate agenda is a required step in the process. As Marcuse (1969) argues, imagination is part of social change and essential for praxis – they are not separate. As we continue to think, imagine, and communicate alternatives, many others will continue to voice their desire for system change. Through this book, it is our hope that these calls for system change will become louder and much more specific.

Conclusion:
The Transformation Has Already Begun

Today we have the capacity to turn the world into hell, and we are well on the way to doing so. We also have the capacity to turn it into the opposite of hell.

– Herbert Marcuse (1967: 1)

*I do not say that these radical transformations will come about...
The means exist, as well as the people who are methodically working towards their realization.*

– André Gorz (2010: 13)

In the introduction, we explain that Herbert Marcuse and André Gorz were key inspirations for this book. While many scholars have been highly critical of capitalism and the associated growth-based social order, those of us hoping for a better future yearn to learn more about alternatives and to specifically identify strategies and pathways for positive social change. Here we return to Marcuse and Gorz for insights and encouragement moving forward. In each of their works, they acknowledge the impediments to reaching a more rational and sustainable post-capitalist society, yet never become fatalistic or defeatist. They call for us to move forward with the goal in sight, arguing that the wheels are already in motion and the journey to transformation has already begun. Both Marcuse and Gorz, especially in their later works, focus on pathways for positive social transformation and examine ways that production, consumption, and work can be changed to increase human and ecological well-being. While Marcuse did write about the relations between social domination and the domination of nature, he focuses more on human well-being and liberation generally. In comparison, Gorz (who examined ecological limitations more in depth and lived several decades longer than Marcuse) also wrote specifically about the climate crisis and how it necessitates social change.

Marcuse's work, especially in *One Dimensional Man* (1964), is rather pessimistic – focusing on how consumption and ideology continue to repress humans' consciousness of their oppression under capitalism. However, much of his other work is more optimistic. This is especially true when compared to his Frankfurt School colleagues Adorno and Horkheimer. The last half of *Eros and Civilization* (1955) examines potentialities for making specific changes to work, production, and consumption that would free humans to have a more creative and fulfilling life. By working and producing less, Marcuse (1955) argues, we can actually be flourishing rather than repressed humans. His later essays, *The End of Utopia* (1967) and *An Essay on Liberation* (1969), return to this discussion of pathways toward liberating humans from the repressive and oppressive conditions of capitalism, offering even more hope. In the 1960s, Marcuse also became a prominent figure among leftist student protesters who resonated with his work. While Marcuse does not provide a clear road map toward liberation, he maintains that positive transformation is possible and desirable. Much of this can be applied to our current time and the threatening manifestations of the climate crisis.

In *The End of Utopia*, Marcuse (1967) makes compelling arguments that, when applied to climate change, are well supported by the evidence in this book. He argues that the idea of utopia is over because we now have the technological means, resources, and capacities to create any world we desire. Although things that are physically impossible may still be called utopian, Marcuse (1967: 3) explains how transformations to a new social order that liberates humans from repression is completely possible with modern knowledge, technologies, and resources:

> All the material and intellectual forces which could be put to work for the realization of a free society are at hand. That they are not used for that purpose is to be attributed to the total mobilization of existing society against its own potential for liberation. But this situation in no way makes the idea of radical transformation itself a utopia.

In the context of climate change, with what we know about the need to downscale overdeveloped economies and with the mitigation tools we already have including renewable energy and carbon capture and storage, it is very possible to reduce the extent of global warming. It is even possible to minimize global warming and the associated harms as much as we can. At the same time, it is also possible to transition to a more just, equitable, and sustainable social order. Yet, the dominant forces prioritizing profit and production continue to stymie these changes.

In *An Essay on Liberation* (1969), Marcuse provides further motivation for action and provides a vision of what a more liberated life might entail. Marcuse states that countering capitalism is indeed possible: "there is a morality, a humanity, a will, and a faith which can resist and deter the gigantic technical and economic force of capitalist expansion." Yet, he also acknowledges that there are many obstacles and challenges: "It would be irresponsible to overrate the present chances of these forces." However, Marcuse (1969) was encouraged by what he saw in the student protest movements of the 1960s. Despite the dominant ideologies of work, overconsumption, and individualism, the students could still *see* human repression:

"they recognized the mark of social repression, even in the most sublime manifestations of traditional culture, even in the most spectacular manifestations of technical progress." Today, we see climate protests, civil disobedience, and other actions increasing in frequency and scope. While this has not yet resulted in the solidarity required to challenge power, it is encouraging that more and more people realize the immorality of climate inaction.

In the end, Marcuse calls for a new sensibility that allows humans to express their true nature rather than living an alienated existence as aggressive and competitive worker-consumers. This new sensibility would also reduce injustice and misery. Yet achieving this new social order and this new form of being human, requires "a moral rebellion, against the hypocritical, aggressive values and goals" of the capitalist system. A radical sense of morality, Marcuse (1969) argues, is necessary for political radicalism and must come from the foundations of morality that exist in human nature. With the climate crisis, the rationality of capitalism may seem increasingly immoral as the devastation of impacts reveals how backwards the system really is. Marcuse states that "social change occurs at a point at which the repressive rationality that has brought about the achievements of industrial society becomes utterly regressive – rational only in its efficiency to 'contain' liberation." We are indeed reaching a point where climate impacts will cause more and more people to question the rationality and the morality of a system that, as Gorz (1980:77) states, is "focused on growth, for the sake of growth."

André Gorz was friends with Marcuse and was even called the "French Marcuse" by some (Lodziak and Tatman, 1997:1). While Gorz agrees with many of Marcuse's ideas about production, consumption, work, and capitalism, he focuses more on ecological thinking and stresses the importance of staying within ecological limits. Therefore, his work more clearly ties together the ideas of ecosocialism and degrowth, calling for both an end to the growth paradigm and an end to the capitalist social relations that drive growth. Thus, he presents a foundation for merging the ideas of ecosocialism and degrowth into actionable climate policies.

Gorz was a realist, having seen the diminishment of a radical labor movement and other forces that might take down capitalism by revolutionary means. Thus, his support for a transition out of capitalism through pragmatic, although catalyzing, "non-reformist reforms" (Gorz 1967). Even more today, we see the absence of an organized, radical proletariat to fight for a livable future. Gorz presents us with a way forward despite the many obstacles and the absence of a revolutionary movement. Social movements already asking for a better future can demand specific policies for meaningful gains that open the door for more radical changes – policies that can shift power dynamics and result in a new social order. In this book, we have outlined a suite of non-reforms reforms—a climate agenda for system change—that could be used as a guide for future policy formation and political struggles. We have also examined pathways for bringing about these changes, highlighting the importance of building a larger climate movement with solidarity around much more *specific* strategies.

In *A Strategy for Labor* (1964), Gorz argues that it is not enough to have a general vision of a better future, as we must specifically show people what this future can bring, what problems it can solve, and what strategies and programs will get us there. In other words, we must show people "not only the overall alternative but also those 'intermediate objectives' (mediations) which lead to it and foreshadow it in the present" (Gorz 1964). Applying this idea to the climate crisis, we must show people who are concerned about social justice and environmental collapse what system change can look like as well as how we can get there. Through specific strategies and reforms, we must articulate what means can get us to our desired destination. The climate agenda discussed in this book represents a step in this direction, identifying and describing specific strategies and programs to forge a more livable future. Now more than ever, implementing "non-reformist reforms" (Gorz 1967) to trigger more radical social change is necessary, as there is little time left to act boldly to minimize global warming. While much was at stake for labor and the environment when Gorz completed his earlier works, his later writing clearly acknowledges that due to climate change, and the relations of capitalism that drive climate change, human survival now clearly depends on a transformation away from capitalism.

This transformation has already begun. In an essay first published the year of his death (2007), titled "The Exit from Capitalism Has Already Begun," Gorz (2010) specifically addresses the climate crisis and how it makes a transition or "exit" out of capitalism inevitable:

> It is impossible to avoid climate catastrophe without a radical break with the economic logic and methods that have been taking us in that direction for 150 years. On current trend projections, global GDP will increase by a factor of three or four by 2050. But, according to a report by the UN Climate Council, CO_2 emissions will have to fall by 85% by that date to limit global warming to a maximum of 2°C.
>
> Negative growth is, therefore, imperative for our survival. But it presupposes a different economy, a different lifestyle, a different civilization, and different social relations. In the absence of these, collapse could be avoided only through restrictions, rationing, and the kind of authoritarian resource-allocation typical of a war economy. The exit from capitalism will happen, then, one way or another, either in a civilized or barbarous fashion. The question is simply what form it will take and how quickly it will occur. (Gorz 2010: 8)

The current struggles, therefore, will determine how this exit from capitalism unfolds. As many ecosocialist and degrowth scholars continue to agree, it is not a matter of *if* the growth-dependent capitalist system will collapse, but *when*, and whether its demise will take civilization with it or result in increased social wellbeing in a new social order. Many also acknowledge that we still have time to direct this transition in ways that can minimize suffering and loss.

Having a specific agenda that illustrates tangible pathways and benefits is key to making this transition civil. The climate movement cannot rely on generic calls for "system change," just as the socialist movement could not and cannot rely on generic calls for socialism (Gorz 1964). It will not be enough. Work is required to continue to identify, articulate, and communicate specific strategies and agendas to drive forward a planned transition. Only a well-thought-out transition can guide us to a new social order and a livable future. This transition, a transition beyond growth centered capitalism, has already begun and will continue. Having specific policies or reforms that radicalize the system and catalyze transformation are necessary. As Marcuse (1969) argues, we need to adopt measures that can create "radical change" and "critically weaken the economic, political, and cultural pressure and power groups." The threat of climate change is not far off, it is now, and this threat will only increase. Yet, there are still many possible ways to effectively reduce and even minimize warming. It remains up to us to direct the change we want to see. As explained by Gorz (2010: 12): "Whether the exit from capitalism assumes a civilized or barbarous form depends on the way this struggle turns out."

References

Adorno, T.W. 1974. *Minima Moralia*. London: Verso.

Adorno, T.W. 1984. *Aesthetic Theory*. New York: Routledge & Kegan Paul.

Adorno, T.W. 1991. "Resignation." In *The Culture Industry: Selected Essays on Mass Culture*, edited by J.M. Bernstein, 171-175. New York: Routledge.

Adorno, T.W. 1998. *Critical Models: Interventions and Catchwords*. New York: Columbia University Press.

Adua, L., K.X. Zhang, and B. Clark. 2021. "Seeking a handle on climate change: Examining the comparative effectiveness of energy efficiency improvement and renewable energy production in the United States." *Global Environmental Change* 70.

Ahmed, N. 2013. "Pentagon bracing for public dissent over climate and energy shocks." *The Guardian* (June 14), 2013. https://www.theguardian.com/environment/earth-insight/2013/jun/14/climate-change-energy-shocks-nsa-prism.

Alcott, B. 2005. "Jevons' paradox." *Ecological Economics* 54 (1): 9-21.

Alexander, S. 2014. *Degrowth and the carbon budget: powerdown strategies for climate stability*. Simplicity Institute Report 14h. http://simplicityinstitute.org/wp-content/uploads/2011/04/.

Alexander, S., and P. Yacoumis. 2016. "Degrowth, energy descent, and 'low tech' living: potential pathways for increased resilience in times of crisis." *Journal of Cleaner Production*.

Almeida, P. 2019. "Climate justice and sustained transnational mobilization." *Globalizations* 16 (7): 973-979.

Almeida, P., and C. Chase-Dunn. 2018. "Globalization and Social Movements." In *Annual Review of Sociology, Vol 44*, edited by K. S. Cook and D. S. Massey, In Annual Review of Sociology, 189-211.

Alperovitz, G., J. Guinan, and T. Hanna. 2017. "The Policy Weapon Activists Need." *The Nation*.

Althusser, L. 1971. "Ideology and ideological state apparatuses." In *Lenin and Philosophy and Other Essays*. New York: Monthly Review Press.

Anderson, K., and A. Bows. 2011. "Beyond 'dangerous' climate change: emission scenarios for a new world." *Philosophical Transactions of the Royal Society a-Mathematical Physical and Engineering Sciences* 369 (1934): 20-44.

Anderson, K., and A. Bows. 2012. "A new paradigm for climate change." *Nature Climate Change* 2 (9): 639-640.

Andreucci, D., and S. Engel-Di Mauro. 2019. "Capitalism, socialism and the challenge of degrowth: introduction to the symposium." *Capitalism Nature Socialism* 30 (2): 176-188.

Andrew, B. 2008. "Market failure, government failure and externalities in climate change mitigation: the case for a carbon tax." *Public Administration and Development* 28 (5): 393-401.

Antonio, R. J., and R. J. Brulle. 2011. "THE UNBEARABLE LIGHTNESS OF POLITICS: Climate Change Denial and Political Polarization." *Sociological Quarterly* 52 (2): 195-202.

Aranoff, K. 2020. "A moderate proposal: nationalize the fossil fuel industry." The New Republic. https://newrepublic.com/article/156941/moderate-proposal-nationalize-fossil-fuel-industry.

Archer, R. 1995. *Economic Democracy: The Politics of Feasible Socialism.* Oxford: Clarendon Press.

Baatz, C., and L. Voget-Kleschin. 2019. "Individuals' Contributions to Harmful Climate Change: The Fair Share Argument Restated." *Journal of Agricultural & Environmental Ethics* 32 (4): 569-590.

Baggetta, M., and D. J. Myers. 2022. "Interpreting Unrest: How Violence changes Public Opinions about Social Movements." *Social Movement Studies* 21 (4): 469-492.

Baik, E., D. L. Sanchez, P. A. Turner, K. J. Mach, C. B. Field, and S. M. Benson. 2018. "Geospatial analysis of near-term potential for carbon-negative bioenergy in the United States." *Proceedings of the National Academy of Sciences of the United States of America* 115 (13): 3290-3295.

Balko, R. 2013. *Rise of the Warrior Cop: The Militarization of America's Police Forces.* New York: Public Affairs.

Barca, S. 2015. "Greening the job: trade unions, climate change and the political ecology of labour." In *The International Handbook of Political Ecology*, edited by R.L. Bryant. Northampton: Edward Elgar Publishing.

Barca, S., E. Chertkovskaya, and A. Paulsson. 2019. "The end of political economy as we knew it? From growth realism to nomadic utopianism." In *Towards a Political Economy of Degrowth*, edited by E. Chertkovskaya, A. Paulsson and S. Barca. Lanham: LRowman & Littlefield.

Barnard, A. 2004. "The legacy of the Situationist International: the production of situations of creative resistance." *Capital & Class* 28 (3): 103-124.

Bayon, D. 2015. "Unions." In *Degrowth: A Vocabulary for a New Era*, edited by G. D'Alisa, F. Demaria and G. Kallis, 181-191. New York: Routledge.

Beck, U. 1992. *Risk Society: Towards a New Modernity*. Translated by Mark Ritter. London: Sage Publications.

Beck, U. 1999. *World Risk Society*. Malden: Polity Press.

Beck, U. 2016. *The Metamorphosis of the World: How Climate Change is Transforming our Concept of the World*. John Wiley & Sons.

Bell, S.E., and R. York. 2010. "Community economic identity: the coal industry and ideology construction in West Virginia." *Rural Sociology* 75 (1): 111-143.

Bellamy, R., and S. Osaka. 2020. "Unnatural climate solutions?" *Nature Climate Change* 10 (2): 98-99.

Bernstein, J.M. 1991. *Adorno: The Culture Industry: Selected Essays on Mass Culture*. Routledge.

Best, S., and D. Kellner. 1999. "Debord, cybersituations, and the interactive spectacle." *Sub-Stance* (90): 129-156.

Biello, D. 2009. "Enhanced Oil Recovery: How to Make Money from Carbon Capture and Storage Today." *Scientific American*.

Biermann, F., J. Oomen, A. Gupta, S. H. Ali, K. Conca, M. A. Hajer, P. Kashwan, L. J. Kotze, M. Leach, D. Messner, C. Okereke, A. Persson, J. Potocnik, D. Schlosberg, M. Scobie, and S. D. VanDeveer. 2022. "Solar geoengineering: The case for an international non-use agreement." *Wiley Interdisciplinary Reviews-Climate Change* 13 (3): 8.

Billings, L. 2019. "Colonizing other planets is a bad idea." *Futures* 110: 44-46.

Bloch, E. 1968. "Man as possibility." *CrossCurrents* 18 (3): 273-283.

Bloch, E. 1986. *The Principle of Hope (Volume 3)*. Cambridge: MIT Press.

Bluhdorn, I. 2007. "Sustaining the unsustainable: symbolic politics and the politics of simulation." *Environmental Politics* 16 (2): 251-275.

Bluhdorn, I. 2017. "Post-capitalism, post-growth, post-consumerism? Eco-political hopes beyond sustainability." *Global Discourses* 7 (1): 42-61.

Boillat, S., J. F. Gerber, and F. R. Funes-Monzote. 2012. "What economic democracy for degrowth? Some comments on the contribution of socialist models and Cuban agroecology." *Futures* 44 (6): 600-607.

Bonneuil, C., and J.B. Fressoz. 2017. *The Shock of the Anthropocene: The Earth, History, and Us*. Translated by D. Fernbach. London: Verso Books.

Bookchin, M. 1990. "The meaning of confederalism." http://theanarchistlibrary.org/library/murray-bookchin-the-meaning-of-confederalism.

Boucher, O., D. Randall, P. Artaxo, C. Bretherton, G. Feingold, P. Forster, V.M. Kerminen, Y. Kondo, H. Liao, U. Lohmann, P. Rasch, S.K. Satheesh, S. Sherwood, B. Stevens, and X.Y. Zhang. 2013. "Clouds and Aerosols." In *Climate Change 2013: The Physical Science Basis*, edited by T. F. Stocker, D. Qin, G.K. Plattner, M. Tignor, S.K. Allen, J. Boschung, A. Nauels, Y. Xia, V. Bex and P.M. Midgley. Cambridge and New York: Cambridge University Press.

Boyer, T. 2019. "Striking the end of the world." The Baffler. https://thebaffler.com/latest/striking-at-the-end-of-the-world-raymond.

Bragman, W. 2021. "Joe Biden is still pushing to expand offshore drilling." Jacobin. https://www.jacobinmag.com/2021/09/joe-biden-administration-offshore-drilling-ipcc-report-fossil-fuel-industry.

Bressler, R.D., 2021. "The mortality cost of carbon." *Nature communications*, 12(1), p.4467.

Breyer, C., M. Fasihi, and A. Aghahosseini. 2020. "Carbon dioxide direct air capture for effective climate change mitigation based on renewable electricity: a new type of energy system sector coupling." *Mitigation and Adaptation Strategies for Global Change* 25 (1): 43-65.

Brossmann, J., and M. Islar. 2020. "Living degrowth? Investigating degrowth practices through performative methods." *Sustainability Science* 15 (3): 917-930.

Brown, D. A. 2003. "The importance of expressly examining global warming policy issues through an ethical prism." *Global Environmental Change-Human and Policy Dimensions* 13 (4): 229-234.

Browne, P. L. 2018. "Reification and passivity in the face of climate change." *European Journal of Social Theory* 21 (4): 435-452.

Bruhn, T., H. Naims, and B. Olfe-Krautlein. 2016. "Separating the debate on CO2 utilisation from carbon capture and storage." *Environmental Science & Policy* 60: 38-43.

Brulle, R. J. 2022. "Advocating inaction: a historical analysis of the Global Climate Coalition." *Environmental Politics*.

Brulle, R. J. 2018. "The climate lobby: a sectoral analysis of lobbying spending on climate change in the USA, 2000 to 2016." *Climatic Change* 149 (3-4): 289-303.

Brulle, R. J., and K. M. Norgaard. 2019. "Avoiding cultural trauma: climate change and social inertia." *Environmental Politics* 28 (5): 886-908.

Bryant, G. 2016. "The politics of carbon market design: rethinking the techno-politics and post-politics of climate change." *Antipode* 48 (4): 877-898.

Buch-Hansen, H., and M. Koch. 2019. "Degrowth through income and wealth caps?" *Ecological Economics* 160: 264-271.

Bui, M., C. S. Adjiman, A. Bardow, E. J. Anthony, A. Boston, S. Brown, P. S. Fennell, S. Fuss, A. Galindo, L. A. Hackett, J. P. Hallett, H. J. Herzog, G. Jackson, J. Kemper, S. Krevor, G. C. Maitland, M. Matuszewski, I. S. Metcalfe, C. Petit, G. Puxty, J. Reimer, D. M. Reiner, E. S. Rubin, S. A. Scott, N. Shah, B. Smit, J. P. M. Trusler, P. Webley, J. Wilcox, and N. Mac Dowell. 2018. "Carbon capture and storage (CCS): the way forward." *Energy & Environmental Science* 11 (5): 1062-1176.

Burke, P. J., M. Shahiduzzaman, and D. I. Stern. 2015. "Carbon dioxide emissions in the short run: The rate and sources of economic growth matter." *Global Environmental Change-Human and Policy Dimensions* 33: 109-121.

Burawoy, M. 2015. "Facing an unequal world." *Current Sociology* 63 (1): 5-34.

Byrne, J., C. Martinez, and C. Ruggero. 2009. "Relocating energy in the social commons: ideas for a sustainable energy utility." *Bulletin of Science, Technology & Society* 29 (2): 81-94.

CarbonBrief. 2019. "Guest post: polls reveal surve in concern in UK about climate change." https://www.carbonbrief.org/guest-post-rolls-reveal-surge-in-concern-in-uk-about-climate-change/.

Carmichael, J. T., R. J. Brulle, and J. K. Huxster. 2017. "The great divide: understanding the role of media and other drivers of the partisan divide in public concern over climate change in the USA, 2001-2014." *Climatic Change* 141 (4): 599-612.

Carrington, D. 2019. "'Climate apartheid': UN expert says human rights may not survive." *The Guardian* (June 25, 2019), 2019. https://www.theguardian.com/environment/2019/jun/25/climate-apartheid-united-nations-expert-says-human-rights-may-not-survive-crisis.

Carrington, D. 2022. "Huge expansion of oil pipelines endangering climate, says report." *The Guardian* (September 27), 2022. https://www.theguardian.com/environment/2022/sep/27/huge-expansion-oil-pipelines-endangering-climate-says-report.

Carrington, D., and M. Taylor. 2022. "Revealed: the 'carbon bombs' set to trigger catastrophic climate breakdown." 2022. https://www.theguardian.com/environment/ng-interactive/2022/may/11/fossil-fuel-carbon-bombs-climate-breakdown-oil-gas.

Carroll, W.K. 2020. "Fossil capitalism, climate capitalism, energy democracy: the struggle for hegemony in an era of climate crisis." *Socialist Studies* 40 (1).

Carson, E. 2018. "Elon Musk wants to preserve humanity in space." Cnet News. https://www.cnet.com/news/elon-musk-wants-to-preserve-humanity-in-space/.

Cassegard, C., and H. Thorn. 2017. "Climate justice, equity and movement mobilization." In *Climate Action in a Globalizing World: Comparative Perspectives on Environmental Movements in the Global North*, edited by C. Cassagard, L. Soneryd, H. Thorn and A. Wettergren, 33-56. New York: Routledge.

Castro-Santa, J., J. van den Bergh, and S. Drews. 2022. "Nudging Low-Carbon Consumption Through Advertising and Social Norms." *SSRN Working Papers* (4045434).

Chalmin, A. 2021. *The fossil fuel industry has a stake in the majority of known CCS and CCUS projects.* Geoengineering Monitor. https://www.geoengineeringmonitor.org/2021/11/fossil-fuel-industry-and-investments-in-ccs-ccus/.

Chancel, L., and T. Piketty. 2015. *Carbon and inequality: From Kyoto to Paris Trends in the global inequality of carbon emissions (1998-2013) & prospects for an equitable adaptation fund World Inequality Lab. 2015.* https://halshs.archives-ouvertes.fr/halshs-02655266/.

Chase, S. 2021. *How agent provocateurs harm our movements: some historical examples and a few ideas on reducing the risk.* International Center on Nonviolent Conflict Press (Washington, DC).

Chen, H., E. A. Tackie, I. Ahakwa, M. Musah, A. Salakpi, M. Alfred, and S. Atingabili. 2022. "Does energy consumption, economic growth, urbanization, and population growth influence carbon emissions in the BRICS? Evidence from panel models robust to cross-sectional dependence and slope heterogeneity." *Environmental Science and Pollution Research* 29 (25): 37598-37616.

Chenoweth, E., and M. Stephan. 2011. *Why Civil Resistance Works: The Strategic Logic of Nonviolent Conflict.* New York: Columbia University Press.

Chertkovskaya, E. 2019. "Degrowth in theory, pursuit of growth in action: exploring the Russian and Soviet Contexts." In *Towards a Political Economy of Degrowth*, edited by S. Barca, E. Chertkovskaya and A. Paulsson. Lanham: Rowman & Littlefield.

Chibber, V. 2022. "Vivek Chibber: "Bad ideas" aren't keeping workers from fighting back." Jacobin. https://www.jacobinmag.com/2022/03/vivek-chibber-class-matrix-materialist-theory-cultural-turn-wright-gramsci.

Ciais, P., C. Sabine, G. Bala, L. Bopp, V. Brovkin, J. Canadell, A. Chabra, R. DeFries, J. Galloway, M. Heimann, C. Jones, C. Le Quere, R.B. Myneni, S. Piao, and P. Thornton. 2013. "Carbon and other biogeochemical cycles." In *Climate Change 2013: The Physical Basis: Contribution of the Working Group I to the Fifth Assessment Report of the Intergovernmental Panel on Climate Change*, edited by T. F. Stocker, D. Qin, G.K. Plattner, M. Tignor, S.K. Allen, J. Boschung, A. Nauels, Y. Xia, V. Bex and P.M. Midgley. Cambridge and New York: Cambridge University Press.

Clark, B., and J. B. Foster. 2001. "William Stanley Jevons and the coal question: an introduction to Jevons's "Of the economy of fuel"." *Organization & Environment* 14 (1): 93-98.

Clayton, S. 2020. "Climate anxiety: Psychological responses to climate change." *Journal of Anxiety Disorders* 74.

Coady, D., I. Parry, L. Sears, and B. P. Shang. 2017. "How Large Are Global Fossil Fuel Subsidies?" *World Development* 91: 11-27.

Cohen, S. 2001. *States of Denial: Knowing about Atrocities and Suffering*. Cambridge: Polity.

Cole, G.D.H. 1953. *A History of Socialist Thought, Volume 1: The Forerunners*, 1789-1850. New York: St. Martin's Press.

Cole, G.D.H. 1954. *A History of Socialist Thought, Volume 2: Marxism and Anarchism*, 1850-1890. New York: St. Martin's Press.

Conley, J. 2019. "Tipping Point: UN Biodiversity Chief Warns Burning of Amazon Could Lead to 'Cascading Collapse of Natural Systems." Common Dreams. https://www.commondreams.org/news/2019/08/30/tipping-point-un-biodiversity-chief-warns-burning-amazon-could-lead-cascading.

Cook, D. 1996. *The Culture Industry Revisited: Theodor W. Adorno on Mass Culture*. Lanham: Rowman & Littlefield Publishers.

Cook, D. 2006. "Adorno's critical materialism." *Philosophy & Social Criticism* 32 (6): 719-737.

Courville, S., and N. Piper. 2004. "Harnessing hope through NGO activism." *Annals of the American Academy of Political and Social Science* 592: 39-61.

Crutzen, P. J. 2006. "Albedo enhancement by stratospheric sulfur injections: A contribution to resolve a policy dilemma?" *Climatic Change* 77 (3-4): 211-219.

D'Alisa, G., and G. Kallis. 2016. "A political ecology of maladaptation: Insights from a Gramscian theory of the State." *Global Environmental Change* 38: 230-242.

D'Alisa, G., and G. Kallis. 2020. "Degrowth and the state." *Ecological Economics* 169.

Daly, H. 2005. "Economics in a full world." *Scientific American* 293: 100-107.

Daly, H. 2008. *A Steady State Economy*. Report to the United Kingdom Sustainable Development Commission. https://www.sd-commission.org.uk/publications.php@id=775.html.

Davenport, C. 1995. "Multidimensional threat perception and state repressions: an inquiry into why states apply negative sanctions." *American Journal of Political Science* 39 (3): 683-713.

de Bruin, W.B. 2022. A majority of people around the world are concerned about climate change, says poll. *https://phys.org/news/2022-07-majority-people-world-climate-poll.html*

de Coninck, H., and S. M. Benson. 2014. "Carbon Dioxide Capture and Storage: Issues and Prospects." In *Annual Review of Environment and Resources, Vol 39*, edited by A. Gadgil and D. M. Liverman, In Annual Review of Environment and Resources, 243-270.

Debord, G. 1971. *A Sick Planet*. Chicago: University of Chicago Press.

Debord, G. 1983. *Society of the Spectacle*. Detroit: Black and Red.

Dello-Iacovo, M., and S. Saydam. 2022. "Humans have big plans for mining in space - but there are many things holding us back." The Conversation. https://theconversation.com/humans-have-big-plans-for-mining-in-space-but-there-are-many-things-holding-us-back-181721.

Demaria, F., G. Kallis, and K. Bakker. 2019. "Geographies of degrowth: Nowtopias, resurgences and the decolonization of imaginaries and places." *Environment and Planning E: Nature and Space* 2 (3): 431-450.

Democratic Socialists of America. 2021. "What is democratic socialism?". Democratic Socialists of America, USA. https://www.dsausa.org/about-us/what-is-democratic-socialism/.

Dentzman, K., R. Gunderson, and R. Jussaume. 2016. "Techno-optimism as a barrier to overcoming herbicide resistance: Comparing farmer perceptions of the future potential of herbicides." *Journal of Rural Studies* 48: 22-32.

DeVito, C. L. 2019. "Getting off planet." *Futures* 110: 54-55.

Dietz, T. 2015. "Environmental value." In *Handbook of Value: Perspectives from Economics, Neuroscience, Philosophy, Psychology, and Sociology*, edited by T. Brosch and D. Sander. Oxford: Oxford University Press.

Dietz, T., G. T. Gardner, J. Gilligan, P. C. Stern, and M. P. Vandenbergh. 2009. "Household actions can provide a behavioral wedge to rapidly reduce US carbon emissions." *Proceedings of the National Academy of Sciences of the United States of America* 106 (44): 18452-18456.

Dodd, V., and M. Taylor. 2019. "Why was the Met's Extinction Rebellion protest ban unlawful?" *The Guardian* (November 6), 2019. https://www.theguardian.com/environment/2019/nov/06/why-was-the-mets-extinction-rebellion-protest-ban-unlawful.

Doherty, B., C Saunders, and G. Hayes. 2020. *A New Climate Movement? Extinction Rebellion's Activists in Profile*. CUSP Working Paper No 25. CUSP Working Paper Series.

Drews, S., and M. Antal. 2016. "Degrowth: A "missile word" that backfires?" *Ecological Economics* 126: 182-187.

EIA (U.S. Energy Information Administration). 2018. *Electricity*. eia.gov/electricity/annual/

Eisen, M. B., & Brown, P. O. 2022. Rapid global phaseout of animal agriculture has the potential to stabilize greenhouse gas levels for 30 years and offset 68 percent of CO_2 emissions this century. PLoS Climate, 1(2), e0000010.

Ernsting, A. 2015. "Renewables cannot sustain the globalized growth economy." Degrowth Web Portal. https://www.degrowth.info/en/2015/02/renewables-cannot-sustain-the-globalized-growth-economy/.

Fajardy, M., S. Chiquier, and N. Mac Dowell. 2018. "Investigating the BECCS resource nexus: delivering sustainable negative emissions." *Energy & Environmental Science* 11 (12): 3408-3430. https://doi.org/10.1039/c8ee01676c.

Fajardy, M., A. Koeberle, N. MacDowell, and A. Fantuzzi. 2019. *BECCS deployment: a reality check*. Grantham Institute Briefing Paper.

Farajzadeh, R., A. A. Eftekhari, G. Dafnomilis, L. W. Lake, and J. Bruining. 2020. "On the sustainability of CO_2 storage through CO_2 - Enhanced oil recovery." *Applied Energy* 261: 12.

Farrell, J. 2016. "Network structure and influence of the climate change counter-movement." *Nature Climate Change* 6 (4): 370-374.

Feinberg, M., R. Willer, and C. Kovacheff. 2020. "The Activist's Dilemma: Extreme Protest Actions Reduce Popular Support for Social Movements." *Journal of Personality and Social Psychology* 119 (5): 1086-1111.

Ferguson, F. 2018. "John Bellamy Foster: Still Time for an Ecological Revolution." REBEL News. http://www.rebelnews.ie/2018/08/24/john-bellamy-foster-there-is-still-time-for-an-ecological-revolution/.

Ferraro, A.J., E.J. Highwood, and A.J. Charlton-Perez. 2014. "Weakened tropical circulation and reduced precipitation in response to geoengineering." *Environmental Research Letters* 9 (1): 014001.

Fisher, D.R. 2022. "AnthroShift in a warming world." *Climate Action* 1 (1): 1-6.

Fisher, M. 2009. *Capitalist Realism: Is There No Alternative?* Winchester: Zero Books.

Fisher, D. R., and A. K. Jorgenson. 2019. "Ending the stalemate: toward a theory of anthro-Shift." *Sociological Theory* 37 (4): 342-362.

Fitzgerald, J. B. 2022. "Working time, inequality and carbon emissions in the United States: A multi-dividend approach to climate change mitigation." *Energy Research & Social Science* 84: 11.

Fitzgerald, J.B., A.K. Jorgenson, and B. Clark. 2015. "Energy consumption and working hours: a longitudinal study of developed and developing nations, 1990-2008." *Environmental Sociology* 3 (1): 213-223.

Fitzgerald, J. B., J. B. Schor, and A. K. Jorgenson. 2018. "Working Hours and Carbon Dioxide Emissions in the United States, 2007-2013." *Social Forces* 96 (4): 1851-1874.

Fitzpatrick, N., T. Parrique, and I. Cosme. 2022. "Exploring degrowth policy proposals: A systematic mapping with thematic synthesis." *Journal of Cleaner Production* 365: 19.

Foer, F. 2019. "Jeff Bezos's master plan." The Atlantic. https://www.theatlantic.com/magazine/archive/2019/11/what-jeff-bezos-wants/598363/.

Foster, J.B. 2000. "The dialectic of organic/inorganic relations: Marx and the Hegelian philosophy of nature." *Organization and Environment* 13 (4): 403-425.

Foster, J.B. 2009. *The Ecological Revolution: Making Peace with the Planet.* New York: Monthly Review Press.

Foster, J. B. 2010. "Why ecological revolution?" *Monthly Review* 61 (8): 1-18.

Foster, J. B. 2015. "The Great Capitalist Climacteric Marxism and "System Change Not Climate Change"." *Monthly Review-an Independent Socialist Magazine* 67 (6): 1-18.

Foster, J.B. 2017. "The long ecological revolution." Monthly Review. https://monthlyreview.org/2017/11/01/the-long-ecological-revolution/

Foster, J.B. 2018. "Making war on the planet: Geoengineering and capitalism's creative destruction of the Earth." Science for the People. https://magazine.scienceforthepeople.org/making-war-on-the-planet/.

Foster, J.B. 2019. "On fire this time." The Monthly Review. https://monthlyreview.org/2019/11/01/on-fire-this-time/.

Foster, J.B. 2020. "The renewal of the socialist ideal." The Monthly Review. https://monthlyreview.org/2020/09/01/the-renewal-of-the-socialist-ideal/.

Foster, J.B. 2021. "Against doomsday scenarios: what is to be done now?". Monthly Review. https://monthlyreview.org/2021/12/01/against-doomsday-scenarios/.

Foster, J.B. 2022. *Capitalism in the Anthropocene: Ecological Ruin or Ecological Revolution*. New York: Monthly Review Press.

Foster, J.B., and B. Clark. 2020. *The Robbery of Nature: Capitalism and the Ecological Rift*. New York: NYU Press.

Foster, J.B., and B. Clark. 2022. "Socialism and ecological survial: an introduction." Monthly Review. https://monthlyreview.org/2022/07/01/socialism-and-ecological-survival-an-introduction/.

Foster, J. B., B. Clark, and R. York. 2010. *The Ecological Rift: Capitalism's War on the Earth*. New York: Monthly Review Press.

Foster, J. B., B. Clark, and R. York. 2010. "Capitalism and the curse of energy efficiency: The return of the Jevons Paradox." *Monthly Review-an Independent Socialist Magazine* 62 (6): 1-12.

Fragniere, A., and S.M. Gardiner. 2016. "Why engineering is not 'Plan B'." In *Climate Justice and Geoengineering: Ethics and Policy in the Atmospheric Anthropocene*, edited by C.J. Preston, 15-32. London: Rowman & Littlefield.

Franzen, J. 2019. "What if we stopped pretending?" *The New Yorker*.

Frase, P. 2011. "Four futures." Jacobin. https://www.jacobinmag.com/2011/12/four-futures/.

Fraser, N. 2014. "Can society be commodities all the way down? Post-Polanyian reflections on capitalist crisis." *Economy and Society* 43 (4): 541-558.

Freeman, R., M. Yearworth, and C. Preist. 2015. "Revisiting Jevons' Paradox with system dynamics: systemic causes andpotential cures." *Journal of Industrial Ecology* 20 (2): 341-353. https://doi.org/10.1111/jiec.12285.

Freire-Gonzalez, J. 2017. "Evidence of direct and indirect rebound effect in households in EU-27 countries." *Energy Policy* 102: 270-276.

Freire-Gonzalez, J. 2021. "Governing Jevons' Paradox: Policies and systemic alternatives to avoid the rebound effect." *Energy Research & Social Science* 72.

Fridahl, M. 2017. "Socio-political prioritization of bioenergy with carbon capture and storage." *Energy Policy* 104: 89-99.

Fridahl, M., and M. Lehtveer. 2018. "Bioenergy with carbon capture and storage (BECCS): Global potential, investment preferences, and deployment barriers." *Energy Research & Social Science* 42: 155-165.

Funk, C., A. Tyson, B. Kennedy, and C. Johnson. 2020. *Concern over climate and the environment predominates among these publics*. Pew Research Center. https://www.pewresearch.org/science/2020/09/29/concern-over-climate-and-the-environment-predominates-among-these-publics/.

Gabriel, C. A., and C. Bond. 2019. "Need, Entitlement and Desert: A Distributive Justice Framework for Consumption Degrowth." *Ecological Economics* 156: 327-336.

Galbraith, J.K. 1958. *The Affluent Society*. New York: Houghton Mifflin Harcourt.

Gardiner, S. M. 2011. "Some early ethics of geoengineering the climate: a commentary on the values of the royal society report." *Environmental Values* 20 (2): 163-188.

Geoengineering Monitor. 2021. *Geoengineering Technology Briefing: Stratospheric Aerosol Injection*. Geoengineering Monitor. https://www.geoengineeringmonitor.org/wp-content/uploads/2018/06/SAI_Eng_v5_LD.pdf.

GFI. 2016. "New report on unrecorded capital flight finds developing countries are not-creditors to the rest of the world." Global Financial Integrity. https://gfintegrity.org/press-release/new-report-on-unrecorded-capital-flight-finds-developing-countries-are-net-creditors-to-the-rest-of-the-world/.

Gifford, R. 2011. "The Dragons of Inaction Psychological Barriers That Limit Climate Change Mitigation and Adaptation." *American Psychologist* 66 (4): 290-302.

Gorton, G., and F. A. Schmid. 2004. "Capital, labor, and the firm: a study of German Codetermination." *Journal of the European Economic Association* 2 (5): 863-905.

Gorz, A. 1967. *Strategy for Labor*. Boston: Beacon Press.

Gorz, André. 1976. Writing as Bosquet, Michel in "Une production destructive" *Le Nouvel Observateur*.

Gorz, André. 1980. *Capitalism, Socialism, Ecology.* Verso, New York

Gorz, A. 2010. "The exit from capitalism has already begun." *Cultural Politics* 6 (1): 5-14.

Gould, K. A., D. N. Pellow, and A. Schnaiberg. 2004. "Interrogating the treadmill of production - Everything you wanted to know about the treadmill but were afraid to ask." *Organization & Environment* 17 (3): 296-316.

Gowan, P. 2018. "A plan to nationalize fossil-fuel companies." Jacobin. https://www.jacobinmag.com/2018/03/nationalize-fossil-fuel-companies-climate-change.

Gramsci, A. 1971. *Selections from the Prison Notebooks.* New York: International.

Granados, J. A. T., and C. L. Spash. 2019. "Policies to reduce CO2 emissions: Fallacies and evidence from the United States and California." *Environmental Science & Policy* 94: 262-266.

Green, B. P. 2019. "Self-preservation should be humankind's first ethical priority and therefore rapid space settlement is necessary." *Futures* 110: 35-37.

Green, A., and M.S. Cato. 2018. "Facts about our ecological crisis are incontrovertible. We must take action." *The Guardian*, October 26. https://www.theguardian.com/environment/2018/oct/26/facts-about-our-ecological-crisis-are-incontrovertible-we-must-take-action.

Green, F., and N. Healy. 2022. "How inequality fuels climate change: The climate case for a Green New Deal." *One Earth* 5 (6): 635-649.

Greenfield, P. 2022. "More than 1,700 environmental activists murdered in the past decade - report." *The Guardian* (September 29), 2022. https://www.theguardian.com/environment/2022/sep/29/global-witness-report-1700-activists-murdered-past-decade-aoe.

Griner, D. 2017. "18 Bullish Stats About the State of U.S. Advertising." Adweek. https://www.adweek.com/agencies/18-bullish-stats-about-the-state-of-u-s-advertising/.

Griscom, B. W., J. Adams, P. W. Ellis, R. A. Houghton, G. Lomax, D. A. Miteva, W. H. Schlesinger, D. Shoch, J. V. Siikamaki, P. Smith, P. Woodbury, C. Zganjar, A. Blackman, J. Campari, R. T. Conant, C. Delgado, P. Elias, T. Gopalakrishna, M. R. Hamsik, M. Herrero, J. Kiesecker, E. Landis, L. Laestadius, S. M. Leavitt, S. Minnemeyer, S. Polasky, P. Potapov, F. E. Putz, J. Sanderman, M. Silvius, E. Wollenberg, and J. Fargione. 2017. "Natural climate solutions." *Proceedings of the National Academy of Sciences of the United States of America* 114 (44): 11645-11650.

Griscom, B. W., G. Lomax, T. Kroeger, J. E. Fargione, J. Adams, L. Almond, D. Bossio, S. C. Cook-Patton, P. W. Ellis, C. M. Kennedy, and J. Kiesecker. 2019. "We need both natural and energy solutions to stabilize our climate." *Global Change Biology* 25 (6): 1889-1890.

Groom, N. 2018. "Big Oil outspends billionaires in Washington state carbon tax fight." *Reuters* (October 31), 2018. https://www.reuters.com/article/us-usa-election-carbon/big-oil-outspends-billionaires-in-washington-state-carbon-tax-fight-idUSKCN1N51H7.

Grumbach, J. M. 2015. "Polluting industries as climate protagonists: cap and trade and the problem of business preferences." *Business and Politics* 17 (4): 633-659.

Gunderson, R. 2017. "Ideology critique for the environmental social sciences: what reproduces the treadmill of production?" *Nature + Culture* 12 (3): 263-289.

Gunderson, R. 2019. "Work time reduction and economic democracy as climate change mitigation strategies: or why the climate needs a renewed labor movement." *Journal of Environmental Studies and Sciences* 9 (1): 35-44.

Gunderson, R. 2021. *Hothouse Utopia: Dialectics Facing Unsavable Futures.* John Hunt Publishing.

Gunderson, R. 2022. Powerless, stupefied, and repressed actors cannot challenge climate change: Real helplessness as a barrier between climate concern and action. *Journal for the Theory of Social Behaviour.* DOI: 10.1111/jtsb.12366.

Gunderson, R., and W. Charles. 2023. "A sociology of 'climatage': the appeal and counterproductivity of property destruction as a climate change strategy." *Environmental Sociology* 9(4): 398-408.

Gunderson, R., B. Petersen, and D. Stuart. 2018. "A critical examination of geoengineering: economic and technological rationality in social context." *Sustainability* 10 (1).

Gunderson, R., D. Stuart, and B. Petersen. 2018. "The political economy of geoengineering as plan B: technological rationality, moral hazard, and new technology." *New Political Economy.*

Gunderson, R., D. Stuart, and B. Petersen. 2019. "Materialized ideology and environmental problems: The cases of solar geoengineering and agricultural biotechnology." *European Journal of Social Theory.*

Gunderson, R., D. Stuart, and B. Petersen. 2020. "The fossil fuel industry's framing of carbon capture and storage: Faith in innovation, value instrumentalization, and status quo maintenance." *Journal of Cleaner Production* 252.

Gunderson, R., and C. Fyock. 2022. "The Political Economy of Climate Change Litigation: Is There a Point to Suing Fossil Fuel Companies?" *New Political Economy* 27 (3): 441-454.

Gunderson, R., D. Stuart, B. Petersen, and S. J. Yun. 2018. "Social conditions to better realize the environmental gains of alternative energy: Degrowth and collective ownership." *Futures* 99: 36-44.

Gunderson, R., and S. J. Yun. 2017. "South Korean green growth and the Jevons paradox: An assessment with democratic and degrowth policy recommendations." *Journal of Cleaner Production* 144: 239-247.

Gunderson, R., and S. J. Yun. 2021. "Building energy democracy to mend ecological and epistemic rifts: An environmental sociological examination of Seoul's One Less Nuclear Power Plant initiative." *Energy Research & Social Science* 72: 9.

Haberl, H., D. Wiedenhofer, D. Virag, G. Kalt, B. Plank, P. Brockway, T. Fishman, D. HauCknost, F. Krausmann, B. Leon-Gruchalski, A. Mayer, M. Pichler, A. Schaffartzik, T. Sousa, J. Streeck, and F. Creutzig. 2020. "A systematic review of the evidence on decoupling of GDP, resource use and GHG emissions, part II: synthesizing the insights." *Environmental Research Letters* 15 (6).

Hale, B. 2012. "The world that would have been: moral hazard arguments against geoengineering." In *Engineering the Climate: The Ethics of Solar Radiation Management*, edited by C.J. Preston, 113-131. Plymouth: Lexington Books.

Hamilton, C. 2013. *Earthmasters: The Dawn of the Age of Climate Engineering*. Padstow: Yale University Press.

Hampton, P. 2018. "Trade unions and climate politics: prisoners of neoliberalism or swords of climate justice?" *Globalizations* 15 (4): 470-486.

Han, H., and C. Barnett-Loro. 2018. "To support a stronger climate movement, focus research on building collective power." *Frontiers in Communication*.

Harnisch, S., S. Uther, and M. Boettcher. 2015. "From 'Go Slow' to 'Gung Ho'? Climate Engineering Discourses in the UK, the US, and Germany." *Global Environmental Politics* 15 (2): 57-78.

Harrington, M. 1989. *Socialism: Past and Future*. New York: Arcade.

Harvard Solar Geoengineering Research Program. n.d. "Geoengineering." https://geoengineering.environment.harvard.edu/geoengineering.

Harvey, D. 2007. *A Brief History of Neoliberalism*. Oxford: Oxford University Press.

Harvey, D. 2014. *Seventeen Contradictions and the End of Capitalism*. Oxford: Oxford University Press.

Harvey, F. 2020. "Lockdowns trigger dramatic fall in global carbon emissions." *The Guardian* (May 19), 2020. https://www.theguardian.com/environment/2020/may/19/lockdowns-trigger-dramatic-fall-global-carbon-emissions.

Harvey, F. 2021. "John Kerry: world leaders must step up to avoid worst impacts of climate crisis." *The Guardian*, 2021. https://www.theguardian.com/environment/2021/jul/20/john-kerry-world-climate-crisis-us.

Harvey, H., and J. Gillis. 2022. *The Big Fix: 7 Practical Steps to Save Our Planet.* Simion & Schuster.

Hedges, C. 2019. "Saving the planet means overthrowing the ruling elites." Trugh Dig. https://www.truthdig.com/articles/saving-the-planet-means-overthrowing-the-ruling-elites/

Heede, R. 2014. "Tracing anthropogenic carbon dioxide and methane emissions to fossil fuel and cement producers, 1854-2010." *Climatic Change* 122 (1-2): 229-241..

Heideman, P. 2020. "Mass politics, not movementism, is the future of the left." Jacobin. https://jacobin.com/2020/04/bernie-sanders-democratic-socialism-mass-politics-left/.

Heikkurinen, P. 2018. "Degrowth by means of technology? A treatise for an ethos of releasement." *Journal of Cleaner Production* 197: 1654-1665.

Herman, E.S., and N. Chomsky. 1988. *Manufacturing Consent: The Political Economy of the Mass Media.* Pantheon Books.

Hickel, J. 2017. "The Paris climate deal won't save us - our future depends on degrowth." *The Guardian*, July 15, 2017. https://www.theguardian.com/global-development-professionals-network/2017/jul/03/paris-climate-deal-wont-work-our-future-depends-degrowth.

Hickel, J. 2019. "Degrowth: a theory of radical abundance." *Real-World Economics Review* 87: 54-68.

Hickel, J. 2021. *Less Is More: How Degrowth Will Save the World.* London: Penguin Random House.

Hickel, J., and G. Kallis. 2019. "Is green growth possible?" *New Political Economy.*

Hoffman, U. 2011. *Some reflections on climate change, green growth illusions and development space.* Discussion paper at the United Nations Conference on Trade and Development, no. 205. United Nations.

Horkheimer, M. 1947. *Eclipse of Reason.* New York: Continuum.

Horkheimer, M. 1993. "Beginnings of the bourgeois philosophy of history." In *Between Philosophy and Social Science: Selected Early Writings*, 313-388. Cambridge: MIT Press.

Horkheimer, M., and T.W. Adorno. 1969. *Dialectic of Enlightenment*. New York: Continuum.

Horton, J. B. 2015. "The emergency framing of solar geoengineering: Time for a different approach." *Anthropocene Review* 2 (2): 147-151.

Horton, J., and D. Keith. 2016. "Solar geoengineering and obligations to the global poor." In *Climate Justice and Geoengineering: Ethics and Policy in the Atmospheric Anthropocene*, edited by C.J. Preston, 79-92. Rowman & Littlefield Publishers.

Hubacek, K., G. Baiocchi, K. S. Feng, R. M. Castillo, L. X. Sun, and J. J. Xue. 2017. "Global carbon inequality." *Energy Ecology and Environment* 2 (6): 361-369.

Hubacek, K., X. Chen, K. Feng, T. Wiedman, and Y. Shan. 2021. "Evidence of decoupling consumption-based CO_2 emissions from economic growth." *Advances in Applied Energy* 4 (19): 100074.

Hunnicutt, T., and J. Mason. 2021. "U.S. calls on OPEC and its allies to pump more oil." Reuters. https://www.reuters.com/article/us-usa-oil-opec-idCAKBN2FC14X.

IEA. 2015. *Storing CO_2 through Enhanced Oil Recovery: Combining EOR with CO_2 storage (EOR+) for profit.* International Energy Agency (Paris, France).

IEA. 2017. "World Energy Outlook 2017." https://www.iea.org/reports/world-energy-outlook-2017.

IPCC. 2012. "Meeting Report of the Intergovernmental Panel on Climate Change Expert Meeting on Geoengineering." In *IPCC Working Group III Technical Support Unit, Postdam Institute for Climate Impact Research*, edited by O. Edenhofer, R. Pichs-Madruga, Y. Sokona, C. Field, V. Barrros, T.F. Stocker, Q. Dahe, J. Minx, K. Mach, G.K. Plattner, S. Schlomer, G. Hansen and M. Mastrandrea, 99. Postdam, Germany.

IPCC. 2014. *Climate Change 2014: Synthesis Report. Contribution of Working Groups I, II and III to the Fifth Assessment Report of the Intergovernmental Panel on Climate Change*. IPCC (Geneva, Switzerland).

IPCC. 2018. "Global Warming of 1.5°C. An IPCC Special Report on the impacts of global warming of 1.5°C above pre-industrial levels and related global greenhouse gas emission pathways, in the context of strengthening the global response to the threat of climate change, sustainable development, and efforts to eradicate poverty." edited by V. Masson-Delmotte, P. Zhai, H.-O. Pörtner, D. Roberts, J. Skea, P.R. Shukla, A. Pirani, W. Moufouma-Okia, C. Péan, R. Pidcock, S. Connors, J.B.R. Matthews, Y. Chen, X. Zhou, M.I. Gomis, E. Lonnoy, T. Maycock, M. Tignor and T. Waterfield.

Ipsos. 2022. *Earth Day 2022: Public Opinion on Climate Change*. https://www.ipsos.com/sites/default/files/ct/news/documents/2022-04/Ipsos%20-%20Global%20Advisor%20-%20Earth%20Day%202022%20-%20Release%201.pdf.

Jackson, T. 2009. *Prosperity Without Growth*. London: Earthscan.

Jacobson, M. Z., M. A. Delucchi, G. Bazouin, Z. A. F. Bauer, C. C. Heavey, E. Fisher, S. B. Morris, D. J. Y. Piekutowski, T. A. Vencill, and T. W. Yeskoo. 2015. "100% clean and renewable wind, water, and sunlight (WWS) all-sector energy roadmaps for the 50 United States." *Energy & Environmental Science* 8 (7): 2093-2117.

Jager, A., and D. Leusder. 2020. "The prophet of inequality." Jacobin. https://jacobin.com/2020/08/the-prophet-of-inequality.

Jaeger, D.A., F.K. Esteban, S.H. Miaari, and D. Paserman. 2015. "Can militants use violence to win public support? Evidence from the Second Intifada." *Journal of Conflict Resolution* 59 (3): 528-549.

Jameson, F. 1990. *Late Marxism: Adorno, or, the Persistence of the Dialectic*. New York: Verso.

Jarvis, H. 2019. "Sharing, togetherness and intentional degrowth." *Progress in Human Geography* 4 (3): 256-275.

Jaramillo, P., W. M. Griffin, and S. T. McCoy. 2009. "Life Cycle Inventory of CO2 in an Enhanced Oil Recovery System." *Environmental Science & Technology* 43 (21): 8027-8032.

Jay, M. 1984. *Marxism and Totality: The Adventures of a Concept from Lukacs to Habermas*. Berkeley: University of California Press.

Jensen, D. 2006. "Beyond hope." *Orion Magazine*.

Jevons, W.S. 1865. *The Coal Question: An Enquiry Concderning the Progress of the Nation, and the Probable Exhaustion of Our Coal-mines*. London: Macmillan.

Johanisova, N., and S. Wolf. 2012. "Economic democracy: A path for the future?" *Futures* 44 (6): 562-570.

Jones, M. 2022. "Now that the IRA is law, the clime movement's fight has just begun." In These Times. https://inthesetimes.com/article/inflation-reduction-act-biden-climate-manchin-fossil-fuels.

Jorgenson, A. K., and B. Clark. 2012. "Are the economy and the environment decoupling? a comparative international study, 1960-2005." *American Journal of Sociology* 118 (1): 1-44.

Jorgenson, A. K., S. Fiske, K. Hubacek, J. Li, T. McGovern, T. Rick, J. B. Schor, W. Solecki, R. York, and A. Zycherman. 2019. "Social science perspectives on drivers of and responses to global climate change." *Wiley Interdisciplinary Reviews-Climate Change* 10 (1).

Jorgenson, A. K., T. Dietz, and O. Kelly. 2018. "Inequality, poverty, and the carbon intensity of human well-being in the United States: a sex-specific analysis." *Sustainability Science* 13 (4): 1167-1174.

Kallis, G. 2017. "Radical dematerialization and degrowth." *Philosophical Transactions of the Royal Society a-Mathematical Physical and Engineering Sciences* 375 (2095).

Kallis, G. 2018. *Degrowth.* Newcastle: Agenda Publishing.

Kallis, G. 2019. "Socialism without growth." *Capitalism Nature Socialism* 30 (2): 189-206.

Kallis, G., F. Demaria, and G. D'Alisa. 2015. "Introduction: Degrowth." In *Degrowth: A Vocabulary for a New Era*, edited by G. D'Alisa, F. Demaria and G. Kallis, 1-17. New York: Routledge.

Kallis, G., C. Kerschner, and J. Martinez-Alier. 2012. "The economics of degrowth." *Ecological Economics* 84: 172-180.

Kaminski, I. 2019. "Dutch supreme court upholds landmark ruling demanding climate action." *The Guardian* (December 20), 2019.

Kartha, S., E. Kemp-Benedict, E. Ghosh, A. Nazareth, and T. Gore. 2020. *The Carbon Inequality Era: An assessment of the global distribution of consumption emissions among individuals from 1990 to 2015 and beyond.* Oxfam (Stockholm). https://oxfamilibrary.openrepository.com/handle/10546/621049.

Kaufman, A.C. 2019. "Senators Not Backing Green New Deal Received On Average 7 Times As Much Fossil Fuel Cash." HuffPost. https://www.huffpost.com/entry/senate-green-new-deal-fossil-fuel-donations_n_5c6dc9b2e4b0e2f4d8a24e83.

Kaup, B. 2015. "Markets, nature, and society: embedding economic and environmental sociology." *Sociological Theory* 33 (3): 280-296.

Keith, D.W. 2013. *Climate Engineering.* Boston: MIT Press.

Keith, D., G. Holmes, D. St. Angelo, and K. Heidel. 2018. "A process for capturing CO2 from the atmosphere." *Joule* 2: 1-22.

Kellner, D. 2002. "Theorizing globalization." *Sociological Theory* 20 (3): 285-305.

Kellner, D. 1984. *Herbert Marcuse and the Crisis of Marxism*. Berkeley: University of California Press.

Kelner, D. 2003. *Media Spectacle*. London: Routledge.

Kenis, A., and E. Mathijs. 2014. "Climate change and post-politics: Repoliticizing the present by imagining the future?" *Geoforum* 52: 148-156.

Kerschner, C., and M. H. Ehlers. 2016. "A framework of attitudes towards technology in theory and practice." *Ecological Economics* 126: 139-151.

Kerschner, C., P. Wachter, L. Nierling, and M. H. Ehlers. 2015. "Special volume: technology and Degrowth." *Journal of Cleaner Production* 108: 31-33.

Kerschner, C., P. Wachter, L. Nierling, and M. H. Ehlers. 2018. "Degrowth and Technology: Towards feasible, viable, appropriate and convivial imaginaries." *Journal of Cleaner Production* 197: 1619-1636.

Keysser, L. T., and M. Lenzen. 2021. "1.5 degrees C degrowth scenarios suggest the need for new mitigation pathways." *Nature Communications* 12 (1): 16.

Kintisch, Eli. 2010. *Hack the Planet: Science's Best Hope - or Worst Nightmare - for Averting Climate Catastrophe*. Hoboken: John Wiley & Sons.

Klein, N. 2011. "Capitalism vs. the climate." *The Nation*, 2011.

Klein, N. 2014. *This Changes Everything: Capitalism vs. the Climate*. New York: Simon and Schuster.

Knight, K. W., E. A. Rosa, and J. B. Schor. 2013. "Could working less reduce pressures on the environment? A cross-national panel analysis of OECD countries, 1970-2007." *Global Environmental Change-Human and Policy Dimensions* 23 (4): 691-700.

Knights, P. 2019. "Inconsequential Contributions to Global Environmental Problems: A Virtue Ethics Account." *Journal of Agricultural & Environmental Ethics* 32 (4): 527-545.

Kokakowski, L. 2005. *Main Currents of Marxism: The Founders, the Golden Age, the Breakdown*. New York: W.W. Norton & Company.

Kountouris, Y., and E. Williams. 2022. "Do protests influence environmental attitudes? Evidence from Extinction Rebellion." *Environmental Research Communications*.

Kovel, J. 2000. "The struggle for use value: thoughts about the transition." *Capitalism Nature Socialism* 11 (2): 3-23.

Kovic, M. 2021. "Risks of space colonization." *Futures* 126.

Kperogi, F. A. 2011. "Cooperation with the corporation? CNN and the hegemonic cooptation of citizen journalism through iReport.com." *New Media & Society* 13 (2): 314-329.

Kretz, L. 2013. "Hope in Environmental Philosophy." *Journal of Agricultural & Environmental Ethics* 26 (5): 925-944.

Kruger, T. 2017. "Conflicts over carbon capture and storage in international climate governance." *Energy Policy* 100: 58-67.

Kunze, C., and S. Becker. 2015. "Collective ownership in renewable energy and opportunities for sustainable degrowth." *Sustainability Science* 10 (3): 425-437.

LaJeunesse, R. 2009. *Worktime Regulation as Sustainable Full Employment Strategy: The Social Effort Bargain.* New York: Routledge.

Larrain, J. 1979. *The Concept of Ideology.* London: Hutchinson & Co.

Larrain, J. 1983. *Marxism and Ideology.* London: Macmillan.

Latouche, S. 2015. "Imaginary, decolonization of." In *Degrowth: A Vocabulary for a New Era*, edited by G. D"Alisa, F. Demaria and G. Kallis. Oxon: Routledge.

Laville, S. 2019. "Top oil firms spending millions lobbying to block climate change policies, says report." *The Guardian* (March 21), 2019.

Lawhon, M., and T. McCreary. 2020. "Beyond Jobs vs Environment: On the Potential of Universal Basic Income to Reconfigure Environmental Politics." *Antipode* 52 (2): 23.

Lawrence, M. 2022. *Planet on Fire: A Manifesto for the Age of Environmental Breakdown.* London: Verso.

Lee, M. S. W., and C. S. Y. Ahn. 2016. "Anti-consumption, Materialism, and Consumer Well-being." *Journal of Consumer Affairs* 50 (1): 18-47.

Leuck, M.A. 2007. "Hope for a cause as cause for hope: the need for hope in environmental sociology." *The American Sociologist* 38 (3): 250-261.

Leung, D. Y. C., G. Caramanna, and M. M. Maroto-Valer. 2014. "An overview of current status of carbon dioxide capture and storage technologies." *Renewable & Sustainable Energy Reviews* 39: 426-443.

Li, C. J., and M. C. Monroe. 2019. "Exploring the essential psychological factors in fostering hope concerning climate change." *Environmental Education Research* 25 (6): 936-954.

Li, M., G. Trencher, and J. Asuka. 2022. "The clean energy claims of BP, Chevron, ExxonMobil and Shell: A mismatch between discourse, actions and investments." *Plos One* 17 (2).

Liberto, D. 2019. "Jeff Bezos wants to colonize the moon." Investopedia. https://www.investopedia.com/news/jeff-bezos-wants-colonize-moon/.

Lichtheim, G. 1967. *The Concept of Ideology and Other Essays*. New York: Random House.

Liegey, V., and A. Nelson. 2020. *Exploring Degrowth: A Critical Guide*. London: Pluto Press.

Lietaert, M. 2010. "Cohousing's relevance to degrowth theories." *Journal of Cleaner Production* 18 (6): 576-580.

Loadenthal, M. 2013a. "Deconstructing "eco-terrorism": rhetoric, framing and statecraft as seen through the insight approach." *Critical Studies on Terrorism* 6 (1): 92-117.

Loadenthal, M. 2013b. "The "Green Scare" and "Eco-Terrorism:" The Development of U.S. "Counterterrorism" Strategy Targeting Direct Action Activists." In *The Terrorization of Dissent: Corporate Repression, Legal Corruption, and teh Animal Enterprise Terrorism Act*, edited by J. Del Gandio and A.J. Nocella, 91-118. New York: Lantern Books.

Lodziak C, Tatman J. 1997. *André Gorz: A Critical Introduction*. Chicago, IL: Pluto Press.

Locke, T. 2020. "Elon Musk on planning for Mars: "the city has to survive if the resupply ships stop coming from Earth." CNBC. https://www.cnbc.com/2020/03/09/spacex-plans-how-elon-musk-see-life-on-mars.html.

Lohmann, L. 2005. "Marketing and making carbon dumps: Commodification, calculation and counterfactuals in climate change mitigation." *Science as Culture* 14 (3): 203-235.

Lohmann, L. 2010. "Uncertainty markets and carbon markets: variations on a Polanyian theme." *New Political Economy* 15 (2): 225-254.

Lorek, S. 2015. "Dematerialization." In *Degrowth: A New Vocabulary for a New Era*, edited by G. D'Alisa, F. Demaria and G. Kallis, 83-85. New York: Routledge.

Lorek, S., and J. H. Spangenberg. 2014. "Sustainable consumption within a sustainable economy beyond green growth and green economies." *Journal of Cleaner Production* 63: 33-44.

Lowe, B. S. 2019. "Ethics in the Anthropocene: Moral Responses to the Climate Crisis." *Journal of Agricultural & Environmental Ethics* 32 (3): 479-485.

Löwy, M. 2007. "Eco-socialism and democratic planning." *Socialist Register* 43: 294-309.

Löwy, M. 2015. *Ecosocialism: A Radical Alternative to Capitalism Catastrophe.* Chicago: Haymarket Books.

Mackintosh, E. 2018. "What the new report on climate change expects from you." CNN News. https://www.cnn.com/2018/10/08/world/ipcc-climate-change-consumer-actions-intl/index.html.

MacNeil, R., and M. Paterson. 2012. "Neoliberal climate policy: from market fetishism to the developmental state." *Environmental Politics* 21 (2): 230-247.

Macy, J., and C. Johnstone. 2012. *Active Hope: How to Face the Mess We're In Without Going Crazy.* Novato: New World Library.

Magdoff, F., and C. Williams. 2017. *Creating an Ecological Society: Towards a Revolutionary Transformation.* New York: Monthly Review Press.

Malm, A. 2021. *How to Blow Up a Pipeline.* London: Verso.

Marcetic, B. 2019. "The democrats are climate deniers." Jacobin. https://jacobin.com/2019/01/climate-change-2020-democrats-green-new-deal.

Marcuse, H. 1964. *One-Dimensional Man.* Boston: Beacon Press.

Marcuse, H. 1967. "The end of utopia." https://www.marxists.org/reference/archive/marcuse/works/1967/end-utopia.htm.

Marcuse, H. 1968. "Industrialization and capitalism in Max Weber." In *Negations: Essays in Critical Theory*, 201-226. Boston: Beacon Press.

Marcuse, H. 1969. *An Essay on Liberation.* Boston: Beacon Press.

Marcuse, H. 1972. *Counterrevolution and Revolt.* Boston: Beacon Press.

Marcuse, H. 1978. "Some social implications of modern technology." In *The Essential Frankfurt School Reader*, edited by A. Arato and E. Gebhardt, 138-162. New York: Urizen Books.

Marcuse, H. 1989. "From ontology to technology: fundamental tendencies of industrial society." In *Critical Theory and Society*, edited by S.E. Bronner and D. Kellner, 119-127. New York: Routledge.

Marcuse, H. 1994. "Ecology and Revolution." In *Ecology: Key Concepts in Critical Theory*, edited by C Merchant. Humanities Press.

Marcuse, H. 2001. "The problem of social change in the technological society." In *Towards a Critical Theory of Society: Collected Papers of Herbert Marcuse*, Vol. 2, edited by D. Kellner and C. Pierce. New York: Routledge.

Marcuse, H. 2011. "On Science and Phemonology." In *Philosophy, Psychoanalysis and Emancipation, Volume 5*, edited by D. Kellner and C. Pierce, 145-154. New York: Routledge.

Marino, L. 2019. "Humanity is not prepared to colonize Mars." *Futures* 110: 15-18.

Markusson, N., F. Ginn, N. S. Ghaleigh, and V. Scott. 2014. "'In case of emergency press here': framing geoengineering as a response to dangerous climate change." *Wiley Interdisciplinary Reviews-Climate Change* 5 (2): 281-290.

Markusson, N., D. McLaren, and D. Tyfield. 2018. "Towards a cultural political economy of mitigation deterrence by negative emissions technologies (NETs)." *Global Sustainability* 1.

Marlon, J., L. Neyens, M. Jefferson, P. Howe, M. Mildenberger, and A. Leiserowitz. 2022. "Yale Climate Opinion Maps 2021." Yale Program on Climate Change Communication. https://climatecommunication.yale.edu/visualizations-data/ycom-us/.

Martinez, C. 2017. "From commodification to the commons: charting the pathway for energy democracy." In *Energy Democracy: Advancing Equity in Clean Energy Solutions*, edited by D. Fairchild and A. Wienrub, 21-36. Washington DC: Island Press.

Marx, G. 1974. "Thoughts on a neglected category of social movement participant: the agent provocateur and the informant." *American Journal of Sociology* 80 (2): 402-442.

Marx, K. 1964. *The Economic and Philosophic Manuscripts of 1844*. New York: International.

Marx, K. 1981. *Capital, Vol. 3*. New York: Vintage.

Marx, K., and F. Engels. 1977. *The German Ideology*. New York: International Publishers.

Mastini, R., G. Kallis, and J. Hickel. 2021. "A green new deal without growth?" *Ecological Economics* 179. https://doi.org/10.1016/j.ecolecon.2020.106832.

Matthews, H. D. 2010. "Can carbon cycle geoengineering be a useful complement to ambitious climate mitigation?" *Carbon Management* 1 (1): 135-144.

Mavar, K. N., N. Gaurina-Medimurec, and L. Hrncevic. 2021. "Significance of Enhanced Oil Recovery in Carbon Dioxide Emission Reduction." *Sustainability* 13 (4).

McCright, A. M., and R. E. Dunlap. 2000. "Challenging global warming as a social problem: An analysis of the conservative movement's counter-claims." *Social Problems* 47 (4): 499-522.

McCright, A. M., and R. E. Dunlap. 2003. "Defeating Kyoto: The conservative movement's impact on U.S. climate change policy." *Social Problems* 50 (3): 348-373.

McCright, A. M., and R. E. Dunlap. 2010. "Anti-reflexivity: The American conservative movement's success in undermining climate science and policy." *Theory Culture & Society* 27 (2-3): 100-133.

McCright, A. M., and R. E. Dunlap. 2011. "The politicization of climate change and polarization in the American public's views of global warming, 2001-2010." *Sociological Quarterly* 52 (2): 155-194.

McCusker, K. E., K. C. Armour, C. M. Bitz, and D. S. Battisti. 2014. "Rapid and extensive warming following cessation of solar radiation management." *Environmental Research Letters* 9 (2).

McFell-Johnsen, M. 2021. "The companies polluting the planet have spent millions to make you think carpooling and recycling will save us." Business Insider. https://www.businessinsider.com/fossil-fuel-companies-spend-millions-to-promote-individual-responsibility-2021-3.

McKibben, B. 2019. "The climate movement: what's next?". The Great Transition Initiative. https://greattransition.org/gti-forum/climate-movement-mckibben.

Mercator Research Institute on Global Commons and Climate Change. 2017. "The Mercator Research Institute." https://www.mcc-berlin.net/en/research.html.

Meyer, R. 2018. "Climate change can be stopped by turning air into gasoline." The Atlantic. https://www.theatlantic.com/science/archive/2018/06/its-possible-to-reverse-climate-change-suggests-major-new-study/562289/.

Milbrath, L. W. 1995. "Psychological, cultural, and informational barriers to sustainability." *Journal of Social Issues* 51 (4): 101-120.

Milman, O. 2022. "Burning world's fossil fuel reserves could emit 3.5tn tons of greenhouse gases." *The Guardian* (September 19), 2022. https://www.theguardian.com/environment/2022/sep/19/world-fossil-fuel-reserve-greenhouse-gas-emissions.

Mol, A.P.J. 1995. *The Refinement of Production*. Utrecht: Van Arkel.

Mol, A.P.J. 1997. "Ecological Modernization: Industrial Transformations and Environmental Reform." In *The International Handbook of Environmental Sociology*, edited by M.R. Redclift and G. Woodgate, 138-149. Northampton: Edwar Elgar.

Mol, A.P.J. 2001. *Globalization and Environmental Reform: The Ecological Modernization of the Global Economy*. Cambridge: MIT Press.

Mol, A.P.J., and D.A. Sonnenfeld. 2000. *Ecological Modernisation Around the World: Perspectives and Critical Debates*. London: Frank Cass.

Molosky, I. 1988. "Reagan vetos bill putting limits on TV programming for children." *New York Times* (November 7), 1988. https://www.nytimes.com/1988/11/07/us/reagan-vetoes-bill-putting-limits-on-tv-programming-for-children.html.

Moran, D., R. Wood, E. Hertwich, K. Mattson, J. F. D. Rodriguez, K. Schanes, and J. Barrett. 2020. "Quantifying the potential for consumer-oriented policy to reduce European and foreign carbon emissions." *Climate Policy* 20: S28-S38.

Mori, A. S., L. E. Dee, A. Gonzalez, H. Ohashi, J. Cowles, A. J. Wright, M. Loreau, Y. Hautier, T. Newbold, P. B. Reich, T. Matsui, W. Takeuchi, K. Okada, R. Seidl, and F. Isbell. 2021. "Biodiversity-productivity relationships are key to nature-based climate solutions." *Nature Climate Change* 11 (6): 543-550.

Mulvale, J. P. 2019. "Social-Ecological Transformation and the Necessity of Universal Basic Income." *Social Alternatives* 38 (2): 39-46.

Munoz, J., and E. Anduiza. 2019. "'If a fight starts, watch the crowd': The effect of violence on popular support for social movements." *Journal of Peace Research* 56 (4): 485-498.

Munoz, J., S. Olzak, and S. A. Soule. 2018. "Going Green: Environmental Protest, Policy, and CO2 Emissions in US States, 1990-2007." *Sociological Forum* 33 (2): 403-421.

Murray, J. 2021. "Half of emissions cuts will come from future tech, says John Kerry." *The Guardian*, 2021. https://www.theguardian.com/environment/2021/may/16/half-of-emissions-cuts-will-come-from-future-tech-says-john-kerry.

National Academies of Sciences, Engineering, and Medicine. 2018. *Negative Emissions Technologies and Reliable Sequestration: A Research Agenda*. The National Academies Press (Washington, DC).

Nerlich, B., and R. Jaspal. 2012. "Metaphors we die by? Geoengineering, metaphors, and the argument from catastrophe." *Metaphor and Symbol* 27 (2): 131-147.

Nielsen, K. S., K. A. Nicholas, F. Creutzig, T. Dietz, and P. C. Stern. 2021. "The role of high-socioeconomic-status people in locking in or rapidly reducing energy-driven greenhouse gas emissions." *Nature Energy* 6 (11): 1011-1016.

Norgaard, K.M. 2011. *Living in Denial: Climate Change, Emotions and Everyday Life.* Cambridge: MIT Press.

Nosek, G. 2020. "The fossil fuel industry's push to target climate protestors in the US." *Pace Environmental Law Review* 38 (53).

Nyberg, D. 2021. Corporations, politics, and democracy: Corporate political activities as political corruption. *Organization Theory,* 2(1), 1-24.

Nyfors, T., L. Linnanen, A. Nissinen, J. Seppala, M. Saarinen, K. Regina, T. Heinonen, R. Viri, and H. Liimatainen. 2020. "Ecological Sufficiency in Climate Policy: Towards Policies for Recomposing Consumption." *Futura* 3: 30-40.

O'Connor, J. 1998. *Natural Causes: Essays in Ecological Marxism.* New York: Guilford Press.

O'Neill, D. W. 2012. "Measuring progress in the degrowth transition to a steady state economy." *Ecological Economics* 84: 221-231.

Obach, B.K. 2004. "New labor: slowing the treadmill of production?" *Organization & Environment* 17 (3): 337-354.

Ollinaho, O.I. 2016. "Environmental destruction as (objectively) uneventful and (subjectively) irrelevant." *Environmental Sociology* 2 (1): 53-63.

Otitoju, O., E. Oko, and M. H. Wang. 2021. "Technical and economic performance assessment of post-combustion carbon capture using piperazine for large scale natural gas combined cycle power plants through process simulation." *Applied Energy* 292: 18.

Oxfam International. 2015. *World's richest 10% produce half of carbon emissions while poorest 3.5 billion account for just a tenth.* Oxfam International. https://www.oxfam.org/en/press-releases/worlds-richest-10-produce-half-carbon-emissions-while-poorest-35-billion-account.

Owen, D. 2011. *The Conundrum: How Scientific Innovation, Increased Efficiency, and Good Intentions Can Make Our Energy and Climate Problems Worse.* New York: Riverhead Books.

Paci, E. 1972. "The Dialectic of the Concrete and the Abstract." In *The Function of the Sciences and the Meaning of Man,* 423-447. Northwestern University Press.

Parrish, W. 2019. "The U.S. border patrol and and Israeli military contractor are putting a Native American reservation under 'persistent surveillance'." https://theintercept.com/2019/08/25/border-patrol-israel-elbit-surveillance/

Parrique, T. 2022. "Degrowth in the IPCC AR6 WGII." https://timotheeparrique.com/degrowth-in-the-ipcc-ar6-wgii/.

Parrique, T., J. Barth, F. Briens, C. Kerschner, A. Karaus-Polk, A. Kuokkanen, and J. H. Spangenberg. 2019. *Decoupling Debunked: Evidence and Arguments against Green Growth as a Sole Strategy for Sustainability*. European Environmental Bureau. https://eeb.org/library/decoupling-debunked/.

Paul, M., C. Skandier, and R. Renzy. 2020. "Out of time: the case for nationalizing the fossil fuel industry." The Next Systems Project. https://thenextsystem.org/learn/stories/out-time-case-nationalizing-fossil-fuel-industry.

Paulson, S. 2017. "Degrowth: culture, power and change." *Journal of Political Ecology* 24: 425-448.

Paulson, S., G. D'Alisa, F. Demaria, and G. Kallis. 2020. *The Case for Degrowth*. Hoboken: John Wiley & Sons.

Perkins, P. E. 2019. "Climate justice, commons, and degrowth." *Ecological Economics* 160: 183-190.

Petersen, B., D. Stuart, and R. Gunderson. 2019. "Reconceptualizing climate change denial: ideological denialism misdiagnoses climate change and limits effective action." *Human Ecology Review* 25 (2).

Phillips, A. 2022. "Biden outpaces Trump in issuing drilling permits on public lands." *The Washington Post* (January 27), 2022. https://www.washingtonpost.com/climate-environment/2022/01/27/oil-gas-leasing-biden-climate/.

Pires, J. C. M., F. G. Martins, M. C. M. Alvim-Ferraz, and M. Simoes. 2011. "Recent developments on carbon capture and storage: An overview." *Chemical Engineering Research & Design* 89 (9): 1446-1460.

Piven, F.F. 2006. *Challenging Authority: How Ordinary People Change America*. Lanham: The Rowman & Littlefield Publishing Group, Inc.

Polanyi, K. 2001. *The Great Transformation: The Political and Economic Origins of Our Time*. Boston: Beacon Press.

Pour, N., P. A. Webley, and P. J. Cook. 2017. "A sustainability framework for bioenergy with carbon capture and storage (BECCS) technologies." *Energy Procedia* 114: 6044-6056.

Pullinger, M. 2014. "Working time reduction policy in a sustainable economy: Criteria and options for its design." *Ecological Economics* 103: 11-19.

Raworth, K. 2017. *Doughnut Economics: 7 Ways to Think Like a 21st Century Economist.* White River Junction: Chelsea Green Publishing.

Realmonte, G., L. Drouet, A. Gambhir, J. Glynn, A. Hawkes, A. C. Koberle, and M. Tavoni. 2019. "An inter-model assessment of the role of direct air capture in deep mitigation pathways." *Nature Communications* 10.

Reich, R. 2016. *Saving capitalism: For the many, not the few.* New York: Vintage.

Reiner, D. M. 2016. "Learning through a portfolio of carbon capture and storage demonstration projects." *Nature Energy* 1.

Ripple, W. J., C. Wolf, T. M. Newsome, J. W. Gregg, T. M. Lenton, I. Palomo, J. A. J. Eikelboom, B. E. Law, S. Huq, P. B. Duffy, and J. Rockstrom. 2021. "World Scientists' Warning of a Climate Emergency 2021." *Bioscience* 71 (9): 894-898.

Robinson, K.S. 2020. *The Ministry for the Future.* Orbit Books.

Robinson, N.J. 2019. *Why You Should Be a Socialist.* All Points Books.

Robock, A. 2008a. "Geoengineering: It's not a panacea." *Geotimes* 53 (7): 58-58.

Robock, A. 2008b. "20 reasons why geoengineering may be a bad idea." *Bulletin of the Atomic Scientists* 64 (2): 14-18. https://doi.org/10.2968/064002006. <Go to ISI>://WOS:000255499200012.

Robock, A., M. Bunzl, B. Kravitz, and G. L. Stenchikov. 2010. "A Test for Geoengineering?" *Science* 327 (5965): 530-531.

Robock, A., A. Marquardt, B. Kravitz, and G. Stenchikov. 2009. "Benefits, risks, and costs of stratospheric geoengineering." *Geophysical Research Letters* 36.

Romm, J. 2010. "Bill Gates disses energy efficiency, renewables, and near term climate action while embracing the magical thinking of Bjorn Lomborg (and George Bush)." Think Progress. http://thinkprogress.org/climate/2010/01/26/205380/bill-gates-energy-efficiency-insulation-renewables-and-global-climate-action-bjorn-lomborg/

Romm, J. 2011. "Pro-geoengineering Bill Gates disses efficiency, 'cute' solar development, deployment - still doesn't know how he got rich." Think Progress. http://thinkprogress.org/climate/2011/05/05/208032/bill-gates-efficiency-cute-solar/.

Rommel, J., J. Radtke, G. von Jorck, F. Mey, and O. Yildiz. 2018. "Community renewable energy at a crossroads: A think piece on degrowth, technology, and the democratization of the German energy system." *Journal of Cleaner Production* 197: 1746-1753.

Rosnick, D., and M. Weisbrot. 2006. *Are shorter working hours good for the environment? A comparison of U.S. and European Energy consumption.* Center for Economic and Policy Research (Washington, D.C.).

Royal Society. 2009. *Geoengineering the Climate: Science, Governance and Uncertainty.* The Royal Society (London). http://eprints.soton.ac.uk/156647/1/Geoengineering_the_climate.pdf?origin=publication_detail

Rushkoff, D. 2009. *Life Inc.: How the World Became a Corporation and How to Take it Back.* Random House.

saed. 2021. "Anti-communism and the hundreds of millions of victims of capitalism." *Capitalism Nature Socialism* 32 (1): 1-17.

Saito, K. 2017. *Karl Marx's Ecosocialism: Capital, Nature, and the Unfinished Critique of Political Economy.* New York: Monthly Review Press.

Samper, J. A., A. Schockling, and M. Islar. 2021. "Climate Politics in Green Deals: Exposing the Political Frontiers of the European Green Deal." *Politics and Governance* 9 (2): 8-16.

Santarius, T. 2012. *Green Growth Unraveled: How Rebound Effects Baffle Sustainability Targets When The Economy Keeps Growing.* Wuppertal Institute (Berlin).

Saunders, H. D. 2014. "Toward a neoclassical theory of sustainable consumption: Eight golden age propositions." *Ecological Economics* 105: 220-232.

Scheetz, M. 2020. "NASA awards contracts to Jeff Bezos and Elon Musk to land astronauts on the moon." CNBC. https://www.cnbc.com/2020/04/30/nasa-selects-hls-lunar-lander-teams-blue-origin-spacex-dynetics.html.

Schmelzer, M. 2016. *The Hegemony of Growth: The Making and Remaking of the Economic Growth Paradigm and the OECD, 1948-2010.* Cambridge: Cambridge University Press.

Schmelzer, M., A. Vansintjan, and A. Vetter. 2022. *The Future is Degrowth: A Guide to a World Beyond Capitalism.* Verso.

Schnaiberg, A. 1980. *The Environment: From Surplus to Scarcity.* New York: Oxford University Press.

Schor, J. 2010. *Plenitude: The New Economics of True Wealth.* New York: Penguin Press.

Schor, J. 2014. *Born to Buy: The Commercialized Child and the New Consumer Cult.* New York: Simon and Schuster.

Schor, J. 2015. "Work sharing." In *Degrowth: A Vocabulary for a New Era,* edited by G. D'Alisa, F. Demaria and G. Kallis, 195-197. New York: Routledge.

Schor, J., and A. Jorgenson. 2019. "Is it too late for growth?" *Review of Radical Political Economics* 51 (2): 320-329.

Schwartz, J. S. J. 2019. "Space settlement: What's the Rush?" *Futures* 110: 56-59.

Schweickart, D. 1992. "Economic democracy - a worthy socialism that would really work." *Science & Society* 56 (1): 9-38.

Sekera, J., and A. Lichtenberger. 2020. "Assessing carbon capture: public policy, science, and societal need." *Biophysical Economics and Sustainability* 5.

Senftle, T. P., and E. A. Carter. 2017. "The Holy Grail: Chemistry Enabling an Economically Viable CO2 Capture, Utilization, and Storage Strategy." *Accounts of Chemical Research* 50 (3): 472-475.

Seyfang, G., J. J. Park, and A. Smith. 2013. "A thousand flowers blooming? An examination of community energy in the UK." *Energy Policy* 61: 977-989.

Siegel, R.P. 2018. "The Fizzy Math of Carbon Capture: Once seen as cost-prohibitive, pulling carbon dioxide out of air could become feasible thanks to a growing secondary market." Grist. https://grist.org/article/direct-air-carbon-capture-global-thermostat/.

Sillman, J., T. M. Lenton, A. Levermann, K. Ott, M. Hulme, F. Benduhn, and J.B. Horton. 2015. "Climate emergencies do not justify engineering the climate." *Nature Climate Change* 5: 290-292.

Simpson, B., R. Willer, and M. Feinberg. 2018. "Does violent protest backfire? Testing a theory of public relations to activist violence." *Socius: Sociological Research for a Dynamic World* 4 (2378023118803189).

Smith, M. 2021. "Concern for environment reaches record high in YouGov top issues tracker." YouGov. https://yougov.co.uk/topics/politics/articles-reports/2021/11/09/concern-environment-reaches-record-high-yougov-top?utm_source=twitter&utm_medium=website_article&utm_campaign=env_tracker_nov_2021.

Smith, R. 2019. "An ecosocialist path to limiting global temperature rise to 1.5°C." *Real-World Economics Review* 87: 149-180.

Solnit, R. 2016. *Hope in the Dark: Untold Histories, Wild Possibilities.* Chicago: Haymarket.

Sorrell, S. 2007. *The Rebound Effect: An Assessment of the Evidence for Economy-wide Energy Savings from Improved Energy Efficiency.* London: UK Energy Research Centre.

Sovacool, B. K., and A. Dunlap. 2022. "Anarchy, war, or revolt? Radical perspectives for climate protection, insurgency and civil disobedience in a low-carbon era." *Energy Research & Social Science* 86: 17.

SpaceX. 2020. https://www.spacex.com/.

Spash, C. L. 2021. "Apologists for growth: passive revolutionaries in a passive revolution." *Globalizations*: 26.

Spash, C. L., and A. Guisan. 2021. "A future for social-ecological economics." *Real World Economics Review*.

Speth, G. 2015. "Getting to the next system: guideposts on the way to a new political economy." *The Next System Project* 31.

Speth, J.G., C.S. Skandier, and J. Bozuwa. 2018. *Taking climate action to the next level*. Next System Project.

Srivastav, S., and R. Rafaty. 2021. *Five Worlds of Political Strategy in the Climate Movement*. Institute for New Economic Thinking at the Oxford Martin School.

Stoddard, I., K. Anderson, S. Capstick, W. Carton, J. Depledge, K. Facer, C. Gough, F. Hache, C. Hoolohan, M. Hultman, N. Hallstrom, S. Kartha, S. Klinsky, M. Kuchler, E. Lovbrand, N. Nasiritousi, P. Newell, G. P. Peters, Y. Sokona, A. Stirling, M. Stilwell, C. L. Spash, and M. Williams. 2021. "Three Decades of Climate Mitigation: Why Haven't We Bent the Global Emissions Curve?" In *Annual Review of Environment and Resources, Vol 46, 2021*, edited by A. Gadgil and T. P. Tomich, In Annual Review of Environment and Resources, 653-689. Palo Alto: Annual Reviews.

Stone, A. 2018. "Negative Emissions Won't Rescue Us from Climate Change." Forbes. https://www.forbes.com/sites/andystone/2018/10/29/negative-emissions-wont-rescue-us-from-climate-change/#88cf13636268

Steffen, W., J. Rockstrom, K. Richardson, T. M. Lenton, C. Folke, D. Liverman, C. P. Summerhayes, A. D. Barnosky, S. E. Cornell, M. Crucifix, J. F. Donges, I. Fetzer, S. J. Lade, M. Scheffer, R. Winkelmann, and H. J. Schellnhuber. 2018. "Trajectories of the Earth System in the Anthropocene." *Proceedings of the National Academy of Sciences of the United States of America* 115 (33): 8252-8259.

Stephens, J. 2009. "Technology leader, policy laggard: CCS development for climate mitigation in the US political context." In *Coaching the Carbon: The Politics and Policy of Carbon Capture and Storage*, edited by J. Meadowcroft and O. Langhelle. Northampton: Edward Elgar.

Stephens, J. C., and K. Surprise. 2020. "The hidden injustices of advancing solar geoengineering research." *Global Sustainability* 3: 6.

Stern, N. 2006. *Stern Review on the Economics of Climate Change*. Cambridge: Cambridge University Press.

Stiglitz, J. 2019. "It's time to retire metrics like GDP. They don't measure everything that matters." *The Guardian*, November 24, 2019. https://www.theguardian.com/commentisfree/2019/nov/24/metrics-gdp-economic-performance-social-progress.

Stone, A. 2018. "Negative Emissions Won't Rescue Us from Climate Change." Forbes. https://www.forbes.com/sites/andystone/2018/10/29/negative-emissions-wont-rescue-us-from-climate-change/#88cf13636268

Stoner, A.M. 2021. "Critical reflections on America's Green New Deal: capital, labor, and the dynamics of contemporary social change." *Capitalism Nature Socialism* 32 (2): 77-94.

Stoner, A.M., and A. Melathopoulos. 2015. *Freedom in the Anthropocene: Twentieth-Century Helplessness in the Face of Climate Change*. New York: Palgrave MacMillan.

Stoner, I. 2017. "Humans Should Not Colonize Mars." *Journal of the American Philosophical Association* 3 (3): 334-353.

Stuart, D. 2022. "Tensions between individual and system change in the climate movement: an analysis of Extinction Rebellion." *New Political Economy* 27 (5): 806-819.

Stuart, D., R. Gunderson, and B. Petersen. 2019. "Climate Change and the Polanyian Counter-movement: Carbon Markets or Degrowth?" *New Political Economy* 24 (1): 89-102.

Stuart, D., R. Gunderson, and B. Petersen. 2020. *Climate Change Solutions: Overcoming the Capital-Climate Contradiction*. Ann Arbor: University of Michigan Press.

Sunkara, B. 2020. *The Socialist Manifesto: The Case for Radical Politics in an Era of Extreme Inequality*. New York: Basic Books.

Surprise, K. 2020. "Solar geoengineering is incompatible with a (radical) Green New Deal." MRonline. https://mronline.org/2020/07/30/solar-geoengineering-is-incompatible-with-a-radical-green-new-deal/.

Swaffield, J., and D. Bell. 2012. "Can 'climate champions' save the planet? A critical reflection on neoliberal social change." *Environmental Politics* 21 (2): 248-267.

Szulecki, K. 2018. "Conceptualizing energy democracy." *Environmental Politics* 27 (1): 21-41.

Taffel, S. 2022. "AirPods and the earth: Digital technologies, planned obsolescence and the Capitalocene." *Environment and Planning E-Nature and Space*: 22.

Tanzer, S. E., and A. Ramirez. 2019. "When are negative emissions negative emissions?" *Energy & Environmental Science* 12 (4): 1210-1218.

Taylor, M. 2021. "Environment protest being criminalised around world, say experts." *The Guardian* (April 29), 2021. https://www.theguardian.com/environment/2021/apr/19/environment-protest-being-criminalised-around-world-say-experts.

Thombs, R. P. 2017. "The Paradoxical Relationship between Renewable Energy and Economic Growth: A Cross-National Panel Study, 1990-2013." *Journal of World-Systems Research* 23 (2): 540-564.

Thompson, A. 2010. "Radical Hope for Living Well in a Warmer World." *Journal of Agricultural & Environmental Ethics* 23 (1-2): 43-59.

Tomassetti, P. 2020. "From Treadmill of Production to Just Transition and Beyond." *European Journal of Industrial Relations* 26 (4): 439-457.

Torchinsky, R. 2022. "Elon Musk hints at a crewed mission to Mars in 2029." https://www.npr.org/2022/03/17/1087167893/elon-musk-mars-2029.

Tracey, M. 2011. "The NYPD's violent crackdown on Occupy Wall Street protestors." Mother Jones. https://www.motherjones.com/politics/2011/10/occupy-wall-street-police-violence/.

Trainer, T. 2010. "Can renewables etc. solve the greenhouse problem? The negative case." *Energy Policy* 38 (8): 4107-4114.

Trainer, T. 2012. "De-growth: Do you realise what it means?" *Futures* 44 (6): 590-599.

Trantas, N. 2021. "Could" degrowth" have the same fate as" sustainable development"? A discussion on passive revolution in the Anthropocene age." *Journal of Political Ecology* 28: 224-245.

Treanor, B. 2010. "Environmentalism and Public Virtue." *Journal of Agricultural & Environmental Ethics* 23 (1-2): 9-28.

Tsagkari, M., J. Roca, and G. Kallis. 2021. ""From local island energy to degrowth? Exploring democracy, self-sufficiency, and renewable energy production in Greece and Spain"." *Energy Research & Social Science* 81.

Turner, P. A., K. J. Mach, D. B. Lobell, S. M. Benson, E. Baik, D. L. Sanchez, and C. B. Field. 2018. "The global overlap of bioenergy and carbon sequestration potential." *Climatic Change* 148 (1-2): 1-10.

United States Department of Housing and Urban Development. 2015. *2015 Characteristics of New Housing*. https://www.census.gov/construction/chars/pdf/c25ann2015.pdf.

United Nations (2023) https://www.un.org/en/climatechange/science/key-findings#health

United Nations Development Programme (UNDP). N.D. "Climate and disaster resilience." http://www.undp.org/content/undp/en/home/climate-and-disaster-resilience/sustainable-energy/renewable-energy.html.

Vaden, T., V. Lahde, A. Majava, P. Jarvensivu, T. Toivanen, E. Hakala, and J. T. Eronen. 2020. "Decoupling for ecological sustainability: A categorisation and review of research literature." *Environmental Science & Policy* 112: 236-244.

Vanderheiden, S. 2008. "Radical environmentalism in an age of antiterrorism." *Environmental Politics* 17 (2): 299-318.

Vaughan, N. E., and T. M. Lenton. 2011. "A review of climate geoengineering proposals." *Climatic Change* 109 (3-4): 745-790.

Vergara-Camus, L. 2019. "Capitalism, democracy, and the degrowth horizon." *Capitalism Nature Socialism* 30 (2): 217-233.

Verma, P. 2022. "There's a carbon-capture gold rush. Some warn better solutions exist." *The Washington Post* (June 23), 2022. https://www.washingtonpost.com/technology/2022/06/23/carbon-capture-climate-change/.

Wallace-Wells, D. 2019. *The Uninhabitable Earth: Life After Warming*. New York: Tim Duggan Books.

Wang, D. J., and A. Piazza. 2016. "The Use of Disruptive Tactics in Protest as a Trade-Off: The Role of Social Movement Claims." *Social Forces* 94 (4): 1675-1710.

Wasow, O. 2020. "Agenda Seeding: How 1960s Black Protests Moved Elites, Public Opinion and Voting." *American Political Science Review* 114 (3): 638-659.

Watson, D.L. 2002. *The Terrorist Threat Confronting the United States*. Testimony Before the Senate Select Committee on Intelligence (Washington DC). https://www.fbi.gov/news/testimony/the-terrorist-threat-confronting-the-unitedstates.

Weber, M. 1978. *Economy and Society, Volume 1*. Berkeley: University of California Press.

Wennersten, R., Q. Sun, and H. L. Li. 2015. "The future potential for Carbon Capture and Storage in climate change mitigation - an overview from perspectives of technology, economy and risk." *Journal of Cleaner Production* 103: 724-736.

Werfel, S. H. 2017. "Household behaviour crowds out support for climate change policy when sufficient progress is perceived." *Nature Climate Change* 7 (7): 512-515.

White, D.F., B.J. Gareau, and A.P. Rudy. 2017. "Ecosocialisms, past, present and future: from the metabolic rift to a reconstructive, dynamic and hybrid ecosocialism." *Capitalism Nature Socialism* 28 (2): 22-40.

Wiedenhofer, D., D. Virag, G. Kalt, B. Plank, J. Streeck, M. Pichler, A. Mayer, F. Krausmann, P. Brockway, A. Schaffartzik, T. Fishman, D. Hausknost, B. Leon-Gruchalski, T. Sousa, F. Creutzig, and H. Haberl. 2020. "A systematic review of the evidence on decoupling of GDP, resource use and GHG emissions, part I: bibliometric and conceptual mapping." *Environmental Research Letters* 15 (6).

Wiedmann, T., M. Lenzen, L. T. Keysser, and J. K. Steinberger. 2020. "Scientists' warning on affluence." *Nature Communications* 11 (1).

Williamson, K., A. Satre-Meloy, K. Velasco, and K. Green. 2018. *Climate Change Needs Behavior Change Making the Case for Behavioral Solutions to Reduce Global Warming: Making the Case for Behavioral Solutions to Reduce Global Warming.* Arlington: Rare.

Williston, B. 2015. *The Anthropocene Project: Virtue in the Age of Climate Change.* Oxford: Oxford University Press.

Wilson, J., and W. Parrish. 2019. "Revealed: FBI and police monitoring Oregon anti-pipeline activists." *The Guardian* (August 8), 2019. https://www.theguardian.com/us-news/2019/aug/08/fbi-oregon-anti-pipeline-jordan-cove-activists.

Wohland, J., D. Witthaut, and C. F. Schleussner. 2018. "Negative Emission Potential of Direct Air Capture Powered by Renewable Excess Electricity in Europe." *Earths Future* 6 (10): 1380-1384.

Wolff, R. 2012. *Democracy at Work: A Cure for Capitalism.* Chicago: Haymarket Books.

Wolff, R. 2019. *Understanding Socialism.* New York: Democracy at Work.

World Inequality Report. 2022. *Executive Summary.* World Inequality Report. https://wir2022.wid.world/executive-summary/.

WHO (2023) World Health Organization. https://www.who.int/news-room/fact-sheets/detail/climate-change-and-health

WorldWatch. 2018. *The State of Consumption Today.* http://www.worldwatch.org/node/810.

Wright, E.O. 2010. *Envisioning Real Utopias.* London: Verso.

Wright, E.O. 2019. *How to Be an Anticapitalist in the Twenty-First Century*. London: Verso.

Yearley, S. 1997. "Science and the environment." In *The International Handbook of Environmental Sociology*, edited by M.R. Redclift and G. Woodgate, 227-236. Northampton: Edward Elgar.

York, R. 2012. "Do alternative energy sources displace fossil fuels?" *Nature Climate Change* 2 (6): 441-443.

York, R. 2016. "Decarbonizing the energy supply may increase energy demand." *Sociology of Development* 2 (3): 265-272.

York, R. 2006. "Ecological paradoxes: William Stanley Jevons and the paperless office." *Human Ecology Review* 13 (2): 143-147.

York, R., L. Adua, and B. Clark. 2022. "The rebound effect and the challenge of moving beyond fossil fuels: A review of empirical and theoretical research." *Wiley Interdisciplinary Reviews-Climate Change* 13 (4): 13.

York, R., and S. E. Bell. 2019. "Energy transitions or additions? Why a transition from fossil fuels requires more than the growth of renewable energy." *Energy Research & Social Science* 51: 40-43.

York, R., and B. Clark. 2010. "Critical Materialism: Science, Technology, and Environmental Sustainability." *Sociological Inquiry* 80 (3): 475-499.

York, R., C. Ergas, E. A. Rosa, and T. Dietz. 2011. "It's a material world: Trends in material extraction in China, India, Indonesia, and Japan." *Nature and Culture* 6 (2): 103-122.

York, R., and J.A. McGee. 2015. "Understanding the Jevons paradox." *Environmental Sociology* 2 (1): 77-87.

York, R., E. A. Rosa, and T. Dietz. 2003. "Footprints on the earth: The environmental consequences of modernity." *American Sociological Review* 68 (2): 279-300.

Yun, S. J. 2018. "Citizen participation-based energy transition experiments in a megacity: the case of the One Less Nuclear Power Plant in Seoul, South Korea." In *Energy Transition in East Asia: A Social Science Perspective*, edited by K.T. Chou, 77-103. New York: Routledge.

Zamora, D. 2017. "The case against a basic income." Jacobin. https://www.jacobinmag.com/2017/12/universal-basic-income-inequality-work

Zehner, O. 2012. *Green Illusions: The Dirty Secrets of Clean Energy and the Future of Environmentalism*. Lincoln: University of Nebraska Press.

Zizek, S. 1994. *Mapping Ideology*. Verso.

Zuboff, S. 2019. *The Age of Surveillance Capitalism: The Fight for a Human Future at the New Frontier of Power*. Public Affairs.

Milton Keynes UK
Ingram Content Group UK Ltd.
UKHW020157231223
434829UK00009B/73

9 781906 948689